WESTERN HUMANISM:
A Christian Perspective

*A Guide for Understanding Moral
Decline in
Western Culture*

John D. Carter, Ph.D.

Photon Publishing
North Canton, Ohio

Cover Images (top to bottom): Charles Darwin, Friedrich Nietzsche, Sigmund Freud, Karl Marx

Printed in the United States of America
First Printing

ISBN 0974005398
Library of Congress Control Number (LCCN) 2004090837

Contents

Dedication and Acknowledgments

This volume is dedicated to Emily, Jane and Brett, the loves of my life. To others, I also owe a full measure of gratitude. My friend from my U.S. Army service, Dr. John Harutunian, is acknowledged for giving me a copy of C. S. Lewis' *Mere Christianity*. Lewis' writings had a profound effect on me, and I think if not for his books, I would have continued to reject the Christianity of my childhood—the influence of which I owe to the lives of my parents. To certain of my undergraduate professors I owe particular thanks for a quality Christian education. Dr. Edward Panosian taught a most excellent course in the history of civilization from a Christian perspective—upon which I have drawn in the writing of this book—and Mr. Paul Brown brought a human touch to scientific topics that often get lost in cold, hard facts. In the brief period of time between my undergraduate and graduate studies, the sermons of the late Rev. Fred Evans of Walnut Grove Chapel in Indianapolis were especially inspiring. Finally, I am grateful to my friends who took the time to read and critique the manuscript of this book, especially Mrs. Vicki Hale and Dr. June Stoll, both professional instructors of the English language. Their many suggestions improved the readability of this book. However, for the errors that remain, only I can be blamed.

Preface

Although laments regarding moral decline in modern society abound, and the conservative voices which offer solutions to the degradation are plethoric, there seems to be little understanding for the true cause of the demise. This work was undertaken to educate the reader towards that understanding. In this book, I elucidate the mechanisms by which humanistic thought has become prevalent in Western culture, a culture where Christianity once had dominate sway.

Because the meaning of the word *humanism* is somewhat ambiguous, I state up front that my use of the word implies a system of thought which teaches that man, in the power of his own nature, can function as a moral being, but, in reality, is a system where that capability does not truly exist. Humanists hold to a system of a perceived morality, but their philosophy actually leads away from true morality because they do not understand that true moral knowledge is only attained when Scripture is recognized as a supernatural revelation of God's mind to mankind. To believe that man can be truly moral—outside of a genuine relationship to the *God of Scripture*— is a gross error in thinking.

Some authors have thus suggested that the term *humanist* should only apply to the Christian.[1] These authors presumably hold to this view because outside of man's reconciliation to the God of Scripture, he cannot be fully human. For illustrative purposes, imagine a beautiful, shiny Rolls Royce parked in front of an elegant home. While the automobile appears to be whole, underneath the "bonnet" (as our British friends would say) is an engine with a cracked block that prevents the engine from firing. The car *appears* to be a whole car but, in reality, it only has the image of one. While it indeed may still be an automobile, it does not function as one—for the "heart" of it (the engine) is not whole. This simple allegory somewhat illustrates the human condition with which this book deals. Man, although he is a creature in the image of God, is morally broken and, therefore, he is not fully human until that brokenness is restored.

Despite the validity for ascribing to *humanism* the definition described in the previous paragraph, I do not feel comfortable attempting to wrest the word back to a meaning which is consistent with that illustration. I am content to let those who call themselves humanists use the term as they wish. Those who call themselves humanists are usually opposed to an interpretation of reality which is consistent with the truth of Scripture. But that is acceptable since the Rolls—in the illustration above—is still a beautiful automobile. My intent in this book is to help the reader understand the extent to which man is broken, because it is in this reality that the decline of morality in Western culture is based.

Since the elevation of Scripture to this supreme position is a foundational presupposition to this work, my primary audience will probably be a Christian one where the term *humanism* is already perceived as a system of thought that is opposed to a scriptural interpretation of reality. This book will hopefully help these readers reconcile their Christian heritage with the world-view that modern humanistic educational systems have thrust upon them. At my son's commencement ceremony a few years ago, a student being recognized for his achievement addressed his audience with the usual lofty idealism for which graduation speeches are noted. When trying to put a Christian spin on his speech, he fashioned a thought beginning with words from Scripture and ending with a quote from Nietzsche, as if the two philosophies were seamlessly compatible. While his mind-set was admirably coming from a Christian perspective, it appeared that he was not cognizant of the extreme nature of Nietzsche's humanism. While some Christians have used the term *humanism* to describe *any* thought process that is incompatible with Scripture, the term is better used to imply a way of thinking that is based on specific errors in perception, and I hope to delineate the sources of those errors.

However, it is also my hope that this work will benefit those non-Christians who might desire to understand why a scripturally based philosophy clashes with both secular and, in some cases, non-secular modern-day thinking. The humanist's error is ultimately based on *his*[2] presupposition that Scripture cannot be relied upon as the absolute source of metaphysical truth. Humanists often presuppose Scripture to be based on half-truths, hearsay and myth, despite the vast amount of historical evidence to suggest—and in many cases prove—otherwise. Although other authors might be better suited to deal with the validity and fallacy of these respective presuppositions, I have, throughout this book, attempted to offer these readers justification for turning from their erroneous views of Scripture.

Humanism in modern Western culture has gone from a position of lesser influence to one of dominance. This is particularly apparent in the field of higher education. In fact, Western systems of higher education must share much of the blame for this cultural evolution. While many prestigious Western universities have their roots in orthodox Christianity, all of them now operate with little or no allegiance to the philosophies on which they were founded. Many of these schools once espoused Scripture to be the absolute source of philosophical and metaphysical truth. It is doubtful that

B. B. Warfield, the noted Princeton theologian, would be offered a teaching position at Princeton Theological Seminary if he were alive today, despite the fact that a chair is still held there in his name. The most prestigious Western universities, are today, for the most part, bastions of humanism and the fruits of this regression are everywhere apparent.³ Likewise, the numerous institutions that hold these schools as role models are turning out legions of graduates who unabashedly tout the humanistic world-views taught there. While remaining vestiges of genuine Christianity yet influence Western culture, very little of that influence is coming from the most respected Western institutions of higher learning. Even many smaller colleges, which likewise were originally based on biblical Christian beliefs, are producing leaders who perpetuate the humanistic philosophies with which this book deals.

Many people incorrectly associate humanism solely with a secular worldview. Indeed, one dictionary even defines humanism as "any system which puts human interests and the mind of man paramount, rejecting religion."⁴ However, humanistic systems of thought often do not exclude the belief in the existence of a supreme being. The term "secular humanism" is used to describe the humanism that excludes a concept of deity. Over time humanism evolves to that secular extreme. But there have always been those who hold to humanistic viewpoints without denying the existence of God. This is especially true in periods of transition where humanism goes from a position of less influence to one of dominance. For example, most of the Enlightenment humanists (discussed in Chapters 6) believed in a transcendent monotheistic God even though their deistic beliefs were far from a view compatible with Scripture. Generally, humanism is any human-generated system of thought that imparts to the human mind a perception of reality that is inconsistent with the truth of Scripture. It may or may not include a concept of deity. If a concept of deity is included, it is one that is in conflict with the God revealed in Scripture. Therefore, when I refer to humanists who call themselves Christian, I am referring to those who wrongly believe that man can achieve moral wholeness apart from *properly* acknowledging the *God of Scripture*.

The reader will note the prolific use of quotations from the many authors whose thinking I bring to bear in this discourse. Quotation is more effective at revealing the mind of an author than simply claiming that so-and-so believed this-or-that. For example, to state that Plato viewed human personality as a three-part entity consisting of the intellectual, the emotional and the volitional, is much less effective than reading his words which directly attribute that concept of human personality to him. Furthermore, it is frustrating to read secondhand knowledge of a historical personality who has shaped the course of either history or philosophical thought, and then find that the author either does not understand the person he represents or he is intentionally misrepresenting that figure to support his own view of reality. I have, therefore, extensively used quotations to prevent, or at least minimize, the likelihood of such error.

This work was not conceived as a means to financial gain. As a somewhat introspective scientist infinitely more comfortable in a laboratory researching the laws of nature than in any limelight of authorship, I began this work only after searching my own soul for a sense of higher purpose. Hopefully, however, the fruit of this work will not validate the shoddy advice given to Ernest, the would-be writer in Samuel Butler's *The Way of All Flesh*, in which Ernest is told

> that the very slender reward which God had attached to
> the pursuit of serious inquiry was a sufficient proof that
> He disapproved if it, or at any rate that He did not set
> much store by it nor wish to encourage it.[5]

A sufficient reward for me would be that this work benefit those who wish to better understand the processes that have shaped—and are shaping—modern Western culture and thereby become more committed to the cause of truth and goodness.

Introduction

In a letter to his father, a young but astute, C. S. Lewis wrote:
Take what point you will for the start of some new chapter in the mind and imagination of man, and you will invariably find that it has always begun a bit earlier: or rather, it branches so imperceptibly out of something else that you are forced to go back to the something else. The only satisfactory opening for any study is the first chapter of Genesis.[1]

And so it is with the study of humanism. In societies where the Hebrew God has been acknowledged as the one true God, the influence of humanism has alternated between periods of dominance and periods where its influence was diminished. Preceding the deluge of Noah's era, humanism abounded, but obviously thereafter abated. Invariably, in those short time periods where humanistic ideas are rendered less potent, over time they again rise to prominence. The dearth of spiritual truth in periods where humanism reigns, as in our modern post-Christian era, results in a quagmire of erroneous ideas. Subsequent to Noah's era, but well before Abraham's, humanism again emerged as a dominant force and its outcome is recorded in the Genesis account of the Tower of Babel.[2]

This book concerns the humanism that has cycled within the rise of Western culture. Generally, humanism is any system of thought that imparts a perception of reality inconsistent with the knowledge of the God revealed in Scripture. I have used the term *humanism* in the preceding paragraph according to this general definition. However, the present book identifies a humanism that is somewhat distinct to Western culture. Western humanism presupposes human personality to possess sovereign power over one's being. From that presupposition proceeds an erroneous perception of self-sufficiency where the belief prevails that one is enabled to move towards that which is good, or towards that which is truly moral, in the sole power of one's being. Therefore, in this work I show that those who hold to a humanistic view of reality put undue emphasis on the self-sufficiency of human personality.

The non-secular humanist acknowledges the existence of a moral good outside of human existence but falsely perceives that he can arrive at that good on the basis of his own terms or through the power of his own personality. In contrast, the secular humanism that often evolves out of non-secular humanism does not acknowledge a morality outside of human existence. Therefore, secular humanists view human personality as completely sovereign in the determination of the moral good. Ultimately, however, all humanists arrive at their concept of morality from within the structures of human personality.

The humanism (in this case a non-secular humanism) of which I am speaking is apparent in the following tribute rendered to a late accomplished macromolecular scientist. A corporate executive paying homage to the deceased, quoting from a well known Rabbi, stated that "any civilized society, if it is to survive and grow in a truly human dimension, must recognize: (1) the reality of purpose with the universe, (2) *the sovereignty of human personality* [italics added], and (3) the sanctity of method."[3] The rabbi's statement clearly reflects the humanistic mind-set to which I here refer. The humanist's perception of personality's sovereignty, however, is a misconstrued one. Human personality, as a created entity, is not of an absolute nature and, therefore, cannot be depended upon to move a person to the moral good.

Understanding the Western model of human personality is beneficial for understanding Western humanism. That model, based on three major distinctions within personality, is first encountered in the ancient Greek philosophers and is also observed in the modern works of Freud. Personality consists of the intellectual, the volitional and the emotional aspects. While Freud's teaching on human personality (discussed in Chapter 7) forms much of the basis for modern Western secular humanism, his concept of personality's structure is basically a traditionally Western one, essentially in line with this three-component model. His concept of the "id" closely parallels the emotional distinction of the conventional Western model. The id, or the emotional part of personality, provides a frame of reference for one's basic nature, since, as Freud taught, the id is the seat of the true psychic reality, i.e., the basic temperament of personality is realized in man's emotional nature. Likewise, the "heart" of man, often referred to in Scripture, has sometimes been identified as the "seat of the emotions."[4,5] Scripture seems to separate the designation of "heart" from the intellectual aspect of man.[6] Furthermore, one who possesses a severely abnormal personality is usually correctly referred to as an "emotionally disturbed" individual. Early Western humanists believed that the potential for human perfection and fulfillment would be realized when the intellect reigned over the emotive and volitional aspects of personality. However, as I show in Chapter 7, Nietzsche, perhaps the most influential of all the modern secular humanists, attempted to shift the controlling aspect of personality from the intellect to that of the will.

In Part One of this two-part work, a chronological (i.e., historical) framework is developed to trace the ideas that birthed the dichotomy between the Western humanistic view of human nature and a view compatible with Scripture. Since human personality is a manifestation of human nature, the differences between a genuine Christian view of reality and the Western humanistic view is centered in their respective teachings on human nature. The first two chapters of Part One are foundational because here I discuss how the ancient Greek ideas of ultimate reality[7] and human nature formed the first Western philosophy of the moral good. I show how these ideas of morality are incompatible with Hebrew Scripture, which forms the basis for Christian morality. Since Western humanism has its roots in the philosophies of ancient Greece, Chapter 1 begins with discussion of a selected few ancient Greek philosophers. Protagoras' declaration that "man is the measure of all things" began a philosophy whose proponents viewed human personality as a sovereign entity. Because one cannot meaningfully discuss Christianity without considering its Jewish heritage, in Chapter 2, I contrast the Hebrew basis of Christian morality with that of the ancient Greek philosophers.

Because this subject is somewhat philosophical in nature, this work is intended for a "thinking" audience, although I have not assumed that the reader will possess even basic levels of knowledge on the many subjects upon which I have touched. Much material will therefore be review to the educated reader. However, I weave that old information into a message that has not yet, to my knowledge, surfaced in the vast body of modern Christian literature. I have purposefully avoided erudite jargon and have sought to remain near the surface of the issues without trivializing them. The treatment, therefore, of philosophy is brief. For example, in the Chapter 1 discussion of the Presocratic philosophers, I do not go further than introducing them as pantheists. To some this brevity will be welcome, but other readers might wish to understand how most Presocratic ideas have the underpinnings of pantheism. The provided references can serve as a starting point for those desiring further understanding of the subjects that, in the reader's opinion, need more treatment. The problems facing an author wishing to appeal to a wide audience on a philosophical subject are many. If he structures the work to be best appreciated by a specialist in philosophy, he risks making the subject unpalatable to most readers. However, if philosophical subjects are ignored due to a misconstrued interpretation of the Apostle Paul's exhortation to the Colossian Christians,[8] little understanding of those subjects would ever be gained. It is with this dichotomy in mind that I discuss the philosophic origins of Western humanism while attempting to communicate to a wide audience. The danger here is in risking the alienation of all, although I think the more likely scenario is the alienation of those at the outer fringes of either pole. Since these are the ones least likely to be accommodated no matter what approach is used, I trust that I have chosen an appropriate strategy.

One further point should be noted regarding the Chapter 2 discussion of the relationship between Christianity and ancient Hebrew culture. Here I have taken all quotes of Hebrew Scripture only from Jewish authorized translations. I could have used Christian translations just as effectively, but to help preclude a perceived Christian bias when discussing text of Hebrew origin, I thought it useful to show (particularly to any non-Christian Jewish readers) that the best Jewish authorized translations render the same message as the best Christian versions. Specifically, I show how a noted and respected Jewish authorized translation overcomes the difficulties of a much inferior Jewish rendition of Genesis 3:15. This is a text that has important implications in Christian theology and, all readers should benefit from this discussion.

Because of the order of the first two chapters, readers should not lose sight of their chronological relationship. The strength of humanism has been cyclical in cultures where the Hebrew God has been acknowledged as the one true God. The days of Israel's greatest glory, i.e., the days of her closest communion with her God, were from an era before Greek humanism became dominant. Malachi, probably the last of the Hebrew prophets, lived about 400 B.C., a time roughly coinciding with that of the Greek Sophists. By then, the state of Israel's spiritual condition, evidenced by the content of Malachi's writing, was again in severe decline. Chronologically, the era of Abraham discussed in Chapter 2 preceded the rise of Greek humanism discussed in Chapter 1. This seeming inversion in chronology is with intent, because Judaism has its ultimate fulfillment in Christianity, and Christianity came on the Western scene subsequent to the philosophers discussed in Chapter 1. Therefore, in this light, the order is chronologically correct.

In Chapter 3, I examine how ancient Western humanistic views of human nature began to again infiltrate the early Western culture in which Christianity triumphed. Here I review Augustine's defense against Pelagius' attack on the scriptural view of human nature and that subject, of necessity, quickly turns to the subject of human volition, a difficult topic to address in Christian circles. The semantics associated with the subject amongst Protestants since the advent of Arminian and Wesleyan theologies have caused misunderstanding between Christians who hold opposing views on the subject. My intent in discussing this complex issue is not to fuel the debate between genuine Christian believers. I think that Christians can honestly disagree on this difficult subject when there is agreement on the basic nature of man, even though it will be apparent to the reader which view I think best fits with a proper understanding of that nature. And by the basic nature of man, I do not mean an academic agreement where there is intellectual assent to the reality of "original sin," but rather an agreement that creates an understanding of what that fallen nature implies. While C. S. Lewis' theology was remote from some of the more distinguishing aspects of Reformed theology, perhaps no other modern author has put forth a keener picture of fallen human nature than he. (I touch on this aspect of C. S. Lewis' thought in Chapters 7 and 10.) Mutual agreement on the scriptural characterization of the relationship between human nature and the nature of God, before and after the fall, usually leads to an underlying philosophical unity. When humanists disagree on the freedom of the will,[9] consistency is found in their views on the basic moral nature of man and that view always runs counter to a proper Christian view. The faulty philosophical basis of humanistic thinking lies in faulty views of human nature and, subsequently, in human personality, since personality is the manifestation of human nature. In the second part of Chapter 3, I briefly discuss the life and work of Thomas Aquinas. Here I show that Aquinas' philosophy, highly influenced by Greek philosophy, is an excellent example of one where an academic acknowledgment of "original sin" existed but where a truly scriptural view of human nature was lacking. It is my contention that much of the humanistic character of the Roman Catholic Church stems from Aquinas' influence.

The humanism of the Renaissance is discussed in Chapter 4. The term humanism originated from this era and, as such, it has a specific meaning separate from the general meaning in which it is commonly used today. However, I will show that Renaissance humanism is not totally divorced from the humanism with which this work is concerned. Although Renaissance humanism was framed in the Christianity of that era, many modern humanists, both those who have strong anti-Christian sentiments and those whose viewpoints might be regarded as nominally Christian, hold the Renaissance humanists in high regard, and in this chapter I show why this is so.

In Chapter 5, I discuss the Reformation and how the Reformer's views of human nature, particularly the aspect of volition, played a major role in its development. I present some of the intense debate regarding that subject between Erasmus, the noted Renaissance humanist, and Martin Luther, the Reformer who literally risked his life for what he knew to be scriptural truth. In light of that revolution, the Catholic Church retreated to the Scholasticism of Thomas Aquinas and essentially remains there to this day.

With the significant successes of the scientific method came the Enlightenment. The humanism of that era is discussed in Chapter 6. This was a humanism that was steeped in the belief of God's existence, but was one that nonetheless stood opposed to a scriptural view of ultimate reality. The Enlightenment served as a bridge to the secular humanism that I treat in Chapter 7. The ideas that I earlier identified with the Western designation of humanism are particularly apparent in the philosophers of the Enlightenment. In Enlightenment philosophy, particularly in the philosophy of Immanuel Kant, is evident the erroneous belief that one is enabled to move towards that which is good, or towards that which is truly moral, in the sole power of one's being.

I close Part One with a discussion of Darwin, Freud, Nietzsche and Marx, the four giants of modern Western secular humanism. Secular humanism is the ultimate end at which Western humanism aims. The desire to determine one's own criteria of morality through the power of one's being is ultimately a quest for independence from God. The foolish belief that God does not exist is the easiest way to free one's psyche from that reality. It is probably better, from a psychological point of view, to believe in no god than to believe in a god that is not real. In either case the beholder is deceived, but one can probably function better in the power of one's personality if he identifies with an atheistic point of view. For this reason secular humanism is growing exponentially in Western culture. These four stalwarts of Western secular humanism have been primarily responsible for instilling in Western man the false notion that he can meaningfully exist apart from God.

While in Part One, I occasionally touch upon modern examples of humanism to illuminate the subject at hand; it is in Part Two where I focus on some of the modern implications of Western humanism. In the first chapter of Part Two (Chapter 8), the focus is on two primary pursuits to which modern Western man has turned for emotional fulfillment. The first of these is his inordinate pursuit of wealth. In his best selling book, *The 7 Habits of Highly Effective People,*[10] I show how Steven Covey presents a humanistic approach to personal change. Secondly, I discuss the destructive effects of modern man's obsession with sexual fulfillment outside the confines of monogamous marriage.

In Chapter 9, I briefly review the effect of modern humanism on the family, society's most basic social entity. Here I discuss some characteristics of the love upon which successful families are built and how modern humanistic views of the sexes are negatively affecting the modern family. I also discuss the issue of abortion and show why the Pro-Life movement is not *always* about morality. Finally, in this chapter I contrast the Christian model of child rearing with the humanistic model that opposes it.

In Chapter 10, I look at humanism in modern religion, discussing why modern Judaism must be regarded as a humanistic system of morality, even though there is frequent agreement between conservative Christians and Jews on modern issues of morality. I also discuss why the issue of homosexuality in the liberal Christian organizations is a symptom of humanistic infiltration. While these liberal Christian denominations of Western culture have long been susceptible to humanistic influence, those influences are now making inroads into more conservative branches of Protestantism. I briefly review the new Open Theism, or Free Will Theism, which has in recent years come to the forefront, and I show why this thinking has a humanistic foundation.

I think that some non-Christian readers might ask about this work, "Is not this author's view of reality too black and white?" and say, "This author sees all reality regimented as either humanistic or Christian." To such a charge I might admit because there are only two basic roads that one can travel in life. There is a broad way, which includes all the ways that leads to separation from the true moral good, and there is a narrow way that leads to a truly moral existence. Jesus plainly stated that no one can come to God unless he comes through Him.[11] That is as black and white a statement as one can find. Jesus is the only door to life. If anyone is to live he must go through that door. There are many ways which *seem* right, but the end of those ways lead to spiritual death.[12] On the other hand, the Christian should realize from reading this work that since humanistic ideas have always attempted to penetrate a scripturally-based Christianity, the demarcation separating a scriptural Christianity from a Christianity that has been influenced by non-secular humanism is not always so black and white.

Without a genuine knowledge of the God of Scripture, humanism is the only option left to the thinking person. As such, humanistic influence always finds its way into any system that strays from an interpretation of reality that is *properly* framed in Scripture. A noted late humanistic American journalist wrote, "When men can no longer be theists, they must, if they are civilized, become humanists."[13] Given the fact that one can be a theist and still a humanist, a better rendering of this same thought might read, "When men refuse to come to a true knowledge of the God of Scripture, they must, if they are civilized, become humanists." As Western man becomes increasingly divorced from the God of Scripture, the prevalence of humanism is growing in like proportion. Let us now begin our study of Western humanism through a Christian perspective.

"There are only two kinds of people in the end: those who say to God, 'Thy will be done,' and those to whom God says, in the end, '*Thy* will be done.'"

C. S. Lewis in *The Great Divorce*

PART ONE

HISTORICAL

1

Historical Humanism: Ancient Greece—The Quest for an Understanding of Ultimate Reality

"Philosophy, like medicine, has plenty of drugs, few good remedies, and hardly any specific cures."
Sébastien-roch Nicolas de Chamfort (1741-94)

Although humanism is as old as humankind, the Western variety was birthed in the ancient Greek world. Ancient Greek humanism stands distinct from the pantheistic thought that preceded it. Greek philosophy is therefore an ideal place to begin an examination of the subject. From the ancient Greeks have come many ideas that, even today, influence Western societies. The Greek Sophists, who lived in the 5th century B.C., introduced secular humanistic ideas that grew out of the pantheism of the Presocratic philosophers. The modern definition of humanism quoted in the introduction, which emphasizes the rejection of the supernatural, aptly applies to the humanism of the Sophists.[1] However, the humanism of Socrates, Plato and Aristotle, the three giants of Greek philosophy who succeeded the Sophists, presupposed the existence of a supreme being. We will briefly examine the secular humanism of the Sophists and then go on to discuss the non-secular humanism of Socrates, Plato and Aristotle. But first, to better understand the conditions that led to Sophistic thinking, we will briefly consider a few aspects of Presocratic pantheism.

The Pantheism of the Presocratic Philosophers

The Greek interest in metaphysics originated in the 6th century B.C. with the Milesian philosopher Thales (ca. 624-546). Western philosophy is generally regarded as beginning with his ideas. Before Thales' era, Greek

ideas on origins and deity were rooted in mythology.[2] The irrational mytho-
logical ideas prevalent before his time yielded no true insight into a working
perception of reality. Thales and the Milesian philosophers who followed
him sought to develop a rational system of thought to comprehend metaphysical reality. Sometimes called the Ionian physicists, they began their
quest to know ultimate reality by attempting to better understand the mysteries of nature.

Thales is best known for his belief that water formed the basis of all
reality.[3] Considering modern scientific knowledge, it is difficult to understand the reasoning that led him to that conclusion. However, it admirably
indicates that he thought a correct perception of reality should consist of a
unifying cause. Understanding that cause, Thales likely perceived, would
lead to an understanding of ultimate reality. Thales' philosophy was therefore a pantheistic one. This deduction is further reinforced in a saying attributed to him by Aristotle. According to Aristotle, Thales believed that all
things were full of gods, and thus, he thought that "soul" was somehow
intermingled with the substance of the universe.[4] Thales' pantheism was
one that stood apart from earlier more simplistic ideas, which simply identified a particular element of nature, such as the sun or moon, with deity.
His pantheism was thus concerned with a hidden reality that he perceived
to be part of the phenomenological universe. Clearly, Thales' significance
lies not in the fact that he made significant contributions to the understanding of nature, but because he was the first Greek to systematically search
for a unifying theme that he thought might give insight into the true nature
of ultimate reality. After Thales, an increasingly sophisticated pantheism
arose in the ideas of his successors.

A more advanced pantheism appeared in the thinking of Anaximander,
Thales' pupil. One definition of pantheism that is particularly appropriate
to enlighten this assertion is from Flint. According to him, "Pantheism is
the theory which regards all finite things as merely aspects, modifications,
or parts of one eternal and self-existent being; which views all material objects, and all particular minds, as necessarily derived from a single infinite
substance."[5] The only actual words of Anaximander that survive are found
in a quote by Simplicius.[6] (Aristotle, however, refers to him on numerous
occasions.[7]) From these references most authors have concluded that
Anaximander believed in the existence of a primary substance which is often
described as boundless, infinite, eternal, unbegotten and indestructible (the
apeiron).[8] Anaximander's *apeiron* identifies with the infinite substance in
Flint's definition of pantheism, though the notion of a *single* infinite substance is not represented in his ideas.

The idea that ultimate reality existed as a single infinite entity appeared in the Eleatic school of thought, which followed that of the Milesians. The Eleatics are thus sometimes referred to as monists. Parmenides pioneered this movement in the 5th century B.C. In this thinking is an even more advanced pantheism than that of the Milesians. The Eleatic philosophers, as did the Milesians, exhibited a strong desire to understand ultimate reality. Parmenides, however, did not view ultimate reality as associated with any macroscopic substance; he viewed ultimate reality as the *ultimate one*. While no connection existed between a macroscopic material entity and Anaximander's *apeiron*, Anaximander did not think of ultimate reality in terms of a single infinite substance, as did Parmenides. Therefore, the ideas of Parmenides better identify with Flint's definition of pantheism than the ideas of Anaximander, although both philosophers held to a pantheistic view of reality. Both philosophers perceived that ultimate reality was contained within the cosmos. Neither philosopher perceived that ultimate reality was distinct from the nature of the macroscopic universe, i.e., they could not conceive of a transcendent God.

Parmenides likely got many of his ideas from Xenophanes, since according to Aristotle,[9] Xenophanes was Parmenides' teacher. Xenophanes' deity was clearly a pantheistic one. Aristotle said that Xenophanes concluded that the unity of the whole material universe was representative of god.[10] Xenophanes' god was, therefore, a cosmic god whose perceived oneness was derived from a diverse world functioning in harmony. One modern author concluded that Xenophanes' god was "unlike mortals in body or in mind" who "is all mind" and who is "supreme and abiding."[11] Xenophanes' god was not identified with any specific macroscopic substance of nature, but he did not divorce the perception of ultimate reality from his perception of the physical universe, i.e., the cosmos.

The Pluralists, who succeeded the Eleatic thinkers, rejected the monistic idea that a single entity existed to unify all reality. Democritus, perhaps the best known of the Pluralists, is usually regarded as the father of the physical sciences because he first had insight into the atomic nature of matter. (He also anticipated the laws of the conservation of energy.) However, his thinking was pantheistic in character, despite his adherence to a rather advanced theory of matter, since he apparently associated the air with deity.[12] It is evident that Democritus, like those Presocratic philosophers preceding him, was not cognizant of a transcendent supreme being.

To help one understand how secular humanistic ideas were ripe for emergence in this atmosphere of pantheistic metaphysical ideas, one should be aware of the Presocratic quest to understand the ethics behind what we today refer to as natural law. In their search for ultimate reality, the Presocratic thinkers did not separate their desire to understand the phenomenological world from their desire to understand human nature and its relationship to ultimate reality. The Presocratic philosophers believed that ultimate reality, the ultimate source of all truth, was contained in the phenomenological, even though the senses could not perceive it. The goal of the Presocratic philosophers was hence to understand ultimate reality by gaining an understanding of the phenomenological world. Therefore, the Presocratic drive for the discovery of truth included in it a desire to understand the basis of the phenomenon that we today refer to as natural law. This desire to understand the basis of moral knowledge is apparent in the writings of both Xenophanes and Democritus. Xenophanes spoke against "luxury, effeminacy, and drunkenness" and especially against corrupt views of god.[13] Sources also credit Democritus with many statements that demonstrate his desire to understand the underlying force behind natural law. Therefore, Democritus' writings deal more with ethics than they do with his more popular ideas on the nature of matter. Statements attributed to him, such as "repentance for shameful deeds is salvation in life" and "the man completely enslaved to wealth can never be honest"[14] indicate that he had a strong interest in discovering a philosophical basis for natural law and moral conduct.

It was the Presocratic inability to establish a consistent philosophical basis of ethics that gave much impetus to the development of the early Western humanistic systems of thought. The problematic philosophical position of pantheism and this system's inability to provide an understanding of the natural system of ethics based on human conscience, gave birth to the secular humanism of the Sophists which evolved into the non-secular humanism of Socrates, Plato and Aristotle.

The Presocratic thinkers, beginning with Thales, were revolutionary in their thinking that it might be possible to understand the phenomenological world through the reasoning processes of the intellect. For this reason some authors attribute the beginning of scientific endeavor to the Presocratic philosophers. These ancient philosophers thought that a yet to be understood ultimate reality existed, although it was not perceived by the senses. They believed that understanding the phenomenological world would lead them to an understanding of this sought after ultimate reality. Moreover, their quest for knowledge included the search for a philosophical basis of the natural ethics of human conscience. Unfortunately, their thinking was faulty because they presumed that the essence of ultimate reality could be found within the substance of nature. The Presocratics could not grasp knowledge of ultimate reality through their attempt to acquire knowledge of the macroscopic world. While knowledge of natural principles is attained through study of the phenomenological, knowledge of ultimate reality is not attained in that manner. And if knowledge of the phenomenological is not sufficient to produce an understanding of ultimate reality it certainly cannot produce an understanding of moral truth which lies in the realm of ultimate reality. One ascertains the phenomenological world by the tools of observation and, therefore, one can use scientific methodology to gain its understanding. However, since one can never gain a sufficient knowledge of ultimate reality by observation of any natural phenomenon, one cannot use the methods of science in pursuit of that knowledge.

Sophistic vs. Socratic Humanism

With the preceding abbreviated introduction into some of the pantheistic aspects of Presocratic thought, we will now briefly consider the Sophists who came on the scene in the mid-5th century B.C. The Sophists were traveling teachers of "wisdom" who instructed their students in worldly ways, often for a fee only affordable by the more affluent members of society. Our modern word *sophisticated* is derived from their influence. The Sophist's teachings marked the beginning of a distinct secular humanistic philosophy in the ancient Greek world.

The two best-known Sophists were Protagoras and Gorgias. Protagoras is best remembered for his conclusion that "man is the measure of all things." Although formulated nearly 2500 years ago, this adage represents a foundational thought of even modern secular humanism. Protagoras' maxim was likely a response to the confusion and contradictions contained in the ideas of the Presocratic philosophers. Protagoras said of the gods, "I am unable to discover whether they exist or not, or what they are like in form."[15] Protagoras challenged the belief in an existence of a reality not perceived by the senses. The Sophists only had interest in what they could literally experience and observe. To them, sensory experience was the sole criteria for the determination of reality. Truth, for the Sophist, was relative to the situation he found himself in. What appeared as real to one person was truth for that person but what appeared as real to another was likewise truth for him. Absolutes, outside humanity, in the thinking of the Sophists did not exist because they considered man to be the standard by which all things were judged. Protagoras taught that all that mattered in life was how to take care of "one's own affairs and the business of the state."[16] In the minds of the Sophists all reality was contained in human experience. Gorgias claimed that a metaphysical ultimate reality simply did not exist. Anything beyond human perception was only a figment of one's imagination. He believed that the ideas of the Presocratic thinkers only led to argument since each thought he had the secrets to the meaning of the universe. Such arguments, thought Gorgias, proved that these ideas were only opinions.[17] The Sophists sought to give the art of debate preeminence, since for them truth was relative. If both sides of an argument had the potential to be equally true, then the one most skillful in persuasion was the one who possessed the correct view of reality. Consequently, the Sophists made the art of rhetoric a primary focus of education. For the Sophists, one could know nothing with absolute certainty. To them, only that which one could perceive with the five senses was real.

In one sense, the Sophistic refusal to acknowledge the existence of a reality apart from the reality perceivable by the senses is understandable. Presocratic thinking had attempted to place *ultimate reality* into the realm of the phenomenological. This perception had made it difficult for realization of truth within that realm. Science would be a chaotic endeavor if forced to operate within a pantheistic system. Nature under such circumstances would likely be whimsical, and it appears that the Sophists had an intuitive understanding of this.

Nevertheless, failure of the Sophists to acknowledge the existence of absolute knowledge brought significant philosophical problems for them as pointed out by Plato. Plato (using the voice of Socrates in dialogue with Protagoras) argued that if truth were relative to a given situation, or if it were only one man's opinion, then for one to have the opinion that truth is absolute would negate any possibility that truth could be relative.[18]

The lack of an absolute basis for moral knowledge in the ancient Greek world resulted in debate between the upholders of *nomos* and the upholders of *physis*.[19,20] *Nomos* represented, in a general sense, thinking which taught that human behavioral standards existed by culture and convention whereas *physis* taught that those standards existed only by nature. The ideas of *nomos* included concepts of both natural and positive law. Natural law is that which is based on an ethic derived solely from human conscience, while positive law is the societal reduction to practice of any law, no matter what its basis. Protagoras held to the principles of *nomos* because he correctly believed that positive law was necessary for a society to properly function.[21] Protagoras did not, however, view law as a God-given institution. Humanists, in the vein of Protagoras, have usually viewed positive law as purely a human institution whose design is solely for a human engineered control of society. Those who held to the *physis* position taught that humanity should live in a natural environment, uninhibited by positive human law. The upholders of *physis* contended that *nomos* was only a means for preventing rule by the strong in the interest of the weak. The distinction between *physis* and *nomos* can be confusing because both systems implicitly acknowledged the value of human conscience as a moral guidance system. Therefore, some proponents of *physis* maintained that "unwritten law" (i.e., natural law) must play a role in human ethics. But most of those holding to the ideas of *physis,* preferred to do away with any positive law or any human imposed restraint, because such restraint, in their minds, had no rational basis. For them, the foundation of positive human-made law was derived from the arbitrariness of the lawmakers. The better system, according to those who held to the *physis* position, was one controlled by a philosophy where nature ruled, one where might made right.

Socrates sought to bring a standard for morality into this sea of relativity. Like the Sophists contemporary with him, he was interested in understanding human nature instead of nature in general. In that sense, one can identify his thinking with the thought processes of the Sophists. But because he believed in the existence of a true ethical good that one could pursue and henceforth attain to, his thought remained distinct from the Sophists. Socrates' well known proclamation that the *"unexamined life is not worth living"* was one with ethical intent. In contrast to Socrates, the Sophists maintained that the only criterion of "the good" was that which would lead to a perceived better life for the one perceiving. Socrates, however, viewed "the good" as a real objective entity that one could attain through rational pursuit. He defined this true "good" as *areté,* commonly referred to as virtue. [22] Since *areté* could be taught, according to Socrates, "the good" was attainable through the acquisition of knowledge and the proper processing of that knowledge through the exercise of the intellect.

Socrates' belief in the existence of a true moral good was a revolutionary concept to the Greek mind of that era. Sophistic ideas of "the good" had been centered entirely in the relativity of the individual. Under the Sophistic system that had acknowledged no absolutes, the political rulers essentially established the norms by which societies and individuals functioned. Standards for human behavior were made according to the dictates of the rule maker's own interests. The driving force behind lawmaking was whatever would seemingly promote "the good life" according to the dictates of the lawmakers. In this system "man was the measure" and, as such, it was one thoroughly built on the assumption of the sovereignty of human personality.

However, the thinking of the Sophists gave preference to the volitional aspect of human personality. As I stated in the introduction, in its natural state, the human psyche exists primarily in the emotional part of human personality. One's natural sense of well-being—or lack thereof—is found in one's natural emotional make-up. The driving force to attain the "good life" in the Sophist's system was centered in the quest to achieve that sense of well-being. In man's basest state, a volitionally controlled drive, often, and usually more often than not, exerts more control over one's emotional sense of well-being than does the intellect.

The philosophy of Socrates was unique in that it forced a shift away from the volitional aspect of human personality to the rational aspect. This new emphasis created the Greek search for meaning in life, the universe, and the consideration that a supreme intelligence could be responsible for the workings of human conscience. Furthermore, that emphasis pointed to an absolute morality. Socrates' failure, however, to successfully delineate the ultimate source of that absolute good was likely why the Sophists held to a philosophy of relativism. Socrates' insistence on the existence of the moral absolute, even though he could not ultimately define its source, better approximated reality. As such, his influence on Western thought is historically greater than that of the Sophists. However, as we will see in Chapter 7, Sophistic ideas are again coming into prominence with the increasing influence of secular humanism in modern Western culture.[23]

The Humanism of Plato and Aristotle

Greek philosophy progressed from Socrates to Plato and, then, to Aristotle. Plato, born in about 428 B.C., was a student of Socrates and what we know of Socrates comes mainly from him. Socrates was approximately forty years Plato's senior. When contrasting Greek humanism against a view of reality that is framed in the truth of Scripture, the important elements to consider are those that bear on the criteria by which the standard for morality is established. The emphasis that Socrates had placed on the power of the human intellect to decipher the moral good was continued and advanced in the works of both Plato and Aristotle. Their notion of morality stemmed directly from their belief in reason's power to enable moral living.

In his *Republic*, Plato first established a communal moral standard that was based on each citizen honorably carrying out his occupation, whatever that occupation might be. He then inferred from this communal standard a similar standard for individual morality. Plato wrote:

> Where each of the constituent parts of an individual does its own job, the individual will be moral and will do *his* own job. ... Since the rational part is wise and looks out for the whole of the mind, isn't it right for it to rule, and for the passionate part to be its subordinate and its ally? ... Isn't it the combination of culture and exercise which will make them attuned to each other? The two combined provide fine discussions and studies to stretch

> and educate the rational part, and music and rhythm to relax, calm, and soothe the passionate part. ... And once these two parts have received this education and have been trained and conditioned in their true work, then they are to be put in charge of the desirous part, which is the major constituent of an individual's mind and is naturally insatiably greedy for things.[24]

That Plato here presented the three major elements of human personality (intellect, will and emotion) with the intellect as the controller of one's moral destiny should be obvious to the reader. And herein is the model that controlled Western humanism until secular humanism began to re-exert its influence in the 19th century A.D.[25] Western humanism has traditionally attempted to establish the intellectual aspect of human personality (usually in conjunction with natural law) as the primary source for the enablement of moral living.

> In characterizing the moral man, Plato described him as one who could have nothing to do with temple-robbery,[26] theft, and betrayal either of his personal friends or, on a public scale, of his country ... Moreover, nothing could induce him to break an oath or any other kind of agreement. ... And he's the last person you'd expect to find committing adultery, neglecting his parents, and failing to worship the gods.[27]

Plato then explained how such a perception of morality was derived. He wrote, "The reason for all of this [is] the fact that each of his constituent parts [i.e., the elements of his personality] does its own job as ruler or subject."[28] Plato here implied that while the human will drives the immoral one towards his immoral acts, the moral person is one who uses knowledge and reason to control those drives. Therefore, the Socratic teaching that one could acquire virtue through the acquisition of knowledge and proper use of the intellect was further developed in Plato's thought. In Plato's system the standard for moral living was further distilled to the belief that the rational aspect of human personality could sovereignly reign over human nature and, through that sovereignty, enable moral living.

Whenever the standard for morality is placed in the functioning of human personality, it becomes dependent on the perspective of the perceiver. To Plato's credit, he understood the difficulty of basing morality and ethics on such relative criteria. He therefore hinted in his "Theory of Forms" that morality must ultimately come from outside the individual. In that theory Plato attempted to tie the idea of a supreme value to his system of ethics.[29] But ultimately Plato was forced back into the system where virtue was yet attained through the acquisition of knowledge using the rational capabilities of human personality. In the *Republic*, (using the voice of Socrates) Plato stated:

> So the summit of the intelligible realm is reached when, by means of dialectic and without relying on anything perceptible, a person perseveres in using rational argument to approach the true reality of things until he has grasped with his intellect the reality of goodness itself.[30]

Thus Plato's system of ethics was yet a relative function of the human intellect. For example, in the *Republic*, he readily justified the use of falsehood (lying) when a situation called for it. In his noted dialogue fashion, Plato stated:

> If it's anyone's job, [lying] then, it's the job of the rulers of our community: they can lie for the good of the community, when either an external or an internal threat makes it necessary. No one else, however, should have anything to do with lying. If an ordinary person lies to these rulers of ours, we'll count that as equivalent in misguidedness, if not worse, to a patient lying to his doctor about his physical condition, or an athlete in training lying to his trainer about his physical condition, or someone misleading a ship's captain, with respect to his ship or crew, by telling him lies about his own state or that of one of his fellow crewmen.[31]

Based on this ethic any statesman could justify his lies with little regard to truthfulness. The actions of Germany's Hitler and even the actions that led to the modern-day political dilemma of American President William Clinton[32] might, by some, be justified using Plato's system of ethics. Whenever the basis of morality is placed into the functioning of the human intellect, it will always remain a relative proposition.

Plato's most famous student was Aristotle, born in 384 B.C., about 15 years after the death of Socrates. Plato was about 44 years the senior of Aristotle. A cohesive succession of ideas over a short period of time is therefore apparent in the thinking of Socrates, Plato and Aristotle.[33] Most of Aristotle's surviving works are more in the form of lecture notes than formal discourse. As such, his writings sometimes appear disorganized and sporadic although they fairly well reveal his thinking in moral philosophy. One work that is of interest to this discussion is his *Nicomachean Ethics*, so named for his son Nicomachus. Here Aristotle further illuminates for us what is meant by the Greek idea of *areté*, i.e., virtue or moral excellence, which he refers to as "the good."

In the tradition of Plato, Aristotle emphasized that "the good" has as its ultimate goal the good of the state and less so that of the individual. Aristotle wrote:

> For even though it be the case that the good is the same for the individual and for the state, nevertheless, the good of the state is manifestly a greater and more perfect good, both to attain and to preserve. To secure the good of one person only is better than nothing; but to secure the good of a nation or a state is a nobler and more divine achievement.[34]

In Greek humanism morality is first concerned with society. Only after the consideration of state morality is individual morality addressed.[35]

Aristotle laid the foundation for a fundamental presupposition of Western humanism when he purported that man has a natural inclination to the true good. As we will see in Chapter 3, during the Middle Ages the idea that man has a natural inclination to know the one and only true God became a central theme in pre-Reformation Christian thought. Thomas Aquinas, who was highly influenced by the writings of Aristotle, introduced this idea into the pre-Reformation Christian Church. While man may possess a natural inclination to 'the good' as Aristotle defined it, the one and only true God, the truly Supreme Good, (discussed in the next chapter) is not the 'true good' defined by Aristotle. The good that Aristotle defined was solely in the functioning of human personality.

Aristotle stated that "Every art and every investigation, and likewise every practical pursuit or undertaking, seems to aim at some good: hence it has been well said that the good is that at which all things aim." Aristotle proposed to give his reader knowledge of the "Supreme Good" because that knowledge will be of "great practical importance for the conduct of life."[36] According to Aristotle, happiness is the highest good that action can achieve, and the "good life" or "doing well" is equated with happiness. Aristotle acknowledged the difficulty with this definition since on the surface, happiness is, as most people view it, a relative proposition. The poor man would likely view wealth as happiness and the sick man might regard health as happiness. Aristotle therefore, defined happiness in terms "of the function of man." Man's function, according to Aristotle was realized through his rational faculties. Aristotle wrote:

> If then the function of man is the active exercise of the soul's faculties in conformity with rational principle ... and if we acknowledge the function of an individual and of a good individual of the same class (for instance, a harper and a good harper, and so generally with all classes)

to be generically the same, the qualification of the latter's superiority in excellence being added to the function in his case (I mean that if the function of a harper is to play the harp, that of a good harper is to play the harp well): if this is so, and if we declare that the function of man is a certain form of life, and define that form of life as the exercise of the soul's faculties and activities in association with rational principle, and say that the function of a good man is to perform these activities well and rightly, and if a function is well performed when it is performed in accordance with its own proper excellence—from these premises it follows that the Good of man is the active exercise of his soul's faculties in conformity with excellence or virtue.[37]

Aristotle equated happiness with "the good" which came only to those who used their rational faculties in such a way to conform to virtue. Aristotle taught that all men sought happiness, i.e., the good, and such happiness would come to only those who used their reason in such a way that would lead to virtuous living. From that process, Aristotle believed that moral virtue would be instilled into one's character as a product of habit. He stated, "The virtues therefore are engendered in us neither by nature nor yet in violation of nature; nature gives us the capacity to receive them, and this capacity is brought to maturity by habit."[38] According to Aristotle, a person's actions, when established by habit in accordance with his rational faculties, enabled him to acquire the goal of moral excellence or moral virtue. Aristotle stated, "We become just by doing just acts, temperate by doing temperate acts, brave by doing brave acts."[39] He further stated in this regard that "this truth is attested by the experience of states: lawgivers make the citizens good by training them in habits of right action—this is the aim of all legislation."[40]

Aristotle's identification of the ultimate good with moral excellence, as we will see in Chapter 2, is not inconsistent *per se* with a Christian interpretation of reality. The philosophical problem for the Christian should come first from Aristotle's definition of the ultimate good and secondly from his belief that one can by his own action move himself into a moral condition. Equating ultimate good with happiness necessitates the ultimate source of good to lie within the functioning of human personality. Happiness is closely linked to the emotional part of personality. There is certainly a natural tendency in man to seek emotional contentment; and, further, there is likewise a natural tendency to associate emotional contentment with happiness. However, to assert from those observations that man by nature seeks the true

Good is problematic. As discussed in the next chapter, the ultimate source of moral excellence does not lie in any aspect of human nature, but it lies in the knowledge of *the ultimate Good* by which all things were created.

Aristotle's concept of virtue or moral excellence stood distinct from that of the Sophists. The Sophists, as all men do, primarily sought the good life through their striving for emotional contentment. But in the Sophistic system essentially any means justified that end. With Socrates, Plato and Aristotle, the means had to pass through the gate of reason. They taught that the true good could only be arrived at through that gate. According to Aristotle, the rational part of personality should exert control over the emotional part by governing one's actions so that the effect of those actions on the emotions was balanced between pleasure and pain. All human behavior had to be judged by the effect which those behaviors produced on that balance. Therefore, Aristotle taught that "pleasures and pains are the things with which moral virtue is concerned." [41] He wrote "We assume therefore that moral virtue is the quality of acting in the best way in relation to pleasures and pains, and that vice is the opposite." [42] Aristotle stated that "pleasure causes us to do base actions and pain causes us to abstain from doing noble actions." [43] For example, in regards to the virtue of courage, Aristotle wrote that a man "is brave if he faces danger with pleasure or at all events without pain, cowardly if he does so with pain." [44] So the intellect, according to Aristotle's system of ethics, had to do its job by finding the mean between excessive pleasure, which for the virtue of courage would yield foolish carelessness, and that of excessive pain, which would yield uncontrollable fear. The mean between these two extremes is what would eventually bring to one a state of true happiness.

However, the morality of an action or thought cannot be identified with its effect on one's apparent sense of well-being. The executive who diverts money to himself from an employee retirement fund because of some loophole in the law may find a sense of contentment and consider himself happy, having reasoned through a seared conscience, that no immoral action was involved. To assign the intellect the role of judge, based on its ability to produce a balance between pleasure and pain, is to assign the absolute standard of morality to the functioning of human personality. Moral virtue, however, must be based on moral absolutes that lie outside of one's person.

In summary, Aristotle believed that a proper functioning intellect would identify the virtuous, and that would enable the will to act properly. Personality would then be perfected through a process of habit, which would lead to a state of emotional contentment—the true good of happiness. Moreover, one should note that the ethical philosophies of Plato and Aristotle differed from the Sophists in mainly the element of human personality that elicited proper action. However, human reason and conscience cannot serve as an absolute standard for determination of good. Often what reason deciphers as good is not the true moral good but is only that which appears as good because of false input from one's emotional state. Therefore, human reason is subject to error and cannot effectively serve as a sovereign absolute in the determination of proper human action. Ultimately, in Aristotle's system of ethics the standard for moral living was yet a relative proposition based on the working of the rational part of human personality and human conscience.

The Greek Understanding of Human Nature

The Greek philosophers struggled with new ideas of deity, morality, physical nature and human nature and how the knowledge concerning them all should come together to form a coherent view of reality. The Presocratic thinkers emphasized physical nature and attempted to find ultimate reality within the confines of the universe. The Sophists realized the futility of this and did away with any attempt to arrive at absolute truth. Socrates believed, as did the Sophists, that to seek absolute knowledge as it related to physical nature was futile. But Socrates insisted on the certainty of knowledge in human nature. Furthermore, it appears that Socrates introduced into the Greek consciousness the idea of a supreme transcendent deity. The Greek interest was in human nature, the Sophists in a purely secular sense and Socrates, Plato and Aristotle in a sense that *attempted* to include a concept of absolute moral truth.

Anyone forced to behave according to a prescribed set of rules has likely internally questioned the reasoning behind those rules. The Greeks sought to discover the source of authority for laws imposed on society. The concept of law is closely associated with human nature, i.e., human behavior, human conscience, morality, and the exertion of external will on one's personal will. Ordered societies have always used law as an integral tool to control human behavior. The law code of the ancient Amorite King Hammurabi (ca. 1750 B.C.), discovered in the early 20th century, reveals man's early use of law to that effect. That code dealt with regulating commerce, the family, and other social institutions. One such law from the Hammurabi code reads, "If a builder has built a house for a man, and has not made his work sound, and the house he built has fallen, and caused the death of its owner, that builder shall be put to death."[45] That law, if Hammurabi enforced it, would have certainly had a significant bearing on the behavior of the ancient house builder. But as we shall see in the next chapter, the ultimate need of human existence is a change in human nature. Law can only be used in an attempt to *control* human behavior; its use cannot *change* human nature.

In considering the relationship of law to the control of human behavior, the Greek Sophists held two opposing ideas. The proponents of *nomos* believed that the final authority for defining behavioral standards for society was centered solely in human political power. But the ideas of *nomos* were inadequate for satisfying man's innate desire to understand the purpose of law. Altering one's behavior solely because a body of rulers perceives it as deficient is contrary to human nature. The behavioral standards that a ruling elite might whimsically perceive as ideal are powerless to change the nature of those it seeks to influence. This is especially so if the ones on whom the legislative system imposes its authority perceive that the personal interests of the ruling elite are primarily at heart. In the ideas of *nomos*, behavioral standards came from only the perspective of those who ruled. A perceived better life for primarily themselves was ultimately, apart from the restraints of conscience, their only basis for determination of "right" behavior.

This relativity, keenly perceived by the Greek mind, is readily observed in the aforementioned ancient Hammurabi code. Under that code if one of noble birth lost an eye because of an assault, the offender was punished with loss of an eye, but if the same misfortune happened to a commoner, the penalty was only "one mina of silver."[46] It is not surprising that this relativity, on which the system of *nomos* was ultimately based, would give rise to the *physis* position.

But if ideas of *nomos* were based on an improper understanding of human nature, those of *physis* were even more faulty. At first glance the ideas of *physis* might appear absurd. However, most Greek thinkers of this era believed that life originated from a warm organic slime,[47] a belief not far removed from that found in modern evolutionary thought. As such, one might suspect that societal order without the institution of law would be no different from that observed in primates who bear some resemblance to the human species. Chimpanzees, for example, obviously do not subscribe to any formally coded system of law; yet, they maintain a societal-like order through mutual respect of the physically strong. Pure physical strength shapes behavior in many biological spheres. However, to infer from such an observation that this approach would be a workable system within the human sphere is simply not to understand human nature. In the human sphere, evil is a reality (as is a true good), and the ideas of *physis* allowed no room for the reality of humanity's moral predicament. Chaotic existence, or at least a substandard civilization, would be the result of a human society without the benefit of some type of legal system based on a principle other than brute force. The idea of natural law did find a place amongst some of the uphold-ers of *physis*. The human conscience holds powerful sway as a natural moral guidance system. Guthrie tells us that Antisthenes, a pupil of Gorgias and an upholder of *physis*, stated that "the wise man in his activity as a citizen will be guided not by the established laws but by the law of *areté*."[48]

With their faulty world-views the Sophists, therefore, did not advance knowledge of either physical nature or human nature. If anything, their refusal to acknowledge any absolute knowledge probably hindered further development of the scientific method of inquiry initiated by the Milesian philosophers and Democritus. Science must operate within a high degree of certainty as it attempts to decipher the physical universe and Sophistic phi-losophy denied that necessary certainty.

Socrates' affirmation of the certainty of knowledge in the area of ethics and morality was a noble one, but he falsely assumed that through the pro-cesses of human reason one could obtain sufficient knowledge of moral truth to affect a change in human nature. His well-touted proclamation to "know thyself" suggests he believed that self-knowledge could effectively change the moral deficiencies that are grounded in human nature. We address the origin of these deficiencies in the next chapter. Socrates essentially taught that ignorance was synonymous with evil and that one could gain virtuous character (*areté*) through self-knowledge. However, as Johnson[49] has recently documented, it is certain that educational level does not effectively bear on one's level of ethical and moral behavior. While knowledge of one's moral deficiencies may be an important first step in coming to terms with ulti-mate reality, knowledge alone cannot alleviate or atone for those deficien-cies.

Socrates laid the groundwork for the ideas of both Plato and Aristotle. Although these philosophers attempted to introduce moral absolutes into their systems of thought, their thinking was yet based in the relativity of human personality. As pointed out by Allen,[50] when Plato and Aristotle referred to morality they brought this subject under the heading of "the good" and not "the right." They did not speak of "the obligations that men are under" but rather of "the ends they seek." This is an important consider-ation that must be kept in mind when referring to any humanistic system of morality. Humanistic morality is always centered in the relativity of the perception of good. It is never centered in an absolute concept of good. In their quest to understand human nature, the major Greek philosophers be-lieved that morality could be deciphered through the rational part of hu-man personality. Western humanism, be it secular or not, is based on the assumption that human personality has within its power the ability to move human nature to "the good" or to moral perfection. That belief is one of the most basic tenets of Western humanism and the implications of this thinking are always present wherever the influence of Western humanistic philosophy is observed. However, because "the good" is often misinterpreted by the emotional nature of personality, reason cannot be relied on as a guide for its establishment. Often what one's emotional nature impresses upon the intellect as "the good" is not the true good.

As we will see in the next chapter, human moral deficiencies are rooted in the very essence of human nature. Just as the laws of physical nature prevent any single human being from physically pushing a 100,000-pound block of steel across a concrete floor (due to the laws of friction and gravity), the laws of human nature, which we address in the next chapter, prevent any man from moving himself, solely within the power of his own being, towards the true moral good. As long as the laws of gravity and friction are in effect, the steel block will remain stationary no matter how strong the pusher's will is to move it (of course, under conditions of lessened gravity and—or—friction one could conceivably move that same steel mass across that same concrete floor.) In the same way, human nature (or human personality), because of its very nature, is powerless, contrary to what the Greek philosophers taught, to address its own moral dilemma. In the next chapter we discuss how human nature *can be* changed making movement to the true moral good a true possibility.

It is interesting that Aristotle acknowledged, somewhat correctly, the moral predicament of human nature. Aristotle wrote in his *Politics*:

> For as man is the best of the animals when perfected, so
> he is the worst of all when sundered from law and
> justice. … Hence when devoid of virtue man is the most
> unscrupulous and savage of animals, and the worst in
> regard to sexual indulgence and gluttony.[51]

But, as shown in the previous section, Aristotle taught that human nature was initially neutral towards good or evil. Human nature in his view had equal capacity for good or bad and it was entirely up to the individual on what the eventual outcome would be. Aristotle stated in regards to this that

> virtues and vices are not capacities; since we are not pronounced good or bad, praised or blamed, merely by reason of our capacity for emotion. Again, we possess certain capacities by nature, but we are not born good or bad by nature.[52]

This statement is in line with his previous quote where he stated that virtue is "engendered in us neither by nature nor yet in violation of nature." (See ref. 38.) According to Aristotle man is born morally neutral and his moral condition will depend on how he uses his reason to direct his will. In the philosophy of Aristotle, man's will was totally free to be moved in whatever direction the intellect so chose. This conclusion is quite obvious in the following words of Aristotle:

> If then whereas we wish for our end, the means to our end are matters of deliberation and choice, it follows that actions dealing with these means are done by choice, and voluntary. But the activities in which the virtues are exercised deal with means. Therefore virtue also depends on ourselves. And so also does vice. For where we are free to act we are also free to refrain from acting ... But if it is in our power to do and to refrain from doing right and wrong, and if, as we saw, being good or bad is doing right or wrong, it consequently depends on us whether we are virtuous or vicious.[53]

According to Aristotle, man was born morally neutral, but possessed solely within the power of his nature, i.e., his personality, the ability to choose whether or not he would be virtuous or vicious. Aristotle believed that man possessed a natural inclination to the true good, a thought that was carried over into the Scholastic theology of Thomas Aquinas (discussed in Chapter 3).

In early Greek humanism one observes some basic principles that remain present even in modern-day humanism. A morality that is based on a drive to acquire "the good" through the dynamics of human personality is commonly observed in humanistic philosophy. Such thinking always translates into a belief that human personality enables one to first understand what the moral good is and, from that understanding, to freely choose that good. According to a humanistic view, movement to the moral good occurs if either the intellect or, as we shall see in Chapter 7, the will, does its job as ruler. Therefore, the elevation of education as a principal means to moral betterment is a foundational principle of humanism. It is these basic principles, stemming from incorrect perceptions of human nature, that we will examine as we continue to contrast a humanistic view of reality with one that is based on principles found in Scripture.

2

Historical Christianity: Ancient Israel

In this chapter we contrast the root ideas of the Western humanism presented in the last chapter with those that form the foundation of Christianity. Orthodox Christians have always acknowledged the Hebrew Scriptures as authoritative; therefore, Christian doctrine has its beginning in those writings. Ultimate reality *is* the God revealed to Abraham, Isaac and Jacob. No better terminology exists to describe ultimate reality than EHEYE ("I AM").[1] This name embodies the absoluteness of God's entity. In the Hebrew Scripture we read that the "I AM" brought the universe into existence by the power of his word. As creator, God is separate from and superior to His creation. Just as Rembrandt is not contained within his paintings, his creations, God is not contained within nature, His creation.[2] God's character and personality are distinct from the nature of His creation. To convey this attribute, we refer to the Hebrew God as transcendent in being. God's transcendency precludes any pantheistic description of Him. While Rembrandt's art may speak of his personality and reveal knowledge of his penetrating intelligence into the human spirit, one cannot know Rembrandt, in the truest sense, from simple observation of, or even the study of, his artistic creation. The same is true of the Hebrew God Jehovah. Ultimately, modern man can only know the Hebrew God through the revelation of Scripture, for reasons discussed later in this chapter. Christianity rests upon the presupposition that the words of Scripture were born of supernatural inspiration and that they alone reveal the nature of the one and only true God.

Modern humanists, of course, reject Scripture as an *absolute* source of truth. This rejection proceeds mainly from the ideas of the Enlightenment (discussed in Chapter 6) where the methods of science became the only criteria for determining reality. Certainly, the complete truth of Scripture cannot be proved according to scientific dictates. The human nature with which Scripture deals is not of the same essence as its habitat (i.e., the physical universe). The creation of man in the image of God has resulted in a spiritual dimension to human nature that renders it elusive to pure scientific scrutiny. The physical sciences deal with reproducible and, therefore, predictable events based on the laws of mathematics which, for example, can predict with pinpoint accuracy the conditions required for a spaceship to travel from the earth to its moon and back. In contrast, the social sciences cannot truly account for the actions of a Jeffery Dahmer,[3] nor could any prior scrutiny of the conditions of his environment have predicted the outcome of his life. The social sciences, therefore, operate with little certainty. They can only attempt an explanation after the facts are revealed. Furthermore, apart from the elusive spiritual nature of man, modern Western man is so rapidly regressing to a secular Sophistic type humanism, where image takes precedence over reality, that the social sciences are even further hampered. Science relies on observation to gather data. But since modern man is a master at disguising his true inner self, the social sciences are even further crippled in their ability to decipher working models of human behavior. Thus the social sciences operate at a different level from the physical sciences. The Scriptures—as a supernaturally inspired record—render a more complete knowledge of human nature than do the social sciences.

While secular humanists usually claim Scripture to be a collection of cultural stories and myths, non-secular humanists often assume Scripture insufficient for knowledge of ultimate reality. Many of these view Scripture as only a supplemental source to human reason. While the non-secular humanist might admit to truth being *contained* within Scripture, he will usually discard the accountings in Scripture that have no scientific explanation. Of course, if only certain aspects of Scripture were true, they would be rendered unreliable at any point to which they speak. Hopefully as the reader progresses through this work he will realize that the basis for a conviction of Scripture's truth is rooted on firmer ground than presupposition. Ultimately Scripture's truth is verified by its effect on the human condition. Therefore, if the evidence for the truth of Christianity is honestly confronted, it will become apparent that the presupposition of Scripture's veracity is born of a faith that does not go contrary to reason. The written word of God was first entrusted to the descendants of Abraham, Isaac and Jacob, and the Christian view of ultimate reality derives first and foremost from that accounting. Accordingly, in the first part of this chapter, we will concern ourselves with examining the content of Hebrew Scripture and how it bears on the foundation of Christianity.

The Faith of Abraham

Abraham, the patriarchal father of the Hebrews, lived in the 21st century B.C. Human civilization was far removed from primitive conditions at this point in history. Many well-developed civilizations preceded Abraham's era by many hundreds of years. "Ur-kasdim," the home of Abraham according to the Hebrew Scripture,[4] was most certainly the Third Dynasty of Ur that existed from about 2100 to 2000 B.C. The site of ancient Ur-kasdim (or Ur), now known as Tell al-Muqayyar, is located in modern Iraq. British Museum archeologists excavated the remains of this ancient Mesopotamian city in 1934. Also noteworthy within this context is that archeologists had only a few years earlier, in 1906, discovered remains of the Hitti (Hittite) civilization. The Hebrew Scripture refers to the Hittites in conjunction with civilizations contemporary with Ur.[5] Secular scholars had once discounted the scriptural record of these people since no archeological evidence prior to the 1906 discovery had been found to support that record. The 1906 discovery proved the Hittites possessed a rather advanced civilization, complete with a sophisticated system of written communication. The dominant religion of Ur was apparently a pantheistic one since Ur was noted for its worship of the moon-god *Sin*. Abraham's immediate ancestors were, therefore, likely involved in that system of worship. Thus, pantheism did not originate with the Greek Presocratic philosophers discussed in the previous chapter. Although pantheism developed in complexity with the ideas of the Presocratic philosophers, more primitive forms of pantheism were in existence much earlier.

The scriptural record tells us how the Hebrew God Jehovah chose Abram to father a line of people through whom He promised to bless all people of the earth. Abram, later called Abraham, is unique in history because his life marked the beginning of a people with whom God sought a special relationship. God chose Abram to be the recipient of a special revelation that had heretofore been absent in the history of humanity. The formation of this relationship between God and Abram reveals two key elements that should help the reader better understand some attributes of this one referred to in the Hebrew Scripture as the "I AM." First, one observes that He wished to make Himself known to Abraham in a distinct and special way. In the first mention of contact between God and Abram we note that the initiative was entirely God's. In Genesis 12 is recorded a description of that first meeting.

Now the Lord said to Avram,* Get thee out of thy country, and from thy kindred, and from thy father's house, to the land that I will show thee: and I will make of thee a great nation, and I will bless thee, and make thy name great; and thou shalt be a blessing: and I will bless them that bless thee, and curse him that curses thee: and in thee shall all the families of the earth be blessed. So Avram departed, as the Lord had spoken to him.[6]

Since God's word had not yet appeared either in written or human form, "the word of the Lord came to Avram in a vision."[7] It is imperative to note that God first chose Abraham as a special object of His affection. The universal and natural condition of humanity involves an ignorance of the God of creation, the reason for which we will discuss in the next section. This is precisely why God had to first specifically reveal himself to Abram. Secondly, we see in Abram a positive response towards God's revelation. Abram's will was a *responsive* will with resolve to obey God's superior will. In the formation of this relationship, the important fact to note is that *Abram's will did not operate determinately*, i.e., his will was not sovereign in the formation of the relationship although it *was* an integral factor. Abram's response demonstrated a unique faith in God's word. This was a faith that God would eventually put to a test of almost unbelievable proportions to demonstrate its genuineness. The result of a genuine faith in God's word is always the imputation of a righteousness that puts the beholder in right standing with the God of the universe—the God of Scripture.

In the Scripture, therefore, we read that Abraham "believed in the Lord; and he counted it to him for righteousness."[8] Abraham responded positively to God's word by submitting his non-sovereign human will to the sovereign will of the creator. The result of that surrender was the imputation of a righteousness that resulted in Abraham's "right-standing" with God. What is the nature of this faith that God recognizes and thus rewards with imputed righteousness? A review of Abraham's offering of Isaac can help one begin to understand the nature of faith that God requires. Abraham's obedience to God's call, evidenced by his willingness to obey God even to the point of sacrificing his only son's life,[9] demonstrated the certainty of God's call and the certainty that Abraham possessed a true knowledge of that calling. Perhaps in no other circumstance could a need for a complete faith in

God have been more required. Abraham's willingness to offer Isaac as a sacrifice was the moral thing to do because, in this instance, it was God's will for Abraham to submit to Him in this way.

Humanists often scrutinize Abraham's offering by projecting the scenario into a modern-day humanistic understanding of ethics. It appears that on this basis, Søren Kierkegaard's[10] understanding of Abraham's offering was flawed. He viewed Abraham's action through *his* idea of the ethical and not through the understanding that it is the will of ultimate reality, as we shall discuss in the next section, that establishes the basis for absolute morality.[11] An even more glaring challenge to this incident, more recently, appeared in *The Humanist*.[12] The author, a Harvard Divinity School graduate, used the Genesis account of Abraham's offering as ammunition for her humanistic agenda. She began her essay with a description of an actual modern-day scenario where a man killed his son because "God told him to do so." The author then inferred that many modern-day societal ills have their roots in the morality induced by the "mythical" teaching of the Abraham-Isaac story. She here proposed that "we should put the Abraham story on trial." The author wanted to use her humanistic understanding of morality to put God on trial. But the answer to the often-asked question, "How could a perfect God ask Abraham to kill his own son?" is the same as in any other situation concerning God's desire for humanity. The "I AM" made his will known and this was reason enough for obedience. When the four-year-old child, in response to a proper parental admonition, rejoins with the familiar, "But why?", the parental response, "Because I said so" is sometimes the most reasonable, considering the gulf that exists between the child's mind and that of his parents'.[13] No reasonable person would subscribe to the view that God would today test anyone's faith in like manner. God is more intelligent than that.

One who seeks knowledge of ultimate reality solely in the power of his own personality will end up in a belief system that excludes the God of Abraham, Isaac and Jacob—the God of the Hebrew Scripture. The example of the major Greek philosophers, discussed in the previous chapter, is primary evidence for this fact. Although the classic Greek philosophers taught the existence of a supreme being, presumably even a transcendent one, their work did not produce a knowledge of the God of Scripture. There is nothing in the historical record to indicate that Socrates, Aristotle or Plato acknowledged the Hebrew God as the one and only true God.[14] In fact, it is quite evident that the god of both Plato and Aristotle was inconsistent with the God of the Hebrew Scripture. One author[15] has pointed out (and most students of Greek philosophy would likely agree) that, while Plato described God as the "supremely good soul," he did not view God as the creator of the universe nor did he view God as necessarily one God. Humanism is always the result of the futile human search to know ultimate reality in the power of human understanding. Ultimately, humanism leads to the false perception that any reality, outside of the perceivable cosmos, simply does not exist. It is out of the disillusionment and hopelessness, birthed by such secular humanistic thinking, that pantheistic philosophies come into existence. The modern New Age movement is essentially a pantheistic system of philosophy, which is emerging in the aftermath of the teachings of modern secular humanism. (Modern secular humanism is discussed in Chapter 7.)

Abraham's emergence of his own will into the will of God is a prime example of the type of personal abandonment that is impossible for the humanist. The humanist's perception of personality's sovereignty precludes his ability to relinquish his will to the sovereign creator of the universe. But it is the type of faith observed in this event of Abraham's life to which genuine Christians aspire. Only such faith in God's revealed word produces true knowledge of ultimate reality and subsequently results in salvation. The dividend of a proper faith is the imputation of a required righteousness. We will discuss in the following sections why the requirement for a genuine knowledge of ultimate reality involves the acquisition of this imputed righteousness.

The Humanistic Greek View of Human Nature Vs. The Christian View

The Christian view of human nature, like the Christian view of ultimate reality, is first and foremost derived from the Hebrew Scripture. Those who hold to views of Christianity consistent with Scripture maintain that only through the consideration of Scripture can one gain a proper understanding of human nature and its relationship to ultimate reality. Christian and humanistic views of human nature are in sharp contrast and are at the very root of the differences between the two systems of thought. Before discussing a proper Christian viewpoint we will briefly expound upon some of the ancient Greek ideas introduced in the previous chapter. This review should be beneficial for gaining an understanding of the proper Christian viewpoint.

i. Review of Ancient Greek views of Human Nature

Early Greek ideas on human nature revolved around the debate between *nomos* and *physis*. Those who held to the ideas of *physis* taught that human nature should not be intruded upon by the application of positive law. Because the ancient Greek *physis* model was unworkable in the strictest sense, the modern day analogue does not now exist. Most thinking people intuitively know that some type of positive law is necessary for any society to function properly.[16] Those who held to the ideas of *nomos* essentially believed that human behavior was shaped through the processes of positive law. The *nomos* position implied that those in governing roles could influence human nature through mechanisms of legal maneuvering. In this system, those who drafted positive law thereby formed the norms by which society functioned, which, in turn, ultimately defined a universal standard of "good." In the system of *nomos*, human personality, along with the dictates of human conscience, controlled the criteria by which the rulers conceived and implemented the positive laws of the state.

Before Socrates, the drive for emotional contentment drove personality without any particular deference to the powers of reason. Human nature, in its basest state, will usually seek its good on the basis of how it can most efficiently reach a perceived state of happiness. Socrates, Plato and Aristotle, however, sought to establish human reason as the primary means of justification for the movement of will in its attempt to satisfy that innate human drive. Reason and conscience, according to them, should rule and guide the will in the pursuit of emotional contentment. This rational justification provided for a system of ethics having a semblance of an absolute moral authority, allowing the ideas of *nomos* to flourish. Plato's idea of the *philosopher king* had its basic concept in the idea of *nomos*, wherein the wise ruler imposed only law that passed the scrutiny of human reason. It was also the ideas of *nomos* that gave rise to the idea of the superiority of societal morality as opposed to individual morality. Both Plato and Aristotle emphasized the moral society over that of individual morality. Aristotle wrote, "The decision of what is just, is the regulation of the political partnership."[17]

The ideals of the principle of *nomos* survive even today. Many humanists in modern Western society believe that legislation is yet the authoritative source of "the good." These often believe that acceptability of human behavior is established by legislative action. For example, in a recently published American medical textbook, the author stated when introducing the subject of medical ethics, "Because legislation determines what is *right* or *good* within a society, legal issues pertaining to psychiatric/mental health nursing are also [herein] discussed."[18]

In human systems of government, the principle and necessity of *natural law* as a moral guidance system is usually recognized. Certainly this was the case in the ancient Greek systems of ethics that we have thus far considered. As we showed in the previous chapter, even some upholders of *physis* believed that adherence to the laws of *areté* was necessary for society to properly function. Every human being is endowed with a natural mechanism, commonly known as the conscience, to point him towards moral responsibility and its effectiveness should not be underestimated. The concepts of natural law are found in the philosophy of Socrates, Plato and Aristotle. The acknowledgment of conscience's power is almost always found in the major philosophical systems of human civilization. The Roman philosopher Cicero wrote:

> For since an intelligence common to us all makes things known to us and formulates them in our minds, honourable actions are ascribed by us to virtue, and dishonorable actions to vice; and only a madman would conclude that these judgments are matters of opinion, and not fixed by Nature.[19]

Despite the obvious power of conscience, however, one should not conclude that an ethical system based on natural law is one that is based on absolute moral principle. Human conscience cannot serve as an absolute source for human morality. Human conscience serves as a natural mechanism (i.e., it is a function of natural law) to point one morally in the right direction. But when repeatedly violated, the conscience will eventually cease to work as intended. It is therefore important to note that human-originated law, in the ancient Greek system of ethics, was based on amoral intentions. The purpose of human-originated law is to shape human behavior in order achieve a human-determined standard. The influence of natural law in the Greek system of ethics often made it congruous with the absolute morality that was established through God's covenant with the Hebrew nation. (This subject is dealt with in the next section.) For example, when speaking of "actions and emotions," Aristotle stated, "Indeed the very names of some [emotions] directly imply evil, for instance malice, shamelessness, envy, and, of actions, adultery, theft, murder."[20] Certainly Aristotle's judgment on many aspects of moral concern was congruous with the morality of ancient Judaism. However, while the humanistic mind-set at some point in history may have acknowledged, through the mechanism of conscience, the evil of adultery, it usually today does not identify the adulterer with the same evil that is implied in the above quote of Aristotle. The modern humanistic view of adultery is often divorced from any concept of morality as was so evident in the blasé public reaction to the American Presidential scandal of 1998-99.[21] Therefore, absolute morality must be based on something other than the mechanisms of human personality and human conscience, and for that consideration we now turn to the Christian view of human nature.

ii.   The Christian View of Human Nature

Unlike law that has its origin in human conscience, and human person-ality, law that makes known the will of ultimate reality is the origin of true moral law. Moral law is that law known through the means of God's word and it is thereby absolute in its nature. Only God-given moral law estab-lishes an absolute basis for morality. We shall discuss in the next section why human nature dictates its necessity. (It is not our purpose here to discuss the entire Mosaic Law and its relationship to Christianity. That subject encom-passes a lengthy study in Christian theology. However, it must first be un-derstood that it was this law that provided to humankind an absolute basis of morality.) The law revealed to the Hebrew people established the basis for absolute morality because it was the explicit will of God made known to man. Even the requirement of circumcision was an issue of morality in the Hebrew system because it was God's explicitly revealed will that established its practice.[22]

All of the ancient Greek humanistic systems of ethics ultimately reduce to an amoral position since the relativism of human personality and human conscience yield these systems independent of an absolute moral authority. If the ancient Greek humanist viewed the act of murder as unethical, it was because he realized that as a potential target of such an action his good was not ultimately served. God's law that states "thou shalt not murder"[23] did not influence his view of morality. The criterion of "the good," for the hu-manist, is from the perspective of self and society. The humanist often con-siders a particular behavior acceptable if it, *in his perception*, does not harm another. It is the humanist's *perception* of good, albeit within the workings of his conscience, that defines his ethical standard. Human personality un-der such a system becomes an amoral, non-absolute standard. Within this context, it should also be here stated that any human-made law that clearly goes contrary to God's will, as revealed in Scripture, must be considered immoral law. Without dwelling specifically on this aspect of law, it is not difficult to witness its practice in modern society. Certainly law that permits a mother and her physician to slaughter an innocent unborn child for no other reason than the mother's convenience must fall into this category.[24] Wherever immoral law exists, it is always the result of some type of human-istic influence within that society.

The Christian view of human nature is distinct from the humanistic perspective. While humanism teaches that mankind can move itself to the ultimate good through mechanisms of human personality, Christianity teaches that humanity, in its natural condition, cannot know ultimate real-ity, the ultimate good. All are, in the power of human personality, incapable of realizing true meaning and purpose. According to the Christian viewpoint, man cannot, solely from the resources of his own being, move himself to a moral condition—to a state of true peace and joy. The Hebrew Scripture addresses the inception of this seemingly hopeless condition. It is here that the reality of sin, the root cause of this hopelessness, must first be understood.

To dispel any misinformed preconceived notions, we should first clarify what is meant by the word *sin*. Even though nearly everyone has formed in his mind a concept of the word's meaning, it is often an ill-conceived definition. Sin is simply the transgression of God's law. Since law is a mechanism by which a will for human behavior is expressed, sin can be viewed as any human activity that God does not will for humanity. Sin need not have any other criteria. The sin of Adam and Eve, and hence their initial act of immorality, occurred when they chose to go against God's desire for them. They chose of their own free will to partake of the forbidden fruit and that act evoked the knowledge of good and evil. As a consequence, human personality was forever changed at that point in history and the evidence for that change is clearly imbedded in the human condition. The Hebrew Scripture tells us that, immediately after they ate of the fruit, "the eyes of them both were opened, and they knew that they were naked."[25] The consciousness of physical nakedness has been a characteristic of human personality ever since that event and its existence cannot be denied. The collective power of all the nudists that have ever existed and are yet to exist will never change this aspect of human nature.

It is important to note that sin might not always be perceived as an "awful" deed, even though in reality it always is. Obviously, the ingestion of an attractive item of fruit does not rationally appear to be an act of immorality. However, in this case, it was the epitome of an immoral act because God, as creator, had made his will known and that was sufficient reason for obedience. As I stated in the previous section, when discussing the ethics of Abraham's offering of his son Isaac, morality must relate to the will of ultimate reality. God's will and morality are the same. Often the term *morality* is used only in reference to sexual sin. But this exclusivity is inappropriate, because all sin represents immorality. The ethical for the Christian simply equates to the will of ultimate reality, the "I AM" revealed to humanity through Scripture.

When C. S. Lewis[26] addressed the issue of whether God commands certain things because they are right or whether certain things are right because God commands them, he stated that he preferred the former scenario. While I agree with Lewis, we should probably question whether we can judge between the two, given our tendency to mis-perceive the mind of

God. Certainly, God's request for Abraham to sacrifice his only son can never appear in human reason as a right act. If Abraham had sought to inject his idea of *right* into the command, might not he have disobeyed?

God chose the Hebrew people to serve as the vehicle for revelation of His will and thereby established an absolute standard for human morality. Therefore, the Scriptures are of utmost importance to the Christian because they are the sole authoritative source for human knowledge of God's will. One's understanding of morality must be based on the knowledge of the reality and nature of sin. One cannot judge the morality of any action or thought without an absolute standard by which to judge it and an absolute standard must have ultimate reality as its source. A coherent view of morality, human nature and the nature of God only becomes possible when one grasps the scriptural concept of sin.

The Christian doctrine of the universality of sin, therefore, plays a primary role in the Christian interpretation of human nature and, hence, in the overall Christian view of reality. One is first introduced to the idea of universal sin in the Hebrew Scriptures, and therefore it is a truth that was first revealed to the descendants of Abraham, Isaac and Jacob. The Hebrew Scriptures are replete with evidence that supports this cardinal doctrine of human nature. In the first few words of the Hebrew Scripture, the concept of sin's universality is plainly stated. In the opening chapters of Genesis, the Scripture very plainly states that "the impulse of man's heart is evil from his youth."[27] In light of these words, how anyone claiming to believe the words of Scripture could yet hold to the belief that the intent of the human heart is naturally bent towards the moral good is beyond understanding. In both II Chronicles and I Kings, the Scripture states plainly that "there is no man who does not sin."[28] King David particularly had a keen sense of sin's universality. He stated in the Psalms:

> God looked down from heaven upon the children of men,
> to see if there were any man of discernment, that did seek
> God. Is every one of them dross? are they altogether filthy?
> is there no one who does good? No, not even one.[29]

David again proclaims in the Psalms, "For in thy sight shall no man living be justified."[30] In the 130th Psalm he asks rhetorically, "If thou, Lord, shouldst mark iniquities, O Lord, who could stand?"[31] Furthermore, Isaiah the prophet wrote: "All we like sheep have gone astray; we have turned every one to his own way."[32] And in the 64th Chapter of Isaiah's prophecy, perhaps the most poignant passage of all these demonstrates remarkably the point. Here we read:

And we are all as one that is unclean, and all our righteousness as filthy rags; and we all do fade as a leaf; and our iniquities, like the wind, take us away. And there is none that calls upon thy name, that stirs himself up to take hold of thee: for thou hast hid thy face from us, and has consumed us, through the force of our iniquities.[33]

It must be emphasized and understood that human nature was drastically changed when Adam sinned. Before Adam's decision to "go his own way," his nature was pure and in harmony with the nature of God. His decision to sin, or to depart from God's will, created a great chasm between God and all of his offspring. A Christianity that is based in Scripture teaches that ultimate reality is hidden from the natural human mind due to the inherited sin nature of Adam from whom all humanity descends. Man's choice to "turn to his own way" resulted in separation from the knowledge of God. As observed in Isaiah's prophecy quoted above, the euphemism often used in Jewish Scripture to convey this thought is the expression of God "hiding His face"[34] from the one who remains opposed to His will. It is only when one is willing to turn from his sin, (or turn from "his own way," or from his predisposition to put his will paramount to that of the creator) that knowledge of ultimate reality becomes possible.

As previously discussed, God has endowed every human being with a natural moral compass known as the conscience. The conscience serves as a basis for the functioning of natural law. C. S. Lewis called this function of conscience "the law of human nature." Lewis clearly pointed out, however, that none of us are completely inclined to obey it.[35] The natural moral darkness and helplessness of unredeemed human nature prevents one from following even the path his conscience dictates. In fact, the theory of natural law in modern times usually holds that self-interest and self-preservation are the driving forces behind its action, the very opposite effect that God intended when He established its function.

The purpose and necessity of God-given moral law becomes apparent when one understands the predicament into which the inherited sin nature has put humanity. Because of man's natural desire to be independent of God's will, he tends to establish for himself the behavioral standards by which he lives. It was thus necessary for God to reveal Himself in a specific and concrete way if mankind was to be redeemed from the curse of sin. The purpose of all law is to make known the will of the lawmaker. God provided through His law a concrete means to make His will known, and He chose the Hebrew people to be the recipients of that law, thereby establishing through them an absolute basis for morality.

Imputed Righteousness

The faith of both Noah and Abraham so pleased God that it was counted to them as righteousness. An imputed righteousness through faith, a particular kind of faith as we discussed earlier, is thus revealed as God's mechanism for the attainment of knowledge of himself which, moreover, translates into personal salvation. An individual's faith in God's revealed truth has always been the means by which one comes into an understanding of ultimate reality. Inherent in the faith of Abraham was his acceptance of God's requirement for the atonement of sin. God requires for the atonement of sin, according to the Hebrew Scripture, a blood sacrifice.[36] It cannot be over emphasized that a misplaced faith is no better than the absence of faith. One observes no better example of this than in the example of Cain and Abel.[37] Cain was truly the first non-secular humanist. He had faith in God but his faith was a misplaced one. His offering to God was on his terms, void of the required blood sacrifice and hence not pleasing to God.

Cain willed to know God but his will was not sufficient because it was not in harmony with God's sovereign will. Cain sought to make his will determinate and, as such, his will was not a *responsive* will to the sovereign will of God. When seeking for understanding on the required relationship between God's will and human will, one should remember that the will to know ultimate reality is necessary but not sufficient. Human volition cannot possess sovereignty over the will of God. Therefore, enablement to moral living only proceeds by human will as it wills to be in line with God's will. Human volition, even when it works through the mechanisms of conscience, cannot establish for its beholder a moral life without the aid of God's sovereign will. The freedom of the will must, therefore, be examined in the light of its moral motive. While one may have true freedom to choose wheat bread over rye for morning breakfast, the same freedom of choice does not necessarily exist for the moral choices that one might make later that day. Because human volition, in its natural state, is *not* morally neutral as Aristotle claimed, in moral choices human volition must function *responsively* to God's sovereign will.

While secular humanists often view the scriptural record as only a collection of traditional and cultural stories, Christians understand that Scripture is a supernatural revelation of God's will to mankind. To question the reasonableness of a blood atonement for sin is to place an imperfect finite judgment onto the infinite. As previously pointed out through the analogy of the child who asks his parent, "But why?" in response to an assertion of parental will, sometimes the best answer, given the gulf that separates the child's mind from the parents', is the "because I said so" answer (see discussions related to notes 13 and 26).

The imputation of righteousness means that God accepts one not on the basis of that individual's merit or on his effort to keep His law but on the basis of faith that one has placed in His revealed word. We will now discuss how God revealed the Messiah to his people Israel. Israel, as a whole, however, did not believe their God and this is why Jehovah, the "I AM" revealed to Abraham, remains hidden from those who refuse to believe that Jesus is the Messiah sent by God for human redemption from the damnation of sin. God requires imputed righteousness, given as a result of personal faith in His revealed truth. Israel's refusal to believe her God is the reason humanism remains the dominant philosophy of the Jewish people today. (The humanism of modern-day Judaism is discussed in Chapter 10.)

Jesus, the Christ

Christians know that in the person of Jesus, God revealed the "anointed one" (Mashiah) and that through this revelation, knowledge of ultimate reality became possible in a way never before in the history of humanity. If the Hebrew Scripture is the revelation of ultimate reality, and if ultimate reality is ultimately revealed in Jesus of Nazareth, then certainly the Hebrew Scripture must have something to say about this one through whom is the embodiment of ultimate reality.

Jesus identified both His purpose and His mission with the use of Hebrew Scripture. Luke showed us this through his description of an episode that occurred in Jesus' hometown synagogue:

> He (Jesus) entered the synagogue on the Sabbath, and stood up to read. And the book of the prophet Isaiah was handed to Him. And He opened the book, and found the place where it was written, "The Spirit of the Lord is upon me/Because He anointed Me to preach the gospel to the poor/He has sent Me to proclaim release to the captives/And recovery of sight to the blind/To set free those who are downtrodden/To proclaim the favorable year of the Lord." And He closed the book, and gave it back to the attendant, and sat down; and the eyes of all in the synagogue were fixed upon Him. And He began to say to them, "Today this Scripture has been fulfilled in your hearing."[38]

Those who make the assertion that Jesus did not claim to be Israel's Messiah simply do not know what Jesus said about himself. Jesus plainly claimed to be Israel's anointed one.[39] The reader should note that Jesus came not to save those who believe in themselves. He came for the spiritually poor, blind and needy. The humanist cannot identify with these traits because he cannot understand the severity of the sin nature with which he came into the world. This ignorance is perhaps *the major factor* underlying the dichotomy between humanism and Christianity.

A major ostensible objection that prevents both the Jew of Jesus' day and the modern Jew from acknowledging the deity of Jesus is the scriptural insistence that Jehovah is one.[40] To acknowledge the deity of Jesus, in many Jewish minds, would violate this inviolate attribute of Jehovah. If one could acknowledge the deity of Jesus, then he obviously could acknowledge Him as the "anointed one" of Israel. The concept of "one God", commonly held by the unbelieving Jew and often cited as cause for rejection of Jesus' deity, however, is a faulty one. The Hebrew Scripture demands that a correct perception of Jehovah include a concept of plurality (at the same time, however, a correct perception of God must meet the Scriptural demand that He is one.) To understand the very first sentence of Hebrew Scripture, one must have a proper perception of this plurality to which we are referring.[41] Here the Hebrew word for God, *Elohim*, is plural. Again in the same chapter, one observes this plurality. Verse 26 of Genesis 1 reads, "Let *us* make Mankind in our image, after *our* likeness [italics added]."[42] And again in the eleventh chapter of Genesis, we read with regard to God's disgust with the humanistic endeavor at the Tower of Babel:

> And the Lord said, Behold, the people is one, and they have all one language; and this they begin to do: and now nothing will be withheld from them, which they have schemed to do. Come, let *us* [italics added] go down, and there confound their language, that they may not understand one another's speech. So the Lord scattered them abroad from there upon the face of all the earth: and they ceased to build the city.[43]

The Hebrew Scripture clearly states that God is indeed one in essence, but it also clearly shows a plurality in His nature.

Some Christians criticize those who use pictorial analogies in attempting to help others understand the three-person nature of God. While some analogies are particularly faulty, others have merit.[44] One does not err in using an analogy to help those who might have intellectual difficulty with acknowledging the triune God. God's creation often mirrors His spiritual truths. The example of water, therefore, can be a legitimate help for one who might honestly struggle with understanding the concept of the trinity. Water is readily observable, on a nearly everyday occurrence, in the three main forms of matter: solid, liquid and gas. A boiling pot of water vents off water in the form of gas (steam) no different in essence from the liquid it once was. The ice in a glass of ice water is no different in essence than the liquid water it eventually becomes. If A (gaseous H_2O)=B (liquid H_2O) and if B=C (ice, solid H_2O), then all equal each other. Water indeed appears to be a simple but valid illustration to show the concept of a single essence that is comprised of three distinctions. While this simple physical illustration obviously cannot provide a complete understanding of the trinity, for no one can fully understand its mystery, it can nonetheless be useful in helping one accept the reality of a single essence, albeit a physical one, which is comprised of three distinctions. (A problem, of course, with this example is that a single molecule of water cannot be in a solid, a liquid and gaseous state simultaneously.)

Hebrew References to Jesus

Very early on, the reader of the Hebrew Scripture finds the first glimpse of Jehovah's plan for human redemption. The first description of a promise for human salvation is found in Genesis 3:15. Here, God is in the midst of cursing the instrument (the serpent) through which sin (opposition to God's will) has entered the world. A proper rendering of this portion of Scripture is critical for understanding how it uniquely refers to the Messiah. A version of the Hebrew Scripture released in 1955 by *The Jewish Publication Society of America* did not correctly render Genesis 3:15 from Hebrew into English. The translators of this edition translated the passage as follows: "I will put enmity between thee and the woman between thy offspring and her offspring. They shall bruise thy head and thou shall bruise their heel."[45] Here the Hebrew word for offspring (seed) assumed to be plural. It implies that the collective offspring of the woman will bruise the head of (kill) the serpent (the symbol of evil) while the offspring of the serpent will collectively bruise the collective heels of the woman's offspring. This faulty translation is actually humanistic in outlook because it implies that collective human effort will eventually destroy evil. A better rendering of Genesis 3:15 is found in the translation that we have used for reference throughout this chapter. This rendering of Scripture is taken from the most accurate Hebrew Masoretic text to appear in print. The English reading here is "and I will put enmity between thee and the woman, and between thy seed and her seed; it shall bruise thy head, and thou shall bruise his heel."[46] The word "it" in conjunction with "his" implies a specific seed of the woman. "It" comes from a

35

Hebrew word that implies male gender. "His" heel is bruised and not "their heel" as the former, less accurate translation has it. Therefore, "it" refers to a specific male offspring of a woman. The fact that the reference is to the seed of the woman is unique because *seed* normally refers to male progeny. Therefore, the reference is to a specific male offspring of a specific woman. One cannot accurately assign the word "offspring" to a collective noun. To do so entirely alters the intended meaning of the text. It is best to interpret the passage literally and then infer from the literal wording the plurality of the word "offspring." When this is done, it becomes apparent the passage refers to the Messiah, who was born not by the seed of a man, but uniquely by the "seed of woman." Jesus is the only one in the history of humanity who is from the seed of woman, i.e., virgin born (discussed in the next few paragraphs). Jesus' heel, not his head because He yet lives, was bruised symbolically in his physical death. By overcoming death, Jesus overcame the power of evil, symbolized by the crushing of the serpent's head.

Isaiah foretold the unique birth of Jesus many years before it came about. The passage relating to the prophecy of Christ's birth is found in Isaiah 7:14-15. In the *Jerusalem Bible* it reads:

> Therefore the Lord himself shall give you a sign; Behold, the young woman is with child, and she will bear a son, and shall call his name *Immanu-el*. Butter and honey shall he eat, when he shall know how to refuse the evil, and choose the good.[47]

Reference to this "sign" was given to the wicked Ahaz by Isaiah after he, in false piety, refused an offer from Jehovah to choose his own sign. This was a sign that would demonstrate to the Jewish people that the God of Abraham, Isaac and Jacob was yet their God and that He would deliver them from their enemies. Israel, during this period in her history, had fallen into a state of severe unbelief and had departed from the will of Jehovah. She had turned to her own way in unrepented sin, prompting the prophet's message of judgment. But here, as throughout Israel's history, we witness a God who was willing to show His chosen people that even though they had turned their backs on Him, He had still not forsaken them. He would yet give his chosen people a "sign" to demonstrate that his love was yet with them. The key in understanding this "sign" is to understand the Hebrew word, *almah*, translated in the Jerusalem Bible as "young woman." As told by Rosen,[48] *almah* can be shown to mean "virgin" in some of its other uses in the Hebrew canon. Even the Jewish translation of the Hebrew Scripture from which this passage is taken translates the plural of *almah* as "virgins" in The Song of Songs.[49] It should be apparent to the unbiased reader that *almah*, as used in this prophecy of Isaiah, can be—and should be—translated as *virgin*. Why can this assertion be made with certainty? The sign involved the birth of a child to a "young woman." It should be apparent to the unbiased mind that ordinarily the birth of a child to a "young woman" could hardly be considered a "sign" since such events have occurred billions of times in the past few thousand years. The use of the word "sign" clearly indicated that a supernatural event would be associated with the birth of this child. Further indication that Isaiah speaks of Jesus in this prophecy is the fact that he would be called *Immanu-el.* This one—of whom Isaiah speaks—would be known as "God-With-Us." No better name could be given to the Messiah, who came to earth from God to provide the ultimate blood atonement for the sins of humanity. The name *Immanu-el* simply indicates that this special child would be one who would be known as "God in the flesh." If there ever was a name which could be used to describe Jesus of Nazareth, then this certainly is that name. Furthermore, we read that this one born as a special sign to the Hebrew people would be one whose nature was not as others. We have just shown that human nature, according to the Hebrew Scripture, is universally afflicted with the malady of sin. Human personality possesses in its nature the desire to be independent from the will of Jehovah and to go its own way. But Isaiah tells us that this special one would not be subject to sin. This would be one who would know how to "refuse the evil and choose the good." He would be one who would possess a unique nature, free from sin, because he was the incarnate God.

From the book of Micah we read that this one, who existed before the world was formed, would come out of Bethlehem of Judah. Micah 5:2 reads:

> But thou, Bet-lehem-efrata [Bethlehem Ephrathah], though thou art little among the thousands of Yehuda [Judah], yet out of thee shall he come forth to me that is to be ruler in Yisra'el [Israel]; and his goings out are from ancient time, from days of old.[50]

That this reference is to the Christ should be obvious. Here is prophesied that one who preexisted would rise out of Bethlehem. Judaism has never been a religion that has held to any belief in reincarnation. Yet, to the causal reader one might suppose that a doctrine of reincarnation is being referred to in this passage. This passage is clearly referring to the incarnation of Jesus Christ, because as God, He existed before the universe was created.

Although examples in the Hebrew Scriptures referring to the Messiah abound, we will look at one additional prophecy concerning Jesus. This prophecy foretold of the mission for which Jesus was sent. The bruising of Jesus' heel (i.e., the shedding of Jesus' blood) met God's demand for the atonement of sin. Isaiah speaks of Christ's atonement in the 53rd chapter. Verses 4 and 5 read:

But in truth he has borne our sicknesses and endured our
pains; yet we did esteem him stricken, smitten of God,
and afflicted. But he was wounded because of our trans-
gressions, bruised because of our iniquities: his sufferings
were that we might have peace, and by his injury we are
healed.

And from verses 8 and 9:

By oppression and false judgement was he taken away;
and of his generation who considered? … For they made
his grave among the wicked, and his tomb among the
rich; because he had done no violence, neither was any
deceit in his mouth.[51]

No better description could be written of the death of Jesus than that found
in these words of Isaiah, hundreds of years before it occurred. Jesus was
unjustly executed with wicked thieves and briefly buried in a rich man's
tomb—a tomb that could not hold Him.

The Christian View of Ultimate Reality

That the Christian understanding of ultimate reality has its roots in the
revelation of Hebrew Scripture is reiterated in this section. A scripturally
based Christianity holds that God imparts a true knowledge of Himself to
only those who have put their faith in his word. The Hebrew Scripture, very
early on, states that Abraham "believed in the Lord and he counted it to
him for righteousness."[8] The faith of Noah and Abraham are excellent examples for understanding the requisites of the faith that reconciles man to
God. One cannot over emphasize the fact that it is only a certain kind of
faith that results in a true knowledge of ultimate reality.

To Adam, Noah, Abraham and even Moses, God's will was not conveyed by His *written* word—it did not exist in their lifetimes. Today, God's
intended message to all mankind is now complete in written form. Essentially the entire literate world has access to a reliable translation of God's
complete written word.[52] In the years between Malachi and Christ, the word
of God, although not yet complete (i.e., the New Testament had not yet
been written) was also in written form, not only in Hebrew but also in
Greek. The Septuagint, the Greek translation of the Hebrew Scripture, was
produced about 250 years before the appearance of Jesus. The authoritative
source of faith for Jewish believers in the era between Malachi and Christ
was His written word, since God's word was no longer spoken directly through
the prophets. No new revelation was given until Jesus, God's Word in the
flesh, appeared to the Jewish people.

Modern people have been so exposed to the secular use of the word "faith" that it has nearly lost its biblical meaning. Consider carefully the faith in God's word that was exercised by Noah when he undertook construction of the ark on dry land. Imagine the ridicule he must have faced. Yet Noah, in the midst of a situation where faith would have been most difficult, believed God. The example of Abraham is even more dramatic. Imagine the faith required of Abraham when God told him to sacrifice the life of his only son. Both Abraham and Noah simply believed God's word and acted in obedience upon that belief. It must be emphasized that the faith of Noah and Abraham was real faith in God's real word and it is only such faith that brought to them, and still brings to the modern believer, knowledge of ultimate reality.

When Jesus as God's promised Messiah came into the world, God's Word appeared in flesh. While the Hebrew prophets spoke God's word and foretold Jesus' coming, a most important distinction is yet made between them and Jesus. Jesus not only spoke God's word, he *was* God's Word. Jesus is God's Word by the very fact that he is God. Jesus' statements "I and the Father are one"[53] and "Truly, truly, I say to you, before Abraham was born, *I AM* [italics added]"[54] affirmed his claim to synonymy with ultimate reality. The Apostle John wrote, speaking of Jesus:

> In the beginning was the Word, and the Word was with God, and the Word was God. He was in the beginning with God. All things came into being through Him; and apart from Him nothing came into being that has come into being. In Him was life; and the life was the light of men. And the light shines in the darkness; and the darkness did not comprehend it. ... And the Word became flesh and dwelt among us.[55]

Jesus claimed to be one with Jehovah, the God of the Hebrews. As C. S. Lewis so eloquently stated in response to those who willingly accept the fact that Jesus was a "great moral teacher," but cannot accept his claim to deity:

> A man who was merely a man and said the sort of things Jesus said would not be a great moral teacher. He would either be a lunatic—on a level with the man who says he is a poached egg—or else he would be the Devil of Hell. You must make your choice. Either this man was, and is, the Son of God: or else a madman or something worse.[56]

When Jesus stood up in the synagogue of Nazareth and identified himself as the Messiah (the anointed one), he read the passage in Isaiah 61:1-2, which reads:

> The spirit of the Lord God is upon me; because the Lord
> has anointed me to announce good tidings to the meek;
> he has sent me to bind up the broken hearted, to pro-
> claim liberty to the captives, and the opening of the prison
> to them that are bound; to proclaim an acceptable year
> of the Lord.[57]

It is interesting to note that Luke's account shows us that Jesus added a phrase to what was in the scroll (see reference 38). The words "recovery of sight to the blind" was, by all indication from existing manuscripts, not in the scroll. Jesus likely added these words during his reading. He could add to Isaiah's rendering of God's written word because He was God's Word. The Scripture is filled with accounts of Jesus opening the eyes of the blind, both in a physical sense and in a spiritual sense. Jesus, as God's Word, was the fulfillment of God's word. What a testimony to those hearing these words that He was indeed God's promised "anointed one."

Jesus, as God's Word, came specifically to the Hebrew people to impute the required righteousness that we spoke of earlier when we discussed the faith of Abraham. Righteousness had to be imputed to Abraham because his nature as a human being was not naturally righteous. "Righteous" means "right standing" with God. There are none who are naturally in right standing with God. The Hebrew Scripture makes plain that there are none without sin. The reconciliation of man to ultimate reality, therefore, requires imputed righteousness. No one can attain true knowledge of ultimate reality outside of imputed righteousness. This is where the Jews' understanding of Jehovah then failed and still fails today. The Jews of Jesus' day believed that favor with God was found on the basis of acknowledgment of God's law. This belief is yet prevalent among the many Jews today who think in a humanistic vein (discussed in Chapter 10). The Hebrews of old, even Abraham, Moses and David, were all made acceptable in God's sight not because of their effort and ability to keep God's law, but because of the righteousness imputed to them because of their personal faith in God's word. God's word, then as now, promised atonement for sin through the shedding of blood. This misunderstanding is precisely why Jesus' message conflicted with the Jewish leaders of His day, those who were outwardly careful about every letter of the Mosaic Law. Jesus denounced their relationship to Abraham[58] because He knew that had they possessed the faith of Abraham, they would have believed Him. The belief that law can change human nature is a humanistic idea. This was essentially the belief of the Greek humanists who held to the idea of *nomos*. Human nature cannot be changed by imposition of any type of law or any effort to uphold existing laws. The Jews of Jesus' day had faith, but their faith was not in God's Word and therefore it was a faith that was contrary to the faith of Abraham.

Jesus had authority to forgive sins because he was sent from God for that purpose. John (the Baptist) when he saw Jesus coming said "Behold, the Lamb of God who takes away the sin of the world!"[59] And when the lame man's caretakers were so persistent as to let him down through an opening in the roof to get him to Jesus for healing, Jesus seeing their faith said to him,

> "Friend, your sins are forgiven you." And the scribes and the Pharisees began to reason, saying, "Who is this man who speaks blasphemies? Who can forgive sins, but God alone?" But Jesus, aware of their reasonings, answered and said to them, "Why are you reasoning in your hearts? Which is easier, to say, 'Your sins have been forgiven you,' or to say, 'Rise and walk'? But in order that you may know that the Son of Man has authority on earth to forgive sins," He said to the paralytic, "I say to you, rise, and take up your stretcher and go home." And at once he rose up before them, and took up what he had been lying on, and went home, glorifying God.[60]

Jesus was sending a sign to the Jews that He was the anointed Messiah of Israel. The fact that the blind received their sight and the paralyzed were healed should have been sufficient evidence that He was who He claimed to be. But for the most part, the Jews refused Jesus' claim. They refused to put their faith in God's Word and, as a result, the righteousness of God was not imputed to them. Instead of believing God's Word they attributed His supernatural works to the evil powers of darkness.

The concept of imputed righteousness has direct bearing on the Christian view of human nature. When Jesus spoke of being "born again,"[61] He was referring to the new nature imparted—as a result of imputed righteousness—to the one who believes. Faith in the word of God conquers the damning nature that every man has inherited from Adam's sin. It is only then that the human will becomes enabled to respond to God's will. As the Apostle John stated,

> For God did not send the Son into the world to judge the world; but that the world should be saved through Him. He who believes in Him is not judged; he who does not believe has been *judged already* [italics added], because he has not believed in the name of the only begotten Son of God.[62]

No man, be he Jew or gentile, can enter into the kingdom of God unless he is "born again," because without the imputed righteousness of Christ he remains under sin's condemnation.

In closing this chapter we will briefly review Episode IV of the television series *Genesis* that aired on the Public Broadcasting System (USA) in 1996. The journalist Bill Moyers hosted the program and subsequently released the program in book form.[63] The content of the discussion is of interest to this work because it reflects a humanistic philosophy framed in the monotheism of Judaism and Christianity. The program featured a diversified group of scholars and thinkers, each possessing impressive academic credentials. Episode IV dealt with the discussion of Noah and the flood. The episode focused on two key elements of the Genesis account of this catastrophic event. The panelists first attempted to come to terms with how a good God could be responsible for the carnage represented by the scriptural account of the flood and secondly to analyze Noah's character and understand why he escaped destruction. Analysis of this dialogue is instructive because it demonstrates modern humanistic philosophy in the context of monotheism.

The scriptural account of Noah touches on many of the truths that have been discussed in this chapter. For the humanist, a most troubling aspect of Scripture is the fact that a God who is commonly portrayed as loving and good is also shown to be a God of wrath.[64] This, in humanistic thinking, is an unacceptable dichotomy and, therefore, the humanistic mind will reach for any tool that can circumvent the acknowledgment of this reality. It was apparent in the *Genesis* dialogue, that in the panelists' attempts to deal with the facts surrounding the Genesis flood, the truth of universal sin was rejected. The humanist, no matter what he believes about God's existence, cannot understand the natural condemnation that all people are under. Although there was an attempt by one of the panelists to rightfully maintain that God had destroyed[65] the world because of human sin, he later acknowledged that he did not believe that God had truly universally destroyed the earth. He stated that the story was only a parable since human sin could not negate the goodness of God. But Scripture makes plain the fact that God detests sin to such an extent that he will destroy those who remain in their sin opposed to Him. The fact that God destroyed the entire world is evidence for the universality of sin. Sin will result in man's ultimate destruction if God does not intervene, as He did in the case of Noah. Some of the panelists, in their humanistic reasoning, purported to believe the unthinkable idea that this story was about the education of God, that God had made a mistake in destroying the world to the extent of even committing evil Himself. One panelist even claimed that here God assaulted humanity to such an extent that human capacity for love and goodness was destroyed.

God makes it plain in his word that while He is a God of love, demonstrated by His willingness to save anyone who will come to Him on *His* terms; He is also a God who will destroy those who remain in their sin. In poetic form, God's word vividly conveys this message:

> Because I have called and you refused
> I have stretched out my hand and no man regarded
> But you have set at nought all my counsel
> And would none of my reproof
> I also will laugh at your calamity
> I will mock when your fear comes upon you
> When your fear comes like a storm
> And your calamity comes like a tempest
> When distress and anguish come upon you
> Then shall they call upon me but I will not answer
> They shall seek me early but they will not find me
> For they hated knowledge
> And did not choose the fear of the Lord
> They would none of my counsel
> They despised all my reproof
> Therefore they shall eat of the fruit of their own way
> And be filled with their own devices
> For the turning away of the simple shall slay them
> And the erring of fools shall destroy them
> But he who listens to me shall dwell safely
> And shall be at ease without fear of evil[66]

Those who claim that the scriptural record of the world's destruction by flood is only a fable that points to an educational process for God should be reminded that while God promised, out of His goodness, to never again universally destroy the world by flood, the heart of God towards the human disobedient spirit remains the same. God is unchanging in His nature. The disobedient "wood gatherer" of Numbers 15:32-36, if he could speak today, would certainly remind us of this.

In their discussion of Noah, not one panelist made the concrete connection between Noah's faith and his salvation. Noah believed God's word and for this he was declared righteous. Noah's faith produced imputed righteousness which resulted in his salvation. Righteousness is never achieved in doing. Righteousness must be imputed because all are naturally opposed to God. As it was in Noah's day, those who today refuse to put their faith in

God's revealed Word will face everlasting destruction. But the one who turns to God, through faith in His Word, His only begotten Son, will not see destruction, but will, as was Noah, be saved.

3

Historical Christianity:
The Early and Medieval Church

How else but through a broken heart
May Lord Christ enter in?
Oscar Wilde (1854-1900)

Christianity triumphed over the Greek and Roman humanistic philosophies of early Western civilization. This is noteworthy
since some Roman authorities had diligently sought to eradicate it. When
recording the extremes to which Nero went in his attempts to destroy Christianity, the Roman historian Tacitus tells us that Nero accused the Christians for the fire that nearly destroyed Rome in 64 A.D. and arrested

> all who pleaded guilty; [to Christianity] then, upon their
> information, an immense multitude was convicted, not so
> much of the crime of firing the city, as of hatred against
> mankind. Mockery of every sort was added to their deaths.
> Covered with the skins of beasts, they were torn by dogs
> and perished, or were nailed to crosses, or were doomed to
> the flames and burnt, to serve as a nightly illumination,
> when daylight had expired.[1]

Diocletian was the last Roman emperor to radically persecute Christians. In
the early fourth century, he too attempted to eliminate Christianity by ex-
ecuting many of its followers.

Some scholars have attributed the success of Christianity to the fact
that many early Christian leaders were highly educated in classical Greek
philosophy. Other modern writers wrongly claim that the orthodox Christian doctrines of God's attributes are corrupted because of an undue influence of Greek philosophy.[2] Those who claim this fail to realize that the
merging of Greek and Roman philosophies with Christian thought during

the early days of Christianity resulted in many false teachings regarding God's nature. Gnosticism, for example, was one such teaching. Many early Christian leaders, including the Apostle Paul, labored diligently to preserve a scriptural concept of God in the midst of these heresies. Some Gnostics falsely taught that the Christian God was a different God from that of the Hebrews. They viewed the *I AM* of Hebrew Scripture as an evil being. The Apostle Paul's letter to the Colossians was written specifically to combat some of these wrong ideas and, as a result, scriptural views of God were strengthened and preserved. Clement of Alexandria (third century A.D.) is another example of an early church leader who was well educated in Greek philosophy. He also spent much of his life defending Christianity against the budding errors of his era. So while many of the early church leaders were well versed in the Greek and Roman philosophies of that day, it is clear that the Christianity they taught and defended stood opposed to those same philosophies.

Greek philosophy, however, probably played a role in creating a desire in the Western mind to better understand human nature and its relationship to a proper view of morality and for accepting the idea of a transcendent ultimate reality. Before the advent of Greek philosophy, nearly all worship practiced outside of Judaism had been to some sort of pantheistic deity. However, Greek humanism ultimately only raised the critical questions. Socrates' claim that the unexamined life was not worth living was indeed a wise entreaty; but against what standard should one's life be examined? Socrates' proclamation that a moral life could be acquired through self-knowledge was only a first step towards a true moral philosophy. Self-knowledge is incomplete unless it is based on an understanding that human nature in its fallen condition is alienated from the one and only true God, the true moral Good. The Greek philosophers simply could not give the answers to the questions they raised. To these questions Christianity offered genuine insight and understanding, which, no doubt, contributed to its widespread acceptance throughout the Western world.

Augustine

Augustine, born in 354 A.D. at Thagaste (alternate spelling, Tagaste), Numidia (modern day Algeria), was influential in defending Christianity against a humanistic assault that developed from within the Church during his lifetime. Here we consider some of the influences instrumental in his conversion and how, subsequent to that conversion, he preserved a scriptural view of human nature in the midst of a threatening humanistic interpretation of the same.

Augustine was the son of a dedicated Christian mother and a pagan father (his father converted to Christianity only shortly before his death). At about the age of fifteen he left Thagaste for Madaura to further his education, and after about two years in Madaura, he moved on to Carthage for further study. It was in Carthage where he was seduced into a life he described as the "filth of concupiscence" and the "hell of lustfulness."[3] While a student in Carthage, Augustine read Cicero's *Hortensius*, (now lost), which he described as an "exhortation to philosophy." This work, Augustine tells us, induced him to a love of wisdom.[4] Thereafter, his philosophical pursuits led him to the Manichaeistic sect named after its Persian founder Mani. But finding no satisfaction in their teachings, he eventually traveled to Milan where he came under the preaching and teaching of Ambrose. He was converted to Christianity as a result of Ambrose's ministry in 386.

Augustine was well versed in Greek philosophy due to many years of its study prior to his conversion. Many authors believe that his knowledge of Plato and the many Neoplatonic writings common to his era contributed to his acceptance of Christianity. In his *Confessions*, Augustine himself fueled these speculations by stating that Simplicianus had congratulated him that he "had not fallen upon the writings of other philosophers, which were full of fallacies and deceits, 'after the rudiments of this world,' whereas they [the Platonists], in many ways, led to the belief in God and His Word."[5] However, Augustine also here made it clear that Greek philosophy could not get him to the God of the Scriptures. He wrote that while in the books of the Platonists he read that "God the Word was born not of flesh, nor of blood, nor of the will of man, nor of the will of the flesh, but of God," he did *not* read that "the Word was made flesh, and dwelt among us."[6]

Augustine's teachings on the human will are of particular interest to this work, since volition is a major constituent of human personality, which, in turn, is a manifestation of human nature. Humanism and Christianity diverge in their respective views of the basic nature of man. From Augustine's early writing on the subject as a new convert, and from the understanding of the subject that he would eventually develop, one can better appreciate how humanistic and Christian viewpoints on human nature differ.

An elementary understanding of two different schools of thought which existed in Augustine's era is beneficial for understanding his writing on the subject. One of these schools was outside of Christianity and the other developed from within the Church. We will first consider the outside one, which, as already mentioned, had substantial influence on him before his conversion to Christianity. Augustine's first hand experience with the Manichees made him particularly knowledgeable of their error prone doctrines. Today, the sect would likely be labeled as a cult. The second school of thought is perhaps even more pertinent to our subject. It was based on the teachings of the British monk Pelagius and came on the scene a few years subsequent to Augustine's conversion. Pelagius taught that a person was not by nature a sinner. He believed, as Aristotle had taught, that a person at birth possessed a morally neutral nature. Pelagius' thought was thoroughly humanistic in that he believed that one was not naturally in wrong standing with God. It is important to remember that Pelagius came on the scene subsequent to Augustine's first writing on the subject of human will.

Augustine's first writing on the subject of human will appeared as the treatise *De libero arbitrio* (*On Free Will*). His original intent in this composition was to respond to the error of the Manichees. The Manichees taught that the source of evil, of necessity, existed co-eternally with God, because if not, God was the originator of evil. In *De libero arbitrio* Augustine attempted to address the origin of evil and the nature of sin. The work was presented in three parts (Books), in the form of a dialogue between Augustine and his colleague Evodius. In Book 1 (written before Pelagius began teaching) Augustine taught that human sin completely originated in the human will. Augustine rightly argued that every man was culpable before God because of his innate willingness to sin and therefore one could not blame God for the condemnation that resulted from that sin. Augustine here wrote:

> Every evil man is the author of his evil deeds. If you wonder how that is, consider what we have just said: evil deeds are punished by the justice of God. They would not be justly punished unless they were done voluntarily.[7]

But Augustine's arguments in Book 1 were based on what at first might appear to be an assumption of personality's sovereignty in the moral affairs of man. Here he asked rhetorically, "For what is so completely within the power of the will as the will itself?[8] Augustine defined a good will as "A will to live rightly and honorably and to reach the highest wisdom."[9] He further stated:

> Whoever has a good will has something which is far better than all earthly realms and all bodily pleasures. Whoever does not have it, lacks that which is more excellent than all the goods which are not in our power, and yet he can have it by willing it simply.[10]

It is important to recall that Augustine's education had been shaped by Hellenistic philosophies, and as such, his concept of human nature had once been grounded in those ideas, particularly in the ideas of Plato. In ancient Greek philosophy, the will was completely free to follow the dictates of a

sovereign human intellect from which all moral action was ultimately derived. But as one editor astutely stated in regards to Augustine's *De libero
arbitrio* :

> In controverting the Manichees with largely Platonist weap-
> ons Augustine had exposed his flank to the Pelagians.
> Pelagius himself was happy to be able to quote from the
> *De Libero Arbitrio* in support of his own views.[11]

A close reading of Augustine's approach on the subject of human volition in Book 1 shows that he attempted to treat the subject from a Christian
viewpoint without including a proper consideration of the effect of Adam's
fall on human nature. Human nature was so drastically changed with Adam's
sin that any consideration of the human will must include the consequences
of Adam's disobedience on human personality. Certainly Adam's will was
free at the time of his disobedience, but the result of that rebellion imputed
sin to all his progeny as we have discussed in Chapter 2. While Scripture is
very clear on this point, humanistic views of human nature always fail to
account fully for the consequences of that rebellion. None of Adam's offspring have inherited the same nature that he originally possessed. In Scripture we read, "Therefore, just as through one man sin entered into the world,
and death through sin, and so death spread to all men, because all sinned."[12]
The death being spoken of here is not only physical death but the eternal
spiritual death of damnation.[13] And again, the Hebrew Scripture plainly
describes the effect that Adam's sin had on human nature. Jeremiah wrote,
"The heart is more deceitful than all else/And is desperately sick/Who can
understand it?"[14] Adam's exercise of his will to sin, a truly free will, created a
chasm between God and man. That separation caused Adam's offspring to
be spiritually dead, and from that incapacitation came the incapacitation of
the will to operate in a purely free way. In other words, with separation from
God, i.e., the true moral good, the will lost its ability, in and of itself, to
move towards that good. Man lost his ability to please God, or to do God's
will, of his own *natural* accord.

An allegorical illustration will help show the light in which the freedom
of the human will must be placed, but one in which Augustine, in his early
writing, failed to place it. For the illustrative purposes of this allegory let us
go into a "science fictional" mode of thinking.

Imagine a person in a mammoth, windowless building with hundreds
of corridors arranged in a complex maze of architecture. Throughout the
building there are speakers where an announcer periodically declares to our
subject that he should always be prepared to exit the building. The walls, all
three-feet thick, have been constructed from a new revolutionary concrete
material of incredible strength. The living conditions in this hypothetical

environment are such that our subject has no desire or reason to ever exit the building. In this building is essentially a self-contained world with every convenience to meet every need of its inhabitants. At the end of every corridor is a door marked with an exit sign. Every exit door leads to another layer of corridors which, like the first, has its own set of exit doors. That layer leads to another layer and the final layer's doors are only unlocked in one direction from the outside in. From the inside they are all securely impenetrable.

Our subject has total freedom on where he can move and what he can do in this massive structure. He believes that he can go to any exit door and leave if he so chooses because he has ventured through many of the layers, although he has never reached the "last layer." So convinced is he that he can exit at will that he now ignores the loud speakers which periodically proclaim the exit warning. He believes that he has no need to worry because he is convinced that he can exit the building if he so chooses. In his thinking he possesses freedom of will and certainly *there is* a freedom associated with his will because in our imaginary building he can seemingly do as he pleases. If he chooses to go into a corridor four layers from his present location he knows that he can freely do so.

However, his freedom is not a *sovereign* freedom because he cannot truly exit the building in accordance with the working of both his will and intellect. His intellect falsely perceives that if he wanted to leave the building he could simply walk through the many exit doors to the final exit.

Now suppose a small fire begins in one remote area of this massive structure and our outside announcer, via the sound system, who happens to be a Nobel Prize winning quantum physicist, warns our occupant that the building must be vacated. Furthermore, our subject is told that there is no escape from the building via the marked exits but if he will go to a certain wing, at a marked point on a certain wall, he will be able to escape by approaching that spot on the wall at a running speed of ten miles per hour. Unknown to our subject is a major breakthrough in quantum physics, which allows a unique concrete of which this spot is constructed to be penetrated by the human body via the quantum tunneling effect when the critical speed of ten miles per hour is reached.

The question is whether or not our subject has freedom to exit the building. Certainly if he has not paid attention to the warning that he must exit, he does not. Furthermore, even if he hears the warning but his intellect dismisses any possibility that he could escape by following the instructions of the announcer, he again has no true freedom to exit the building. Even if he believes the accuracy of the announcer's information and acts upon it accordingly, his ability to leave the structure is only because his will acted *responsively* (not sovereignly in accordance with his own knowledge of the situation) to the knowledge and will of a higher power. In this instance that higher power is represented by the knowledge and will of the physicist who has provided a means for his escape.

In this allegorical example, reconciliation with God (and therefore salvation) is represented, of course, by the quantum exit. To believe that the subject of this example possesses the freedom to will his exit *of his own accord* would be, of course, a faulty conclusion.

The ancient Greek philosophers had created a system of morality where the human will appeared to be free to follow the lead of the intellect to attain the true moral good. But in reality, that freedom was not a true freedom because Greek philosophy had forced the intellect to operate on the false premise that human nature is morally neutral at birth.

To use the constructs of the above allegory, Augustine originally failed to sufficiently confine the will to the "impenetrable building" which represents the sin nature that every human being has inherited from Adam. Because of this failure, Pelagius used Book 1 of Augustine's *De libero arbitrio* to support his grossly erroneous teaching on human nature. The human will is only free within certain boundaries. The human will does not possess a sovereign freedom that is able to separate its owner from the nature that condemns him. In other words, as we have already emphasized in Chapter 2, while the human will has freedom in many areas that do not involve moral choice, that freedom is limited in its ability to choose of its own accord the moral good i.e., in its *stand-alone* ability to please God. Adam originally possessed a nature that was not confined to the "the building" of our allegory. But Adam's decision to enter that building through the "one-way locked-doors" put all of his posterity into that prison of sin.

Because of Augustine's approach to the human will in Book 1 of his *De libero arbitrio*, some authors have concluded—as did Pelagius—that he was a proponent of a free will congruous with a humanistic understanding of reality. However, it must be understood that the free will of which Augustine here spoke was not the same free will as that spoken of by the ancient Greek philosophers nor of that currently spoken of by modern humanists. In reality, Augustine's view of human will was inconsistent with a humanistic viewpoint because he eventually came to understand that the will was severely incapacitated because of Adam's sin, even though at the time the first two Books were written, his understanding of that incapacitation was not yet fully developed.

It is in Book 3 of the same work where it becomes clear that the free will of which Augustine wrote is different from the free will of the Greek humanists. Book 3, written a few years after Books 1 and 2, reflects a matured

Augustine. It is apparent that at this point Augustine had begun to deal with the consequences of the fall on human nature and hence of its effect on the human will. Augustine wrote in Book 3:

> It is not surprising that man, through his ignorance, does not have free choice of will to determine what he ought to do; or that, through the resistance of carnal habits, which have become second nature as a result of the element of unrestraint handed on in human heredity, he sees what he ought to do and wills it, but cannot accomplish it. It is an absolutely just punishment for sin that a man should lose what he refuses to use rightly, when he could do so without any difficulty if he wished. This is a man who knows what he ought to do and does not do it, loses the knowledge of what is right, and the man who has refused to act rightly when he could, loses the power when he wishes to have it.[15]

Augustine attempted to make his reader aware that the nature with which one is born is void of a natural ability to will the moral good. Augustine came to understand that moral free will, in the purest sense, applied only to Adam, the first man, and not to his offspring. Augustine states this plainly in the same section, writing:

> When we speak of a will free to act rightly, we speak of the will with which man was created [i.e., Adam's will]. … The wrong actions which are done in ignorance, and the right actions which cannot be done in spite of a good will, are called sins because they draw their origin from the first sin which was committed freely, and which brought about these effects as a due consequence. … So too we use the word "nature" properly speaking of the nature which men share in common, and with which at first man was created in a state of innocence. We also use nature to mean that nature with which we are born mortal, ignorant and slaves of the flesh, after sentence has been pronounced on the first man.[16]

It is this line of thinking that emerges in Augustine's later works. A more mature Augustine is evident in the *Confessions* and for this reason this is perhaps his best known work. When the *Confessions* were penned, his thinking had gelled into a more consistent theology. In the *Confessions*, one reads of the effect of his early schooling on his view of human nature and particularly on that of his own nature. In speaking of the state of his mind before his conversion, Augustine stated:

For it still seemed to me "that it was not we that sin, but that I know not what other nature sinned in us." And it gratified my pride to be free from blame, and, after I had committed any fault, not to acknowledge that I had done any ... but I loved to excuse it, and to accuse something else (I wot not what) which was with me, but was not I.[17]

Although Augustine acknowledged the reality of sin before his conversion, his pre-Christian thought processes regarding personal responsibility for sin were typically humanistic in that he could not understand the extent to which sin controlled *his* nature. One's "slate" is not clean at birth. One is not free, independent of God's working, to will the moral good because human nature is incapacitated, in its natural condition, to move itself to the moral Good. Augustine elsewhere stated of his pre-Christian condition:

I was descending into hell burdened with all the sins that I had committed. both [*sic*] against Thee, myself, and others, many and grievous, over and above that bond of original sin whereby we all die in Adam. For none of these things hadst Thou forgiven me in Christ, neither had He "abolished" by His cross "the enmity" which, by my sins, I had incurred with Thee.[18]

Augustine's awareness that God had to first supernaturally awaken his dead sinful conscience is apparent in the testimony of his *Confessions*. Influenced by his devout Christian mother, Augustine tells us that in his seeking for wisdom, he initially turned to the Scripture that he had often heard read as a child, but states that he could not understand the things of God due to his proud and sinful natural mind. In Augustine's own words:

And behold, I perceive something not comprehended by the proud, not disclosed to children, but lowly as you approach, sublime as you advance, and veiled in mysteries; and I was not of the number of those who could enter into it, or bend my neck to follow its steps. For not as when now I speak did I feel when I turned towards those Scriptures, but they appeared to me to be unworthy to be compared with the dignity of Tully; for my inflated pride shunned their style, nor could the sharpness of my wit pierce their inner meaning. Yet, truly, were they such as would develop in little ones; but I scorned to be a little one, and, swollen with pride, I looked upon myself as a great one.[19]

In the *Confessions* Augustine prolifically expressed his gratitude to God for removing that natural blindness to spiritual truth that has befallen all men because of Adam's sin. Augustine came to know that God must first move on one's personality before he can come to know the God of the universe. He stated that "Thou sendedst Thine hand from above, and drewest my soul out of that profound darkness."[20] And later again in the same work when speaking of a dark depression induced by the death of a friend before his conversion, Augustine stated concerning his soul,

> To Thee, O Lord, should it have been raised, for Thee to lighten and avert it. This I knew, but was neither willing nor able; all the more since, in my thoughts of Thee, Thou wert not any solid or substantial thing to me. For Thou wert not Thyself, but an empty phantasm, and my error was my god.[21]

The mature Augustine became keenly aware that the will had to be empowered through a supernatural enlightenment of one's mind, allowing it to move *responsively* to God's will. In the treatise *Grace and Free Will* he wrote:

> Certainly, in willing anything, it is we who will, but it is He who enables us to will what is good. And the words I quoted a short while ago refer to Him, namely: "The will is prepared by the Lord." It is further said of Him: "The steps of a man are directed by the Lord and He it is who wills his way"; and, "It is God who works in you even to will." [22, 23]

The Pelagian controversy was one of immense importance in the early establishment of Christianity within the Western world. Augustine's successful effort against the Pelagians was instrumental in keeping Christianity, at least for a few hundred years, free from man's perennial gravitation towards that mind-set which is ever forgetful of man's natural standing before God. It is difficult to preserve the knowledge and understanding that all men are *already judged guilty*, or, are *already condemned*. Pelagius' view of human nature was consistent with Aristotle's view, where immorality was simply the result of bad habits and bad example. They both believed that one could correct these deficiencies, if in fact they existed, through the exertion of human will. Such thinking renders the human will as a sovereign entity in the scheme of moral philosophy. Whenever any aspect of human personality is allowed to become sovereign in one's thinking, one has resorted to a humanistic philosophy, no matter what one claims to believe about God. When humanism creeps into societies that have been established in biblically based viewpoints of reality, it always gains a foothold through error-prone views of sin's effect on human nature. These same issues always come back to the forefront. The issues resurfaced in the Catholic Church (see next section), and helped to trigger the Reformation, and they are yet present in our own era (see Chapter 10).

In his later years, Augustine published a retraction to his *De libero arbitrio* to better delineate his views on the Pelagian controversy. Pelagius and his proponents had used the early part of that work to defend their humanistic position. In the *Retractions,* Augustine reiterated that his initial writing on the subject (Book 1) was intended to refute the Manichees' position that introduced "a being, evil in nature, which is unchangeable and coeternal with God."[24] Augustine here wrote:

> As this was why we raised the problem, these books contain no reference to God's grace ... Hence the recent Pelagian heretics, who hold a theory of free choice of will which leaves no place for the grace of God, since they hold it is given in accordance with our merits, must not boast of my support. ... The Pelagians think, or may think, that I held their views. They are wrong, however in thinking so. It is the will by which we sin ... Unless, therefore, the will itself is set free by the grace of God from that slavery by which it has been made a servant of sin, and unless it is given help to overcome its vices, mortal men cannot live upright and devout lives. If this gift of God, by which the will is set free, did not precede the act of the will, it would be given in accordance with the will's merits, and would not be grace which is certainly given as a free gift. ... But, though man fell through his own will, he cannot rise through his own will.[25]

Augustine was here making it clear that the free will of which he wrote was one only assignable to man in a state of supernatural grace and one that is not associated with unredeemed human nature.

Pelagius was excommunicated in 412 A.D. as a result of Augustine's vigorous defense of the scriptural view of sin. In so doing, Augustine relied on the teachings of the Apostle Paul who had addressed the same issues regarding similar error in Jewish thinking during the Apostle's era. The Apostle wrote:

> Sin entered into the world, and death through sin, and so death spread to all men, because all sinned ... [The] Gentiles, who did not pursue righteousness, attained righteousness, even the righteousness which is by faith; but Israel, pursuing a law of righteousness, did not arrive at that law.

Why? because they did not pursue it by faith, but as though it were by works. They stumbled over the stumbling stone,[26] just as it is written, "Behold, I lay in Zion a stone of stumbling and a rock of offense, And he who believes in Him will not be disappointed."[27]

Aquinas

The demarcation from a Christianity with a diminutive humanistic influence to one that became oppressed by humanistic thought is indistinct, as expected, from a process that occurred over many years. Certainly the processes that precipitated the humanism of the Renaissance were well underway before the time usually marked by historians as the beginning of that era. Before discussing the Renaissance and Reformation, we here discuss how Thomas Aquinas' teachings contributed to the advent of humanistic thinking in the pre-Reformation Christian church. Aquinas is the predominate figure of Scholasticism, the major school of theological and philosophical thinking of the Middle Ages. The Roman Catholic Church, even today, recognizes Aquinas as an authority on many matters of philosophical and theological importance and, his writings are therefore responsible for many of the Roman Catholic beliefs and practices that exist today.

Aquinas was born in either the latter part of 1224 or the early months of 1225 in the town of Roccasecca, Italy. His father there was a public servant (a count) under the Emperor of Sicily. His early education was steeped in the Catholic tradition but at about the age of 15 he began study in the liberal arts at the University of Naples. At about the age of 20, against the wishes of his family, he became a Dominican friar and thereafter entered into Dominican study, first at Paris, and later at Cologne. During this period he came under the teaching of Albertus Magnus, a noted authority on Aristotle. The influence of Magnus on the young Aquinas was monumental. Because of that influence, the teachings of Aristotle would become the focal point of much of his subsequent work. Aquinas took an advanced degree in theology from the University of Paris in 1256, and thereafter became a member of its faculty in philosophy.

Some historians wrongly believe that Aquinas' era, often referred to as the Dark Ages, was one of little academic progress. Those years, however, brought advancements in many areas of learning. Roger Bacon, for example, was then actively researching topics in both chemistry and physics, although, of course, somewhat crudely by modern standards. The writings of Aquinas clearly reflect that the scientific period was already in its infancy. His works contain scientific terminology used yet today. Understandably, then, Aquinas was concerned with the Church's views on, and its relationship to, this new developing scientific methodology. As one concerned with knowledge, Aquinas understood the importance of acknowledging the power of reason. A main objective of his academic endeavor was to show compatibility between Christianity and reason. Because scientific endeavor was gaining momentum, Aquinas turned to the writings and teachings of Aristotle whom he perceived to be an authority in that area.

In his theological discussions, Aquinas ventured into scientific topics. In the *Summa* he discussed the nature of light when speaking of the creation account of Genesis. On the nature of light, Aquinas stated:

> It is impossible for light to be a body; this is apparent for three reasons. The first is an argument from place. For the place of any one body is different from the place of any other body, nor is it naturally possible for two bodies to be in the same place at the same time, no matter what kind of bodies they may be, because contiguity demands a difference in position. Secondly, the same conclusion follows from an analysis of motion. For if light were a body, illumination would be the translational motion of a body. But no translational motion of a body can occur instantaneously, since everything that moves translationally must first pass over the midpoint of the length before reaching the end. Yet illumination takes place instantaneously.[28]

That Aquinas spoke on the physical sciences demonstrates a bold approach to epistemology. Of course Aquinas was wrong regarding his statements on the nature of light. While light is a complex phenomenon still not fully understood, we know today that it does indeed possess properties of a body. Illumination *does not* take place instantaneously.[29] We will see in Chapter 6 how the Catholic Church got into trouble when it spoke on scientific topics where it had no expertise.[30]

Aquinas taught that certain truths about God were a form of science and, as such, they could be defended through scientific methodology. He brought those truths under the heading of Natural Theology. Under this topic he drew much on the thought processes and terminology of the Greek humanistic philosophers in his attempt to rationally prove the existence of God. Aquinas, therefore, sought to establish reason as a primary mechanism for the attainment of knowledge, even spiritual knowledge, although to his credit, he acknowledged that certain spiritual truths could only be known through revelation.

If one is to trace the influence of humanism on modern Western thought, one should conclude that Aquinas erred in his attempt to reconcile Christianity to the philosophies of the ancient Greek humanists. Aquinas attempted to place knowledge acquirable through the intellect on par with that which can only be attained through that light of supernatural election referred to centuries earlier by Augustine. Aquinas' sincerity and academic integrity cannot be doubted. However, in his attempt to show compatibility between reason and Christianity, (and they *are*, again to Aquinas' credit, compatible) he erred in not sufficiently differentiating between the knowledge of the physical universe obtainable through the intellect by the scientific method and the knowledge which is available only to those who have been given to Christ by the Father.[31] Therefore, a major error of Aquinas was his inversion of the relative importance of reason versus the knowledge that comes to one through only that type faith demonstrated by Abraham, spoken of in Chapter 2.

In his effort to establish compatibility between Aristotle and Christianity, Aquinas essentially equated Aristotle's god to that of the God of Scripture. Aristotle's *first principle* cannot be equated with the God of Scripture. Believing in the existence of a *prime-mover* does not get one to the truth of God. Many believe in the so-called "supreme being" without truly knowing the God of Holy Scripture. That Aristotle's god was not the same God as Abraham's, defeats one of Aquinas' main thesis. Reason can decipher the physical truths of nature but it cannot decipher a true knowledge of the God who created that nature. As I stressed in Chapter 1 when discussing the Presocratic philosophers, the scientific method cannot decipher the truth of ultimate reality because ultimate reality, to again use mathematical terminology, is not a subset of the universe. The universe is a creation of ultimate reality. One might successfully argue that through the scientific method, i.e., pure logic, one might arrive at the ultimate physical truth of the universe, although even this argument would probably break down with sufficient depth of consideration. However, the ultimate physical truth of the universe is not truth by which one can deduce the principles of ultimate reality. This is not to say that knowledge of God goes against reason. Truth by its very nature cannot be irrational, and it was this fact from which Aquinas was attempting to generate his arguments. Scripture makes plain the fact that reason *should* enable one to be convinced of God's existence. However, Scripture[32] also tells us that human reason has become darkened (not subject to truthful conclusions in the spiritual realm) because of prior rejection of already revealed spiritual truth. As a result of the fallen nature that each and every human being has inherited, pure human reason is subject to error and cannot therefore be relied upon to get one to the absolute truth of ultimate reality.

Aquinas did not clearly communicate to his audience that knowledge of the God of Scripture is unattainable to the ordinary person solely in the power of human reason. I use the word *ordinary* here for shock effect because it makes the claim a rather bold one, and perhaps to some, an even preposterous one. I do not use the term in the same sense that C. S. Lewis used it when he stated that "there are no ordinary people."[33] But here I use the term *ordinary* to mean the natural person. The Apostle Paul wrote, "But a natural man [the ordinary man] does not accept the things of the Spirit of God; for they are foolishness to him, and he cannot understand them, because they are spiritually appraised."[34] The ordinary one according to human standards might be extraordinary with God, or a person ordinary by God's standards might be extraordinary according to human standards. If the greatest scientist who has ever lived (or is yet to live), no matter the power of his intellect and reasoning ability, never attained (or attains) a personal knowledge of the truth of Jesus Christ, through faith, he is an ordinary human in God's sight. The natural or ordinary person is one who has yet to reconcile his will to the will of the God of the universe. He is one who either has not understood his will to be naturally contrary to the will of God or if he understands it to be so, has chosen to remain in rebellion against God by remaining at the helm of his life and directing his own paths. Scripture makes it plain that the natural man (or the ordinary man) cannot even begin to understand the God of Scripture—the God of the universe—because the things of the Spirit of God are not discerned by reason. Aquinas' teaching appears to be irreconcilable with Scripture on this point.

Therefore, it appears that Aquinas did not fully understand the effect of Adam's fall on human nature. Although Aquinas clearly taught the concept of "original sin," he failed to understand the natural enmity between God and man brought about by that sin. Aquinas stated wrongly in the *Summa* that man has a natural inclination towards knowing the truth of God. He wrote:

> Therefore the order of the precepts of the natural law is according to the order of natural inclinations. Because in man there is first of all an inclination to good in accordance with the nature which he has in common with all substances; that is, every substance seeks the preservation of its own being, according to its nature. And by reason of this inclination, whatever is a means of preserving human

life and of warding off its obstacles belongs to the natural law. …There is in man an inclination to good, according to the nature of his reason, which nature is proper to him; thus man has a natural inclination to know the truth about God, and to live in society. And in this respect, whatever pertains to this inclination belongs to the natural law.[35]

Aquinas believed that all men, through the power of the human conscience, were naturally moved towards the one true God and the moral good. In other words, all humans, in Aquinas' view, have a natural inclination to know the God of Scripture because of the influence of natural law. Aquinas had been so influenced by the philosophy of Aristotle that he let Aristotle contaminate his thinking in this area. Aristotle, as we have discussed in the previous chapter, taught that "the good" was that at which all things aimed. Aquinas rightfully acknowledged God's goodness, but falsely concluded that human nature had a natural inclination to know the truth of God. While it may be true that God has put into the human spirit a desire that can only be filled by Himself, this is not the same as saying that in human nature is a natural inclination to know God in a personal way. As we discussed in Chapter 1, the power of the conscience to suggest the moral good cannot be denied. But to imply that the human conscience has the power to activate the will towards God appears to go against the precepts of Scripture. The drive towards self-preservation that Aquinas evoked as a function of natural law to drive the will towards the moral good, in reality, is usually the drive that separates him from the moral good. The natural man tends to believe that his survival depends upon himself to engineer it, and as such, he will use immoral means in his human attempt to insure that survival.

Although Aquinas correctly said that one could not see God, unless God by his grace made himself intelligible to that mind,[36] he did not clearly delineate to whom God bestows that grace. The grace of God is only available to the one who has seen his innermost being and understands that it is *his* heart (i.e., *his personality*) to which the Scripture refers when it says that the human heart is deceitful and desperately sick.[37] Grace is bestowed on the one who realizes that he is naturally in rebellion against the God of the universe and understands the consequence of that rebellion: separation from ultimate reality resulting in ultimate destruction. But he is also the one who understands that if he will repent of that rebellion, God's grace provides for him a way to be reconciled to God. The Scripture tells us that God made Jesus "to be sin" on behalf of those believing in Him so that they could "become the righteousness of God in Him.""[38] One simply cannot come to the true moral good without first understanding how his fallen nature has separated him from any possibility of attaining, in the power of his own personality, a true knowledge of the God of Scripture. Humanistic thought will always creep into a system of Christian thought when this point is not fully comprehended.

The concept of the new birth is closely associated with this naturally lost condition of which we are speaking. The nature with which every human being is born (Jesus, of course, excluded) is one that is in rebellion against God and, therefore, is one that prevents everyone from naturally understanding the truth of God. The *new birth* is God's impartation of new nature, by his grace, through faith, that reconciles the sinner to Himself. The ordinary one then becomes the extraordinary one. Unless one experiences spiritual birth, he can never truly know the God of the universe. Spiritual birth and a true knowledge of God are one and the same. Only when one sees himself as he naturally is, that is, one who by nature is opposed to the will of God, and understands that this natural condition will lead him to everlasting destruction, can he understand that he must, as Jesus stated, be "born again." That means he must have new nature imparted to him before he can "see the kingdom of God," or to use the terminology that we have been using, before he can know, or understand, ultimate reality.

Aquinas appears to have lacked understanding of the meaning of spiritual birth even though his writings often refer to Scripture that involves it. A quote from his *Summa* illustrates this point. In his discussion of miracles he makes a most revealing statement that readily demonstrates his lack of understanding of the natural vs. the new man. Here he states,

> Creation and the justifying of the sinner, while they are acts of God alone, are strictly speaking not miracles, because they are acts not meant to be accomplished by other causes. Thus they do not occur as exceptions to the pattern in nature, since they are not part of that pattern.[39]

Aquinas apparently failed to understand that salvation is certainly a departure from the natural order. The salvation of a sinner is not in nature's power, but the absence of the miracle of salvation will certainly result in nature taking its course. If the ordinary man does not experience the miracle of salvation, his end will be one of damnation. When one comes into a personal knowledge of ultimate reality, one indeed departs from the natural order. Scripture states that if any man is in Christ he is a new creature.[40] The process that produces the "new creature," referred to here, is synonymous with the new birth that Jesus referred to when he told Nicodemus that "unless one is born again, he cannot see the kingdom of God."[41] The new birth implies that the one who has come into an understanding of ultimate reality, through faith in the work of Jesus, is set free from the nature he inherited through Adam's sin. The nature that every man has inherited from Adam is subject to the law of sin and death[42] but the imparted new nature becomes free from the dominion of sin. Scripture states that most people (the ordinary) follow the humanistic way that leads to destruction.[43]

When Aquinas discussed sin's definition, he rightly included Augustine's definition. Aquinas reminded his reader that Augustine defined sin as any word, deed or desire, which is against eternal law.[44] This definition is in accord with the scriptural definition that was discussed in Chapter 2. Sin is simply the transgression of God's law, or the transgression of God's will, since law is always given to make known the standard, or will, of the lawgiver. But Aquinas, in seeking to defend Augustine's definition, actually modifies it in order to accommodate his own view of sin. Aquinas wrote:

> As has been said, sin is nothing else but a bad human act. A human act is human because it is voluntary, whether it is internal, e.g. to will or to choose; or external, e.g. to speak or to act. A human act is evil because it does not meet the standard for human behavior. Standards are nothing other than rules. The human will is subject to a twofold rule: one is proximate and on his own level, i.e., human reason; the other is the first rule beyond man's own level, i.e., the eternal law which is the mind of God.[45]

Here, Aquinas is further developing the "human reason" thesis of which we have been speaking. To allow human reason to play a role in determining the moral standard is opening the road to disaster, no matter if it is an immediate standard or an ultimate standard. Human reason simply cannot be trusted as an absolute in the establishment of a moral standard.

It is therefore apparent that Aristotle's erroneous views of human nature had a strong influence on Aquinas. In the humanism of Aristotle, human nature was morally neutral, i.e., every human being possessed at birth a clean moral slate. In Aristotle's view, human personality—man's intellect, will and emotion—was responsible for moving him to the moral good. The will, according to Aristotle, functioned to move an individual to the moral good if the intellect did its job as ruler over his emotional nature.

Aquinas' view of human will was consistent with the way in which he viewed human nature, the nature of sin and the extent to which sin has affected human nature. His thinking was not far removed from humanistic pattern of Aristotle, who viewed human personality as sovereign in its ability to move its possessor towards the true moral good. Aquinas stated in his *Summa*:

> Man has free choice. Otherwise counsels, exhortations, commands, prohibitions, rewards and punishments would be in vain. In order to make this evident, we must observe that some things act without judgment, as a stone moves downwards; and in like manner all things which lack knowledge. ... But man acts from judgment because by his knowing power he judges that something should be avoided or sought. But because this judgment, in the case of some particular act, is not from a natural instinct, but from some act of comparison in the reason, therefore he acts from free judgment and retains the power of being inclined to various things. ... And since man is rational man must have free choice.[46]

An interesting observation here is Aquinas' use of the natural law of gravity to illustrate his point. And yet it is a law of human nature (i.e., the law of sin and death) that determines why, in the final analysis, that man, solely within the power of his personality, lacks the ability to know, and to do, the true moral good. Man cannot solely in the power of his will do God's will. Man's will is already operative at birth against his Creator due to the nature he inherited from Adam. Without the power of Christ to spiritually revive one's fallen nature, the natural man has no more power to redeem himself than the stone (which Aquinas used for illustrative purpose) has to defy gravity and move itself upward. It must be remembered that God first chose to reveal himself to Abraham. Without God first moving, Abraham would have been lost in the pantheism of his ancestors. Abraham's will moved in *response* to the sovereign will of God.

Finally, as a result of faith in God's word, Abraham certainly became aware of his election. Concerning predestination Aquinas stated, "Even were predestination revealed to some by special privilege, it were better not revealed to everyone; that would breed despair in the non-predestined, and negligence in the predestined."[47] While this position might initially appear to be a reasonable one, it is in total opposition to what the Scripture teaches. This statement totally undermines a foundational truth of the Christian faith. A product of one's faith in Christ should be the assurance of the new birth, or of one's election. The Apostle John stated, "These things I have written to you who believe in the name of the Son of God, *in order that you may know* [italics added] that you have eternal life."[48] Aquinas' teaching on the subject of human will and predestination resulted in placing into Christian thinking uncertainty on how one could be justified before God. This uncertainly, subsequently, opened an opportunity for humanism to gain a foothold in Christian thinking. We shall see in the following chapters how this issue again became a factor in the era of the Renaissance and Reformation.

4

Historical Humanism: The Renaissance

My lawgivers are Erasmus and Montaigne, not Moses and St. Paul.
E. M. Forster (1879-1970)

Historians attempting to understand modern Western civilization usually scrutinize the Renaissance, the period generally considered to span the mid 14th century through the mid 16th century. The era encompasses a complex and important period in Western history. That complexity has sometimes caused historians to misinterpret it. An error in perception, which can lead to a misinterpretation, arises from modern connotations of humanism. When speaking of Renaissance humanism, one does not speak of a secular humanism since the movement was yet framed in the Christianity of that era.

The Renaissance began in 14th century Italy with a renewed interest in the writings of certain ancient Greek and Roman authors. As stated by Kristeller and Randall, the emphasis of the Renaissance humanists

> was an educational and cultural program based on the study of the classical Greek and Latin authors. ... They emphasized the ideal of literary elegance and considered the imitation of the Roman authors the best way of learning to speak and to write well in prose and in verse.[1]

Renaissance humanism is better identified as an academic discipline than with any particular philosophy. Today, when we speak of "the humanities" in academic training, we are closer to the meaning of "Renaissance humanism" than when we identify it with modern connotations of secular humanism. Nonetheless, it is generally correct to say that the period generated an interest in ancient literature in such a way that caused the emphasis in human learning to shift from a vertical plane to a horizontal plane. The relationship between God and man, as stressed in the Scholasticism of Aquinas, became less important in the thinking of the Renaissance humanists than did their endeavor in the literary arts.

Although there is a distinction between Renaissance humanism and the humanism with which this work is concerned, the two are not unrelated. The challenge for the modern thinker is to understand why Renaissance humanism not only was derived from the Christianity of that day, but also, in a sense, contributed to the development of the worldview that now stands opposed to true Christian faith. In this chapter I briefly address two primary factors responsible for this evolution.

Certainly a connection between the humanism of the Renaissance and the ideas that led to the Reformation can be shown. Yet, nearly all scholars would agree that the two movements, although they shared some of the same roots, remain very distinct. This distinctness will become more apparent in the next chapter when we examine how Erasmus, one of the best-known Renaissance humanists (discussed later in this chapter) was eventually forced to deal with Luther, the undisputed leader of the Reformation. Understanding the positive role that Renaissance humanism played in the development of the Reformation—and how, from that development, divergent ideas arose in the thinking of those involved in those movements—gives one a better appreciation of this critical period in Western history.

Renaissance humanism, therefore, has somewhat of a duel nature. One aspect of Renaissance humanism is positive since the learning it spawned was instrumental in freeing the human spirit from the negative effects of the Scholasticism that was dominant in the official Church thinking of the Middle Ages. Humanism is often superior to the skeletal remains of that which it replaces. For example, to revert to a topic of Chapter 1 for illustrative purposes, the secular humanism of the Sophists should probably be considered superior to the pantheism of the Presocratics. Although neither view was a correct one, it is probably better to believe, from a practical standpoint, in the absence of God rather than believe the air itself is God, as perhaps did Democritus.[2] Therefore, when Renaissance humanism is presented in a favorable light, the Christian need not oppose that view. This era represented, for the most part, a positive period of learning into areas where prior Scholastic philosophy had poisoned knowledge. At the same time, it is important to understand why humanists (i.e., those in the vein of which this work is concerned), both secular and non-secular, often claim the Renaissance as foundational to some of their ideals and why the Christian aspects of this period are not usually considered by them to be pertinent.

In a sense, the Renaissance led to three divergences. Certainly, the Reformation was a child of the Renaissance. Furthermore, Renaissance humanism contributed to the development of Enlightenment humanism, which is basically a continuation of the Western humanism of which this book deals. This is the humanism birthed in Greek philosophy which is based on the idea that man, outside of a genuine relationship with the God *of Scripture*, can move himself, in the power of his own personality, towards the true moral good. Perhaps the most complex divergence of the Renaissance was in its effect on the Catholic Church. Theologically, the Catholic Church retreated to the Scholasticism of Aquinas, in spite of the Renaissance movement against it, and it remains affected by that move to this day. Because the humanism birthed in ancient Greek philosophy was already present in the Catholic Church before the Renaissance began, the Church therefore did not relinquish the effect of that humanism. Although the Catholic Church did not throw off Scholastic theology, Renaissance humanism was yet influential in the so-called Counter Reformation of the Catholic Church.

It is the negative influences of this era, for example its influence on the birth of Enlightenment deism, that one should be aware of, while at the same time remembering that were it not for the Renaissance, Luther and Calvin perhaps would not have uncovered the understanding of Scripture that Scholastic theology had suppressed and that humanists, both secular and non-secular, continue to reject.

Petrarch

The beginning of the Renaissance is usually associated with the life and work of Francesco Petrarch (or Petrarca). He was born in Arezzo, Italy, in 1304, and moved with his family to France when he was eight years of age, remaining there for about eight years. He returned to Italy to study law but, before finishing those studies, moved back to France and there entered the service of the Church.

From study of Petrarch's life and work one can begin to understand the transition that Renaissance humanism brought to the Western mind. Before the Renaissance, the Scholasticism of the Middle Ages dominated the intellectual climate. The Renaissance humanists threw off the tenants of Scholasticism and, thereby, introduced into the Western consciousness a new understanding of reality.

Petrarch is today recognized as the father of Renaissance humanism due to his pioneering interest and expertise in the literature of the ancients. Most Renaissance scholars admire him as the first modern poet. His conception and perfection of the sonnet form is believed to have influenced even

Shakespeare's work. Cicero, the noted Roman poet, was without question the author that exerted the greatest influence upon Petrarch's literary style. As the father of Renaissance humanism, Petrarch sought to turn academic thinking from abstract theological and scientific endeavor to real academic problems of language and written communication.

It is important to note that Petrarch did not divorce himself from Christianity. He remained a devout Roman Catholic his entire life. Much of his writing exhibits a rather strong framework of Catholicism. For example, Petrarch called Averroes a "ranting dog . . . who, excited by hellish wrath, abused and blasphemed the holy name of Christ and the Catholic faith by his sacrilegious insults and cursing."[3] Petrarch's writings show that he had more than a cursory knowledge of Scripture since he often referred to scriptural passages when defending his philosophical views.

A common theme observed in Renaissance humanism is the disdain of Scholasticism. Petrarch believed that the Scholastics were trying in vain to penetrate a world inaccessible. In his words:

> There are fools who seek to understand the secrets of nature and the far more difficult secrets of God, with supercilious pride, instead of accepting them in humble faith. They cannot approach them, let alone reach them. These fools imagine they can grasp the heavens with their hands. Moreover, they are content with their erroneous opinion and actually imagine to have grasped truth. They are quite happy in their illusion. Not even the telling words addressed by the Apostle to the Romans are able to deflect them from their lunacy: "Who knows the secrets of God? Who is a party to His counsels?"[4]

A short work of Petrarch, which demonstrates how he sought to move Christianity away from its Scholastic influences, is his *De sui ipsius et multorum ignorantia* (*On His Own Ignorance and That Of Many Others*). In this work—written late in life—Petrarch defends an attack by four former friends who had evidently accused him of ignorance for holding too much allegiance to the ancient pagan authors—especially to Cicero. Petrarch was, at that time, one of Italy's foremost scholars and was probably insulted by that charge. His response was written in a rather sarcastic tone to defend his honor on the pretense of admitting to the ignorance of which he is accused. The work instead served as a showcase for his vast knowledge and was a rather effective repudiation of his attackers. In this work, Petrarch demonstrated a good knowledge of philosophy (which he attempted to put into perspective of overall truth), and of Cicero, whom, as before mentioned, he greatly admired. The work also shows a familiarity with Scripture, which he used sparingly to defend himself. But more importantly, this work shows his misgivings concerning the philosophical foundations of Scholasticism.

Petrarch here revealed that his primary criticism of Scholastic thought was its reliance on the ancient Greek philosophers. Petrarch wrote:

> No wonder human arrogance meets countless rugged cliffs when it unfolds its unfledged wings to the wind in this penury of knowledge. How copious and how ridiculous are the vanities of philosophers, how many contradicting opinions show up; how great is their obstinacy, how great their impudence! Innumerable are the sects, innumerable the differences. How many quarrels break out, how ambiguous are all matters, how great and entangled is the confusion of words! Deep and inaccessible are the caverns where truth is hidden, and sophists lay countless ambushes which completely obstruct the road to truth, as it were, with briars and thorns, so as to make it impossible to distinguish which way leads straight to truth.[5]

These words show how the roots of Renaissance humanism positively contributed to the development of the Western mind. Ultimately, the Reformation has its beginnings in these same misgivings because Scholastic thought is ultimately responsible for the conditions that led to the Reformation.

When writing of Aristotle's *Nicomachean Ethics*, Petrarch commented on Aristotle's statement, "We learn ... philosophy not with the purpose of gaining knowledge but of becoming better." He wrote in response:

> I see virtue, and all that is peculiar to vice as well as to virtue, egregiously defined and distinguished by him [Aristotle] and treated with penetrating insight. When I learn all this, I know a little bit more than I knew before, but mind and will remain the same as they were, and I myself remain the same. It is one thing to know, another to love; one thing to understand, another to will. He teaches what virtue is, I do not deny that; but his lesson lacks the words that sting and set afire and urge toward love of virtue and hatred of vice or, at any rate, does not have enough of such power. He who looks for that will find it in our Latin writers, especially in Cicero and Seneca, and, what may be astonishing to hear, in Horace, a poet somewhat rough in style but most pleasing in his maxims.[6]

It is interesting to note here that while Petrarch identified a major problem with the philosophy of Aristotle (i.e., the lack of a means to a true moral remedy), in order to resolve that problem, he first pointed his reader to authors whose philosophies were yet divorced from Scripture. He only turned his reader to the subject of Christ almost as an afterthought. Accordingly, Petrarch goes on to write:

> I know but too well that all this cannot be achieved outside the doctrine of Christ and without His help: no one can become wise and good who has not drunk a large draught—*not* [italics added] from the fabulous spring of Pegasus in the folds of Mount Parnassus—but from the true and unique source which has its origin in heaven, the source of the water that springs up in eternal life. Those who drink from it no longer thirst.[7] However, much is achieved also by the authors of whom I have just spoken. They are a great help to those who are making their way to this goal.[8]

Petrarch's criticism of Greek philosophy ultimately came from the influence of his Christian education. Petrarch was intuitively aware that simply understanding certain aspects of virtue, based on the workings of human conscience, could not change human nature. Petrarch stated that

> the true moral philosophers and useful teachers of the virtues are those whose first and last intention is to make hearer and reader good, those who do not merely teach what virtue and vice are and hammer into our ears the brilliant name of the one and the grim name of the other ... Therefore, those are far wrong who consume their time in learning to know virtue instead of acquiring it, and, in a still higher degree, those whose time is spent in learning to know God instead of loving Him.[9]

Petrarch placed greater emphasis on loving God than on knowing God. This admonition demonstrated his bias towards the emotive aspect of human personality. This was a reaction against the Scholastic philosophy that had improperly exalted human reason. However, knowing God properly and loving him properly are inseparable. Merely understanding the qualities of virtue cannot make one virtuous because to be truly virtuous (or righteous) one must have imparted to him that new nature of which we have previously spoken—which only Christ can impart.

Although it often appears that Petrarch possessed a genuine Christian faith, one cannot be sure that he understood the impact of genuine faith on human nature. This doubt is not only evident from the last sentence of his words quoted above—for one cannot love God properly without properly knowing Him—but it is also reinforced from the following statement. Petrarch wrote in this same work:

> My incorruptible treasure and the superior part of my soul is with Christ; but, because of the frailties and burdens of mortal life, which are not only difficult to bear but difficult merely to enumerate, I cannot, I confess, lift up, however ardently I should wish, the inferior parts of my soul, in which the irascible and concupiscible appetites are located, and cannot make them cease to cling to earth. I call upon Christ as witness and invoke Him: He alone knows how often I have tried again and again, sadly and indignantly and with the greatest effort, to drag them up from the ground and how much I suffer because I have not succeeded. Christ will perhaps have compassion on me and lend me a helping hand in the sound attempt of my frail soul, which is weighted down and depressed by the mass of its sin.[10]

These words of Petrarch so well demonstrate that one cannot achieve any degree of righteousness through one's own effort. Outside of man's responsive will to God's will, imposition of human will cannot, in a saving way, affect one's nature. One who seeks to move himself, on his own accord, towards that which is truly moral will always fail. Humanistic philosophy cannot grasp that truth. The righteousness, from which all true moral action springs, is always imputed as a result of one's faith in the God of Scripture. No amount of human effort, in and of itself, can achieve it.

The struggle between Petrarch's desire to live as a Christian and yet engage the world apart from his faith is particularly well pointed out by E. H. Wilkins, an authority on the life and works of Petrarch. Wilkin's words, when emphasizing that struggle, give further insight into Petrarch's complex personality. He characterized Petrarch's character as one who intensely desired to be loved and tells how this trait manifested itself in his love for Laura—the subject of much of his poetry—his love for family, and the love he had for his many friends.[11] As a young man Petrarch sought intensely the fame he achieved and he readily expressed that drive in his work.

Wilkins points out this conflict when discussing the years of 1344-45. Of Petrarch's *canzone l' vo pensando* (*I live and move in thought*) Wilkins writes:

> It voices an intense conflict between the thought of salvation, on the one hand, and the thoughts of glory and of love on the other hand—thoughts that are in reality de-

sires infused with thought. After an introductory stanza, the thought of salvation, speaking in direct discourse, attacks the thoughts of glory [desire for fame] and of love; Petrarch then defends them as best he can; and the concluding stanzas depict the plight from which he cannot free himself. The stanza devoted to the defense of the thought of glory reads in part: 'A thought that is sweet and sharp abides in my soul, a wearying and a delightful burden. It fills my heart with desire and feeds it with hope, for when I think of glorious and generous fame I know not whether I freeze or burn, or whether I be pale and gaunt; and if I slay it, it springs up again stronger than ever. This thought has been growing in me ever since I slept in swaddling clothes, and I fear that it will go down with me into the tomb.'[12]

These words illustrate the battle that raged within Petrarch's psyche between his desire to please God and his desire to live to self. Thus, the conflict between his desire for salvation and the desire to find himself through his humanistic pursuits became painfully internalized.

While some historians claim that the Renaissance was a period of great scientific advancement, that characterization is somewhat misconceived. Significant gains in science did not come until after the Reformation. Petrarch met the emerging scientific methodology with scorn. Aquinas' attempt to make theology stand primarily on reason was recognized by the Renaissance humanists as a problematic union. In the previously given quote (ref. 4), where Petrarch was shown to attack the Scholastics, we also see his negative attitude towards the sciences. His declaration that "there are fools who seek to understand the secrets of nature" shows how little regard he had for scientific endeavor. Petrarch was keen on attacking the medical profession. Petrarch's address to a group of physicians, quoted by Garin from Petrarch's *Senilia*, included the statement, "It is your business to look after bodies. Leave the care and the education of the mind to genuine philosophers and orators."[13] As in the Sophistic humanism of the ancient Greek world, Renaissance humanism, in a certain sense, actually resulted in a de-emphasis of scientific study.

So while Petrarch was privy to the bankruptcy of Scholasticism and the ancient Greek philosophy that influenced it, he did little to address the problems that Scholastic philosophy had produced. Petrarch, as a humanist, was chiefly a man of letters. His primary focus was to express himself in poetry and it was through this channel that he enjoyed much of the fame that he so intensely sought. Tarnas has summarized Petrarch's mission with the following words:

> While Dante and the Scholastics were focused on theological precision and scientific knowledge of the natural world, Petrarch was instead engaged by the depths and complexities of his own consciousness. Rather than spiritual and scientific system building his focus was psychological, humanist, and aesthetic.[14]

The Roman Catholic Church was then well established in the corrupt practices which Erasmus would soon rail against. One should remember that only a few years after Petrarch's death, the Church burned John Huss alive, the fiery reformer educated at the University of Prague (M.A. 1396). Huss had dared to espouse the truth that Scripture was the ultimate spiritual authority and that Christ, not the Pope, was the true head of the Church. Petrarch's answer to the abuses of the Church was to simply turn away from contemplation of those problems. He was instead absorbed in his literary pursuits. His primary mission was not to exalt theological truth but was to immerse himself in the humanism of his poetry, which served as his vehicle to his own exaltation.

Valla

Like Petrarch, Lorenzo Valla (ca. 1406(7)?-1457) was an Italian humanist whose philosophy was also based in the Christian tradition of that day. Valla, noted for his philological exegesis of both ancient literature and Scripture, was also known for a brazen argumentative style, which over the course of his life made him many enemies.

The work that particularly set Valla at odds with the Roman Catholic establishment was his *De voluptate* (*On Pleasure*) which was judged by the Church as heretical. Valla later preferred to call the work *De vero bono* (*On the True Good*) probably because of misconstrued inferences derived from the original title. *De vero bono* was written in the form of a dialogue between three voices. The first voice represented the philosophy of the Stoics, the second the philosophy of the Epicureans, and the third voice of one who presented a Christian view of the two preceding voices.

Some modern scholars, who have wished to divorce the works of Valla from their Christian perspectives, have taken this work, much like his ecclesiastical contemporaries, to represent a defense of pro-Epicurean philosophy.[15] However, as pointed out by Kristeller,[16] in his own peculiar way, Valla was defending Christianity by attempting to show that pleasure, in the truest sense, was derived from a relationship with God. Valla thus believed the Epicureans to be closer to truth than the Stoics. Since Roman Catholic teaching had been somewhat influenced by Stoic philosophy, the church authorities judged this work as an attack on the Church. Scholasticism had set up the ancient Greek philosophers as ideals from which much of Stoic philosophy had been derived. In the preface, Valla claims the third voice to be his own position.

> Do you really say that pleasure is the true good? Yes, I do; and I shall assert that nothing but pleasure is good, and I have decided to assume and to prove its cause. Yet this true good is of two kinds, one in this life, the other in the future life. We prefer the latter to the former, but the former to the virtue of the philosophers. We shall set out to refute the Stoics, the defenders of virtue, and assume the defense of the Epicureans, and in this way we shall also defend the Christian religion.[17]

In the usual tradition of the Renaissance humanists, Valla was here attacking the methods of Scholasticism. He, like Petrarch, was especially suspect of the reliance Christianity had developed on those methods. The criticism of Scholastic thought is further evident in the opening few lines of his *De libero arbitrio* (On Free Will).[18] Here he wrote:

> I would prefer … that … those who are called theologians would not depend so much on philosophy or devote so much energy to it, making it almost an equal and sister … of theology. For it seems to me that they have a poor opinion of our religion if they think it needs the protection of philosophy. The followers of the Apostles, truly columns in the temple of God, whose works have now been extant many centuries, used this protection least of all. In fact, if we look carefully, the heresies of those times, which we understand were many and not insignificant, derived almost entirely from philosophic sources, so that philosophy not only profited our most sacred religion little but even violently injured it. But they of whom I speak consider [philosophy] a tool for weeding out heresies, when actually it is a seedbed of heresy.[19]

But more importantly, *De libero arbitrio* is an especially interesting work because here Valla laid the groundwork that questioned the meaning of free will in the traditional sense that Scholasticism had defined it and, thus, set the stage for one of the issues of the Reformation. In this discourse, Valla attempted to convince a friend that the will of man is not in conflict with the foreknowledge of God, because if this were the case then knowing something "is" would make the same thing "be." In regard to the case of Judas' betrayal of Jesus, Valla stated:

> Something that can happen and something that will happen are very different. I can be a husband, I can be a soldier or a priest, but will I right away? Not at all. Though I can do otherwise than will happen, nevertheless I shall not do otherwise; and it was in Judas' power not to sin even though it was foreseen that he would, but he preferred to sin, which it was foreseen would happen. Thus foreknowledge is valid and free will abides. … It is possible for you to do otherwise than God foreknows, nevertheless you will not do otherwise.[20]

While Valla attempted to show that human volition was not in conflict with God's foreknowledge, he acknowledged that there was difficulty in understanding how human free will could exist in conjunction with God's sovereign will. To address this issue Valla quoted from the Apostle Paul's letter to the Romans where it is written:

> I will have mercy on whom I will have mercy, and I will have compassion on whom I will have compassion. So then it is not of him that willeth, nor of him that runneth, but of God that showeth mercy. For the scripture saith unto Pharaoh, Even for this same purpose have I raised thee up, that I might show my power in thee, and that my name might be declared throughout all the earth. Therefore hath he mercy on whom he will have mercy, and whom he will he hardeneth. Thou wilt say then unto me, Why doth he yet find fault? For who hath resisted his will? Nay but, O man, who art thou that repliest against God?[21]

Valla maintained that even in this example of Scripture, human volition is preserved, even though he believed that its understanding was not possible. Valla stated, "His hardening one and showing another mercy does not deprive us of free will since He does this most wisely and in full holiness."[22] But as the translator pointed out, Valla's position here is an ambiguous one because if we are "hardened and, therefore, unable not to sin; or are shown mercy and thereby enabled to do good," then free will comes not as a "natural possession" but as a "gift of grace." Nonetheless, one observes in Valla's thought a meaning of free will that is distinct from that of the Scholastic theologians in the vein of Aquinas who held to a free will more in line with the ancient humanism of the Greek philosophers. Valla had essentially rediscovered a will more in line with that of Augustine, that is not, by nature, in human capacity. Yet Valla, probably did not yet fully understand the full effect of Adam's fall on human nature. Valla stated, "For God poured into us, on account of the disobedience of the first parent in whom all of us have sinned, the penalty of death, not the guilt which comes from hardening."[23]

It is here appropriate to further consider why Valla and the many other Renaissance humanists, although Christian in name, have traditionally been identified with a humanism that goes beyond the literary humanism of the Renaissance. The Renaissance humanists, as pointed out in these examples of Petrarch and Valla, were quite strongly identified with their Christianity. Yet, modern humanists whose positions can be described as anti-Christian have championed these Italian Renaissance humanists. How can this apparent dichotomy be accounted for?

First, during this era, the influence of Scholastic thinking had conditioned those in influential positions of the Roman Catholic Church to seek spiritual truth primarily through mechanisms of reason. The proverbial intellectual exercise of determining how many angels could dance on the head of a pin so well demonstrates the ludicrous extremes to which Scholastic theology had taken Christian thought. Through the influences primarily of Aquinas, the Catholic Church came to value the idea that through human reason, natural revelation could pave a path to a true knowledge of God. This view yet survives in Roman Catholic Theology. Such teaching was proclaimed as infallible church doctrine at the Vatican Council of 1870 where it was stated that "God could be known with certainty from that which had been created *through the natural light of reason.*"[24] As emphasized in the previous chapters, reason is the primary mechanism by which scientific truth is attained, but reason alone cannot get one to the truth of ultimate reality because ultimate reality is not *contained* within the physical universe. The successes of modern science have shown the flaws in Aquinas' primary thesis. Some of the greatest minds of modern science have been, and continue to be, atheists. (Likewise, many noteworthy scientists have been, and continue to be, dedicated Christians, which is evidence that there is no *conflict* between faith and reason.) Natural Theology, if true, should result in bright minds (i.e., minds that show great powers of reason, characteristic of many of the great scientific minds) always concluding, through the light of Natural Theology, the certainty of God's existence. But we know that this is not true. Moreover, as Berkouwer pointed out, "Even in Roman Catholic circles some voices say that the Roman Catholic proofs mean little or nothing *for those who do not already believe.*"[25]

The Renaissance humanists are, therefore, often considered champions by modern humanists because they sought to remove the correlation between reason and religion that theologians in the vein of Aquinas had attempted to establish. The Renaissance humanists perceived the problems resulting from that integration. Therefore, railing against Scholasticism is a common characteristic of Renaissance humanism. But instead of addressing the theological and philosophical problems of Scholasticism, the Renaissance humanists, for the most part, chose to ignore the issue. They instead turned to perfecting literary techniques and new forms of literary expression. It should not be hard for the modern person to understand the essence of this change in direction. Public education in most parts of the world today follows this humanistic tradition. Many of those controlling public education today consider any subject having philosophical and religious importance as unnecessary to a good education. These have generally been content with steeping their students in only the "humanities" and the natural sciences. The concept of the "humanities" in secular education today stems from the philosophy of Renaissance humanism; and, hence, there is a subtle connection between the inculpable humanism of the Renaissance and the more sinister modern secular humanism which teaches that morality can be divorced from the God of Scripture.

Secondly, an even more important characteristic of Renaissance humanism which finds compatibility with the Western humanism of which this work is concerned, is the view that many of the Renaissance humanists had of Scripture. In the thinking of Petrarch, Valla, and Erasmus, one observes an approach towards Scripture that distinguishes them from the Reformers which followed them. (Erasmus is discussed in the next section and the humanistic approach to Scripture is discussed further in the next chapter.) The Renaissance humanists appear to have treated Scripture as if it were only another cog in the wheel of the academic literature of the day. They did not seem to have a keen awareness of Scripture's supernatural character. The supernatural character of Scripture equips it as *the* only authoritative source for Christian doctrine and practice, and the Renaissance humanists appear to have been ignorant of this. The stage for these inferior views of Scripture was set in Scholasticism. Bromiley stated that the Scholastics were most "interested in defining the status of the Bible in relation to that of the other authorities in the Church."[26] Roman Catholicism since the Middle Ages has usually viewed tradition and the voice of the Church (the Pope) as having an authority on par, if not superior, to the authority of Scripture. Ridderbos stated, "According to the Roman Catholic view, the [Scriptural] Canon *viewed in itself* (*quoad se*) possesses undoubted inherent authority. But *as it concerns us* (*quoad nos*), the recognition of the Canon rests upon the authority of the Church."[27] At this point in Church history, Scripture was treated somewhat subjectively, not as objective truth coming direct from the mind of God. The philosophy of Renaissance humanism was subtlety merged with a viewpoint that failed to recognize the special place that Scripture holds for the attainment of a proper perception of reality.

Valla's specialty was one of philology and he brought to this subject not only matters of secular interest but more importantly, for the subject at hand, his views of Scripture. To Valla's credit in the area of philology, in about the year 1440, he proved the *Donation* of Constantine to be a forgery (the *Donation* of Constantine was a document supposedly issued by Constantine to proclaim Pope Sylvester I sovereign over the whole Western European continent). But it was Valla's apparent belief in the unreliability of Scripture that points to an attitude toward Scripture that associates him with the negative aspects of humanism with which this work is concerned.

As emphasized in Chapter 2 regarding the meaning of Genesis 3:15, accuracy in the translation of Scripture is important to convey its true meaning. Christians have always sought to insure the accurate translation of Scripture from the original-language manuscripts. But obviously, given the fact that imperfect humans have always had a hand in the translation and copying processes, it should not be surprising that certain types of error have occurred throughout the centuries. Nonetheless, orthodox Christians have always stressed that God has supernaturally protected the intended meaning of the copied original manuscripts. J. I. Packer wrote in this regard:

> It is sometimes suggested that … we can have no confidence that any text we possess conveys to us the genuine meaning of the inspired Word. … But faith in the consistency of God warrants an attitude of confidence that the text is sufficiently trustworthy not to lead us astray. If God gave the Scriptures for a practical purpose—to make men wise unto salvation through faith in Christ—it is a safe inference that He never permits them to become so corrupted that they can no longer fulfill it. It is noteworthy that the New Testament men did not hesitate to trust the words of the Old Testament as they had it as a reliable indication of the mind of God. This attitude of faith in the adequacy of the text is confirmed, so far as it can be, by the unanimous verdict of textual scholars that the biblical text is excellently preserved, and no point of doctrine depends on any of the small number of cases in which the true reading remains doubtful. Professor F. F. Bruce expressed the verdict of scholarship as well as of biblical faith when he writes: "By the 'singular care and providence' of God the Bible text has come down to us in such substan-

tial purity that even the most uncritical edition of the Hebrew or Greek ... cannot effectively obscure the real message of the Bible, or neutralize its saving power."[28]
The orthodox Christian position is that any errors that have occurred from
copy processes are insignificant in matters of doctrine and communication
of God's word to humanity.

Valla, however, apparently did not comprehend this. Some of the words
from his last major work, entitled *Annotations to the New Testament*[29] reveals
how he probably viewed the nature of Scripture. According to Garin, Valla
here stated (in his *Annotations*) that "none of the words of Christ have come
to us, for Christ spoke in Hebrew and never wrote down anything."[30] Valla
apparently believed that the existing Latin versions of Scripture could not
be trusted to render the true meaning of Jesus' actual spoken Aramaic and
Hebrew words. And commenting on Jerome's assertion of corrupt Biblical
manuscripts Valla wrote:

> If after only four hundred years the river had become too
> murky, need we be surprised that after a thousand years—
> for we are separated from St. Jerome by that many years—
> that river, never having been purged, carries both mud
> and refuse?[31]

These words of Valla demonstrate the view of Scripture that was then prevalent among the Renaissance humanists. In their minds there appears to be
little cognizance of Scripture's supernatural character. Similar views of Scripture are prevalent in both secular and non-secular modern humanism and it
is these views of the Renaissance humanists that command the respect of
even modern-day secular humanists.

The discovery of the Dead Sea Scrolls has, however, shown how well
the message of the Hebrew Scripture has been preserved. The nearly 2000-
year old manuscripts found in the Qumran caves represented copies at least
1000 years older than the oldest previous existing copies (the Masoretic
scrolls) when they were discovered in 1947. The Isaiah scroll found in 1947
was found to be essentially identical to the much newer Masoretic text, the
differences being insignificant.[32]

One additional characteristic of many Renaissance humanists that must
be considered is the personal lives that many of them led. Unfortunately
many of them appear to have manifested life-styles which were inconsistent
with genuine Christian faith. For example, Durant wrote,

> The humanists were as morally corrupt as the clergy they
> criticized. ... An impressively large minority of the men
> whom resurrected Greek and Roman literature lived like
> pagans who had never heard of Christianity. Their mobil-

ity deracinated them; they passed from city to city seeking laurels and fees, and sank no roots in stability. They were as fond of money as any moneylender or his wife. They were vain of their genius, their income, their features, their dress. They were coarse in their speech, ungenerous and disgraceful in their controversies, faithless in their friendships and transient in their loves.[33]

While Durant admits exceptions to this generalization, he unfortunately puts Valla in that "impressively large minority."

Erasmus

Desiderius Erasmus was the foremost player in the so-called northern humanism, which was essentially an extension of the humanism that had originated earlier in Italy with the work of Petrarch. The Dutch born Catholic priest lived contemporary with Luther in the 15th and 16th centuries. From study of his life and work one can better appreciate how Renaissance humanism diverged into the distinct paths that were outlined in the introduction to this chapter.

The details of Erasmus' early life are sketchy. Erasmus probably desired to conceal the circumstances surrounding his birth. He was evidently born out of wedlock, and such circumstances had greater implications on one's prospects for success than would be the case today. It is generally believed that he was born in either 1466 or 1467; however, one author says with confidence that he was born in 1469.[34] (If this is true, Erasmus was deceitful regarding his birth-date.) His father, Roger Gerard, was either a priest at the time of his birth or a soon-to-be priest.[35] His mother, Margaret, was a physician's daughter. Desiderius and his older brother Peter were orphaned in their teens and their guardians eventually committed them to monastery life. This choice was likely made to rid their caretakers of responsibility, and not one born from the brothers' desire.

By this time in the history of the Church, the monasteries were often vile pits of corruption, and it was the influence of this environment that would set the tone for many of Erasmus' later works. At the monastery, Erasmus exhibited a fondness for books and learning. He particularly showed a precociousness for composing both verse and prose, and it was those literary skills that would propel him to fame as one of the foremost humanists of the Renaissance. As an ambitious young intellectual, Erasmus escaped monastery life by convincing his superiors that he could best serve the Church by immersing himself in the intellectual climate of the University of Paris. After his ordination he was allowed to study in Paris, and there his humanistic thinking matured into the strong influence for which he would become famous. Erasmus used those early years of study to build a strong network of influential friends, and as a result of those contacts, his fame accelerated rapidly.

In all, Erasmus made about four trips to England, beginning in the latter part of the 15th century and continuing into the early part of the 16th century. While in England, Erasmus mastered the Greek language and was instrumental in contributing to the humanistic movement through his many friendships with some of England's most influential scholars including Thomas More and John Colet.

Erasmus left a large volume of correspondence addressed to many friends and professional acquaintants. To better understand the mind of Erasmus, we will examine some of these letters since they provide better insight into his mind than could any biographer. A good source (in English) for much of that correspondence comes from the lectures of Froude, delivered at Oxford in 1893.[36] The quotes we will consider here have been taken from these lectures. A letter Erasmus composed to a friend from the Paris period illustrates certain telling aspects of his character. He was about thirty years of age when the following words were penned:

> Vain is wisdom if a man is not wise for himself. Admire learning as much as you will, but fill your pockets as well. Always have a good opinion of yourself. Nothing more improves the appearance. Care above all things for your own skin. Let all else stand second to your own advantage. Choose your friends for the service which they do for you. Do not seek to be over-learned. Study moderately, and love ardently. Be liberal of your words and careful of your money.[37]

This worldly attitude of self-preservation remained with him throughout his entire life as we will see in the next chapter when we discuss his confrontation with Luther.

The works of Valla apparently had a strong influence on the thinking of Erasmus. For example, after Erasmus discovered Valla's dormant *Annotations*, the work so impressed him that he took it on himself to publish the long forgotten manuscript.[38] The following excerpt from a letter composed in defense of Valla, to an acquaintance who had attacked Valla's work, demonstrates the high regard which Erasmus had for Valla.

> Is it to be peace or war between us? Will you dare to speak as you do of such a man as Valla—Valla, who has been well called *Suadæ medulla*. And you to call him a chattering magpie. Oh! if he was alive he would make you skip

for it. He is in his grave now and you think that dead men do not bite, and that you can say what you please. Not quite. I will stand as his champion, and this *cartel* is my challenge. Apologise or look to your weapons.[39]

It is thus not surprising that the Renaissance philosophy of Scripture, previously identified when we considered the writing of Valla, is also readily observed in the writings of Erasmus. As told by McGrath, Erasmus (as did Valla) regarded Scripture as

> the primary instrument in an educative and formative process. It was, however, only one of several such sources, and could not be regarded as the sole authoritative source of doctrine and ethics. For the Reformers, scripture was the sole means by which access might be had to the Word of God.[40]

We also learn from Faludy of Erasmus' view of Hebrew Scripture. Faludy tells us that Erasmus had the desire to master Hebrew, but soon abandoned that goal because

> he did not much care for the Old Testament, considering its impact upon Christianity much too 'shadowy'. The stories of Jewish history struck the budding humanist as 'barbarous and savage' … Indeed, he once confessed that he would not have minded if the whole of the Old Testament had been lost to posterity.[41]

If these words are reliable, then it is certain that Erasmus did not possess a proper view of Scripture. Jesus' many references to the Hebrew Scripture demonstrated convincingly that he viewed that Scripture as inspired and absolutely authoritative.[42] It is apparent that Renaissance humanism perpetuated faulty views of Scripture and it was this thinking which the Reformers had to overcome.

Perhaps the most characteristic and distinguishing mark of Erasmus' work was his incessant criticism of the sinister conditions then prevalent within the Roman Catholic Church. Erasmus well understood the many problems the Church was then facing. He knew her practices and beliefs were far from what they should have been, and he used that knowledge as a springboard to the fame he enjoyed. In speaking of the conditions of worship within the Church during those dark days, Froude tells us that it

> consisted of the Mass and the Confessional, of elaborate ceremonials, rituals, procession, pilgrimages, prayers to the Virgin and the saints, with dispensations and indulgences for laws broken or duties left undone. Of the Gospels and Epistles so much only was known to the laity as was read

in the Church services, and that intoned as if to be purposely unintelligible to the understanding. Of the rest of the Bible nothing was known at all, because nothing was supposed to be necessary ... Copies of the Scripture were rare, shut up in convent libraries, and studied only by professional theologians; while conventional interpretations were attached to the text which corrupted or distorted its meaning.[43]

Even the practice of astrology, while somewhat prevalent during the Middle Ages outside of Christendom, had by this time found its way into the Church. In his famous work on the Renaissance, Burckhardt[44] told us that Marsilio Ficino[45] drew the horoscope of Lorenzo the Magnificent's children and subsequently promised Giovanni (Lorenzo's child) that he would one day be pope. As predicted, Giovanni grew up to become Pope Leo X.[46] Leo X would be the one to come to Erasmus' defense when the monks, at whom much of Erasmus' criticisms were aimed, sought revenge.

Erasmus' writing against Church corruption began, in a somewhat systematic way, at the turn of the century, about the same time as his visits to England began. Soon after his first stint in England, Erasmus published the *Adagia*, a work instrumental in further establishing his fame. The *Adagia* was a light work of collected "popular sayings, quotations, epigrams, proverbs, anecdotes, anything amusing which came to hand, with his own reflections attached to them."[47] In this work he began to subtlety criticize the Church's many improprieties, and these criticisms later turned into more bold harangues when praises from the *Adagia* were forthcoming. One quote from the *Adagia* illustrates its tone: "Priests ... are said in Scripture to devour the sins of the people, and they find sins so hard of digestion that they must have the best wine to wash them down."[48]

Not surprisingly, the churchmen who were the objects of Erasmus' scorn met this work with derision. The monks of Erasmus' attacks intuitively knew that if learning in the tradition of the humanists was to turn toward the study of Scripture, their doom was sure. Froude said of the monks:

They were children of darkness, and they dreaded daylight like bats and owls. The revival of learning, the growing study of the classical poetry and history and philosophy, they knew instinctively would be fatal to them. They fought against it as if were for life or death, and, by identifying knowledge with heresy, they made orthodoxy synonymous with ignorance.[49]

But Erasmus was unrelenting in his criticisms of the monks, and they, in turn, increasingly grew to despise him. One letter of Erasmus read:

Obedience (he says) is so taught as to hide that there is any obedience due to God. Kings are to obey the Pope. Priests are to obey their bishops. Monks are to obey their abbots. Oaths are exacted that want of submission may be punished as perjury. It may happen, it often does happen, that an abbot is a fool or a drunkard. He issues an order to the brotherhood in the name of holy obedience. And what will such order be? An order to observe chastity? An order to be sober? An order to tell no lies? Not one of these things. It will be that a brother is not to learn Greek; he is not to seek to instruct himself. He may be a sot. He may go with prostitutes. He may be full of hatred and malice. He may never look inside the Scriptures. No matter. He has not broken any oath. He is an excellent member of the community. While if he disobeys such a command as this from an insolent superior there is stake or dungeon for him instantly.[50]

Because of the *Adagia's* success, Erasmus followed it with his work *Praise of Folly* where the Church was again the frequent object of his attacks. First published in 1509, it perhaps is the writing for which he is most noted. The work is a satirical comment on many aspects of Renaissance life. On the mendicant friars, Erasmus here wrote:

They pretend to resemble the Apostles, and they are filthy, ignorant, impudent vagabonds. They have their rules, forsooth. Yes, rules—how many knots, for instance, there may be in a shoe-string, how their petticoats should be cut or coloured, how much cloth should be used in their hoods, and how many hours they may sleep. But for all else—for conduct and character, they quarrel with each other and curse each other. They pretend to poverty, but they steal into honest men's houses and pollute them, and, wasps as they are, no one dares refuse them admittance for fear of their stings. They hold the secrets of every family through the confessional, and when they are drunk, or wish to amuse their company, they let them out to the world. If any wretched man dares to imitate them they pay him off from the pulpits, and they never stop their barking till you fling them a piece of meat.[51]

Even in Erasmus' 1516 translation of the New Testament direct from Greek manuscripts, he provided along with the translation, additional stunning commentary on Church corruption. Two examples of his commentary show his continual pounding of the Church he represented. His commentary on Matthew 19:12 reads as follows:

> Men are threatened or tempted into vows of celibacy. They can have license to go with harlots, but they must not marry wives. They may keep concubines and remain priests. If they take wives they are thrown to the flames. Parents who design their children for a celibate priesthood should emasculate them in their infancy, instead of forcing them, reluctant or ignorant, into a furnace of licentiousness.[52]

His commentary on Matthew 23 further demonstrated the depths to which Catholicism had fallen. Here Erasmus wrote:

> What would Jerome say could he see the Virgin's milk exhibited for money, with as much honor paid it as to the consecrated body of Christ; the miraculous oil; the portions of the true cross, enough if they were collected to freight a large ship? Here we have the hood of St. Francis, there Our Lady's petticoat or St. Anne's comb, or St. Thomas of Canterbury's shoes; not presented as innocent aids to religion, but as the substance of religion itself—and all through the avarice of priests and the hypocrisy of monks playing on the credulity of the people. Even bishops play their parts in these fantastic shows, and approve and dwell on them in their rescripts.[53]

Upon careful analysis of Erasmus' criticisms of the Church, one notes that he attacked only the behavior of the churchmen without getting to the root cause of the problem. The ugly realities he so well exposed followed on the heels of Scholastic philosophy. Erasmus believed that change would come from abandoning the deficiencies of Scholasticism in favor of humanistic learning. But to get to the root of the Church's problems, the nature of sin and its subsequent effect on human nature would have to be addressed. This Erasmus either could not or would not do and the responsibility was left to Luther, a contemporary of Erasmus. Luther's leadership would shake the very foundation of Christianity. We will now turn our attention to the Reformation, but in so doing our study of Erasmus will continue, because in the persons of Luther and Erasmus, Renaissance humanism and Christianity became further delineated in a way that distinctly marked the course of history for both trains of thought.

5

Historical Christianity: The Reformation

Change is not made without inconvenience, even from worse to better.
Richard Hooker (1554-1600)

In the Middle Ages, the Church's concern for knowing and practicing scriptural truth became suppressed in relationship to its political and otherworldly concerns. By the turn of the 16th century, the Roman Catholic Church had reached a point where the vernacular cliché "something has to give" could appropriately be used to describe its dire situation. While our purpose here is not to expound on the spiritual failure of the Roman Church, any honest student of history must acknowledge that it was then found wanting in its spiritual obligation to the Christian world. In his classical work on the Renaissance, Burckhardt tells us that "Italy at the beginning of the sixteenth century found itself in the midst of a grave moral crisis, out of which the best men saw hardly any escape."[1] He further stated in this regard:

> When the Church became corrupt, men ought to have
> drawn a distinction, and kept their religion in spite of all.
> But this is more easily said than done. It is not every people
> which is calm enough, or dull enough, to tolerate a last-
> ing contradiction between a principle and its outward
> expression. But history does not record a heavier respon-
> sibility than that which rests upon the decaying Church.
> She set up as absolute truth, and by the most violent
> means, a doctrine which she had distorted to serve her
> own aggrandizement. Safe in the sense of her inviolabil-
> ity, she abandoned herself to the most scandalous profli-
> gacy, and, in order to maintain herself in this state, she
> levelled [*sic*] mortal blows against the conscience and the

intellect of nations, and drove multitudes of the noblest spirits, whom she had inwardly estranged, into the arms of unbelief and despair.[2]

The Reformation follows so closely on the heels of the Renaissance that it is best to view the movements as overlapping. The emergence of the Renaissance cannot be divorced from the effects that Scholastic theology had perpetuated on the intellectual climate of Europe. The Reformation, like the Renaissance, was a response to Scholastic philosophy, but while the response of the Renaissance was literary, the response of the Reformation was theological. Whether the Church's moral failure gave rise to Scholasticism, or whether Scholasticism was primarily responsible for the Church's decline is difficult to ascertain, but certainly that failure cannot be denied.

The Reformers stood against the Church's error because of what they had learned from their own intensive study of Scripture. Many of their followers were excommunicated as heretics because of their dedication to the truth of Scripture. Some were even executed. One such atrocity occurred on July 1, 1523, in Brussels, when the Church burned alive two Augustinian monks for holding to those teachings of Luther of which we will here briefly summarize. So, where under Augustine the Church had excommunicated those espousing non-scriptural views of sin and human nature, the Church was now excommunicating and even killing some who were espousing scripturally correct views of the same doctrines. The Reformation stands as a definitive pivotal point in the history of Western thought. Out of it came a freedom that empowered those who were concerned with knowing and understanding the truth of Scripture. While the Reformation profoundly influenced Christianity, it also notably and positively affected the institutions of education and government.

Luther

Martin Luther is inextricably associated with the emergence and success of the Reformation. He was born in Eisleben in 1483, the son of a copper miner. He graduated from the University of Erfurt with a bachelor's degree in 1502, and in 1505, he earned the master's degree. Luther originally wanted to study law but a short time after taking his master's degree a fierce thunderstorm nearly killed him. In the midst of that terrifying event, the young Luther made a vow to God that compelled him into the service of the Church. Soon after that encounter with nature's wrath, he entered the Augustinian Convent at Erfurt.

It was in 1510 when traveling to Rome on official Church business that his eyes were opened to the debauchery prevalent within the ranks of Roman Catholicism. Luther here observed a majority of Church officials conducting Church affairs in manners indistinguishable from the ordinary corrupt ways of the world. This experience triggered in him a contemplation of the genuineness of his own relationship to God and the genuineness of the Christianity taught by the Church.

After obtaining the doctorate in theology (1512), he joined the faculty at the University of Wittenburg. Here Luther began an intense study of the Apostle Paul's letter to the Romans because of incessant doubts regarding his own standing with the God he perceived to be represented in that Scripture. The God described in Scripture appeared to Luther a different God than the one taught by the Church. As one author wrote, certain passages struck Luther with irreconcilable terror.

> One of these [passages] was "Save me in thy righteousness and thy truth." "I thought," said he [Luther], "that righteousness was the fierce wrath of God, wherewith he punishes sinners." Certain passages in the Epistles of St. Paul haunted him for days. The doctrine of grace was not indeed unknown to him, but the dogma that sin was at once taken away by it produced upon him, who was but too conscious of his sins, rather a sense of rejection—a feeling of deep depression—than of hope. He says it made his heart bleed—it made him despair of God.[3]

The learning that the Renaissance humanists had long pushed for and corrupt monks had long dreaded blossomed in the mind of Luther. However, instead of using his education to propagate a humanistic agenda, an agenda more concerned with the pursuit to know and imitate the writings of the ancient philosophers and poets, Luther turned his attention towards matters of theological doctrine. Luther applied the education he acquired in the humanistic tradition, which emphasized the mastery of philological exegesis of Greek, Hebrew and Latin, to better understand the truth revealed in Holy Scripture.

Throughout the Middle Ages, most of those identifying themselves as Christian fell prey to the idea—as had the Hebrews of old—that one gained salvation simply by living in good standing within the realm of one's ecclesiastical organization. From study of the Apostle Paul's writings to the Romans, Luther came to understand that one could not gain salvation through one's effort to live according to the dictates of the Roman Church. Luther came to realize that the true Church was not a human made organization but was that body of believers who had been justified for salvation solely on the basis of personal faith in God's word. The truth that one is saved only by the grace of God, through faith,[4] made an indelible impression on him in a way that all the many years of previous "religious" training had not been able to accomplish. The truth that God imputes righteousness because of personal faith in His word had passed over the Catholic consciousness the same way in which it had passed over the Hebrew consciousness hundreds of years prior. To correct that misconception, the prophet Habakkuk[5] had made known the same message to the Jews that Luther, through the Apostle Paul's letter to the Romans, attempted to communicate to the Catholic Church. Furthermore, Luther came to understand that Scripture was a supernaturally inspired revelation direct from the mind of God and that it was the only means for conveying God's will to fallen humanity, and subsequently as such, one had to rely upon it as the sole authority in matters of doctrine and Christian practice.

The selling of indulgences was the Church practice that instigated Luther's rebellion. Luther could not reconcile its practice with Scripture. The practice of indulgences had originated in medieval times as a by-product of the sacrament of penance. The indulgence was originally administered in a congregational setting where the parishioner would publicly confess his sin and then perform a subscribed act of penance to obtain "satisfaction" and, subsequently, would be reinstated into good standing with the Church. The indulgence was the performance of the penitent act. Public penance, however, eventually gave way to the practice of private penance and the indulgence in this system came to be administered by the clergy under the authority of the Pope. This eventually led to the selling of indulgence letters by papal officials. By purchasing the indulgence letter the sinner was performing the penitent act and thereby obtaining his required "satisfaction."[6]

To understand the indulgence system, one needs to understand the extra-biblical views of sin and punishment that Scholasticism had successfully perpetrated on the Church. If a Church member was near death and thus could not perform an act of penance, he could be granted absolution to keep him from eternal judgment. However, penance was required to keep him from purgatory. Scholastic theologians had essentially fabricated a theological system to accommodate a justification that could be obtained by earthly means. An intricate and confusing entanglement of extra-biblical concepts concerning plenary indulgences, partial indulgences, absolution, penance, temporal punishment, eternal punishment, satisfaction, venial sins, mortal sins and purgatory created a system whereby the indulgence made "rational" sense. Therefore, the system was able to entangle the scripturally misinformed masses into its destructive weave. Faulty doctrines of atonement, based largely on human systems of thought, had resulted from the Scholastic theology of the Middle Ages. Luther came to understand that the indulgence system had evolved into a system whereby an evil clergy had schemed to fatten the coffers of the Church and, even in some cases, to line their own pockets.

The fire was ignited when Luther posted the now famed "Ninety-Five Theses" on the door of the Wittenburg Church. The posted document began as follows.[7]

> Ninety-five Theses: Disputation on the Power and Efficacy of Indulgences
> Out of love and zeal for truth and the desire to bring it to light, the following theses will be publicly discussed at Wittenberg under the chairmanship of the reverend father Martin Luther, Master of Arts and Sacred Theology and regularly appointed Lecturer on these subjects at that place. He requests that those who cannot be present to debate orally with us will do so by letter.

While a listing of all 95 theses is not practical here, a few will give the general gist of Luther's proclamation.

> 1. When our Lord and Master Jesus Christ said, "Repent" [Mat. 4:17], he willed the entire life of believers to be one of repentance.
> 2. This word cannot be understood as referring to the sacrament of penance, that is, confession and satisfaction, as administered by the clergy.
> 3. Yet it does not mean solely inner repentance; such inner repentance is worthless unless it produces various outward mortifications of the flesh.
> 5. The pope neither desires nor is able to remit any penalties except those imposed by his own authority or that of the canons.
> 6. The pope cannot remit any guilt, except by declaring and showing that it has been remitted by God; or, to be sure, by remitting guilt in cases reserved to his judgment. If his right to grant remission in these cases were disregarded, the guilt would certainly remain unforgiven.
> 27. They preach only human doctrines who say that as soon as the money clinks into the money chest, the soul flies out of purgatory.
> 30. No one is sure of the integrity of his own contrition, much less of having received plenary remission.

32. Those who believe that they can be certain of their salvation because they have indulgence letters will be eternally damned, together with their teachers.

37. Any true Christian, whether living or dead, participates in all the blessings of Christ and the church; and this is granted him by God, even without indulgence letters.

Luther was here proclaiming to the world the uselessness of the entire indulgence system.

With this daring challenge to a spiritually darkened Church, Luther broke the humanistic tradition that heretofore had only superficially criticized the methods and practices of the Church. The movement that wicked monks and priests had feared would develop as a result of humanistic learning in the vein of Erasmus had come to fruition in Luther. Erasmus talked about the symptoms, but Luther sought to expunge the root cause, not in a selfish way to bring recognition to himself, but in a way to bring glory to God through the exposition of the eternal truths of God's word. The monks stated that "Erasmus laid the egg and Luther hatched it" to which Erasmus replied, "Yes ... but the egg I laid was a hen, and Luther hatched a gamecock."[8]

In a letter from Luther to Erasmus, one observes a humble Luther asking for Erasmus' support. He wrote:

But I trust that you will let me look on you as a brother. My fate is a hard one. I, a poor ignorant creature, fit only to be buried in a corner out of sight of sun and sky, have been forced forward into controversy against my natural will.[9]

From Erasmus' response to that plea for support we can better understand the dichotomy between the humanistic thought of the Renaissance, represented by Erasmus, and a Christianity that sought to propagate the truth of salvation through faith in Jesus Christ, represented in the efforts of Luther.

Luther's approach of taking the controversy directly to the top had forced Erasmus into a dilemma. Erasmus knew that Luther's attack on the Pope would draw vehement scrutiny from the entire ecclesiastical system. Erasmus had spent a lifetime learning how to criticize the Church while maintaining the favor of its higher powers. Pope Leo X certainly had not felt threatened by Erasmus' criticisms of the Church. While Erasmus aimed serious criticisms at the Church, he demanded no change. The Pope had often come to Erasmus' defense when the monks, at whom his criticisms were primarily aimed, rebuked Erasmus. Therefore, Erasmus initially chose the politically safe route and attempted to divorce himself from any contact with Luther.

However, based on the content of his own writings, Erasmus knew that to totally disagree with Luther would be philosophically inconsistent. He was forced, at least initially, to maintain a civility toward Luther. A letter written by Erasmus a few months after Luther's bold move at Wittenburg is instructive and interesting to peruse. The letter shows us Erasmus' reaction to the news of Luther's action. Erasmus addressed it to the rector at the University of Erfort, where Luther had been trained. Perhaps that rector still held some influence over Luther. A portion of the letter reads as follows:

> That frigid, quarrelsome old lady, Theology, had swollen herself to such a point of vanity that it was necessary to bring her back to the fountain, but I would rather have her mended than ended. I would at least have her permitted to endure till a better theology has been invented. Luther has said many things excellently well. I could wish, however, that he would be less rude in his manner. He would have stronger support behind him, and might do real good. But at any rate, unless we stand by him when he is right, no one hereafter will dare to speak the truth. I can give no opinion about his positive doctrines; but one good thing he has done, and has been a public benefactor by doing it—he has forced the controversialists to examine the early Fathers for themselves.[10]

But Erasmus' neutrality did not last long. As Froude so succinctly put it, Erasmus "was ready and willing to fight angry monks and scholastics. But he had none of the passionate horror of falsehood in sacred things which inspired the new movement."[11] And it was for this reason that Erasmus made it clear that his allegiance would remain with the Pope and the Roman Catholic Church. In a letter to a cardinal he wrote, "Erasmus will always be found on the side of the Roman See, and especially of its present occupant."[12] Indeed, many letters of correspondence that followed show that Erasmus was desperate to distinguish himself from Luther. Many in the Church were attempting to blame Erasmus for the outbreak of Luther's rebellion. In another letter to a bishop Erasmus wrote:

> Christ I know: Luther I know not. The Roman Church I know, and death will not part me from it till the Church departs from Christ. I abhor sedition. Would that Luther and the Germans abhorred it equally. … I approve of those who stand by the Pope, but I could wish them to be wiser than they are. They would devour Luther off hand. They may eat him boiled or roast for all that I care, but they mistake in linking him and me together, and they can fin-

ish him more easily without me than with me. ... They pretend that Luther has borrowed from me. No lie can be more impudent. He may have borrowed from me as heretics borrow from Evangelists and Apostles, but not a syllable else.[13]

In 1520 the Pope issued a bull (an official papal document) against Luther which was the first step leading to his excommunication. In Luther's written answer (*Assertions*)[14] to the official Church condemnation, Luther asserted that man, in his natural sinful condition, could not of his own free will, outside of God's grace, move himself into a redeemed state.

From the many years of contemplation and study of Scripture, Luther procured the theological understanding that laid the foundation for the break from the Roman Church. Separation from the Church, however, was not Luther's intent. Luther had hoped that those in positions of Church authority would welcome the truth of Scripture. He attempted to show Church authorities that justification before God came to the believer solely from God's declaration of righteousness based upon one's faith in the work of Jesus, the Christ, for the atonement of one's personal sin.

But Luther's message fell on deaf ears. On April 18, 1521, Luther appeared in Worms in response to a summons by the Emperor Charles V. Here Luther was asked to recant. Luther closed his defense with the following, now famous, two sentences: "I cannot and will not recant anything, for to go against conscience is neither right nor safe. Here I stand, I can do no other, so help me God. Amen." Luther was certainly aware that those two sentences could have meant his death at the stake. Nevertheless, because he feared God rather than man, we today have the benefit of a Christianity that has empowered the believer to stand against the humanism that is in constant struggle with the teachings of Scripture.

With Luther's position on the issue of human volition made known in his official reply to the Church (*Assertions*), Erasmus now had a subject on which he could write against him. It is interesting that Erasmus finally picked up his pen against Luther when Luther wrote on this subject. Erasmus knew that he could not attack Luther's whole theology from a scriptural standpoint. But the issue of the role of human will in salvation has always been, and is yet to this day, a difficult issue. While human volition must obviously play a role in one's decision to turn to Christ for salvation, the ultimate issue is the relationship between a non-sovereign human will and the sovereign will of God. On the subject of the role of human will in salvation, Erasmus could attack Luther using Scripture and then subtly infer that Luther's whole approach to change was wanting. And this is what he did.

Erasmus' response to Luther's *Assertions,* was entitled *Diatribe seu collatio de libero arbitrio (A Diatribe or Sermon Concerning Free Will).* In the introduction, Erasmus wasted no time going on the offensive when he stated his aversion to assertions, the very title of Luther's writing to which he was responding. Here he stated:

> So great is my dislike of assertions that I prefer the views of the sceptics [*sic*] wherever the inviolable authority of Scripture and the decision of the Church permit—a Church to which at all times I willingly submit my own views, whether I attain what she prescribes or not. And as a matter of fact, I prefer this natural inclination to one I can observe in certain people who are so blindly addicted to one opinion that they cannot tolerate whatever differs from it. Whatever they read in Holy Scripture, they distort to serve the opinion to which they have once and for all enslaved themselves.[15]

In Erasmus' response to Luther's *Assertions* he attempted to cast Luther as an intolerant and closed-minded bigot.[16] Erasmus stated that he only wanted

> to analyze and not to judge, to inquire and not to dogmatize. I am ready to learn from anyone who advances something more accurate or more reliable, though I would rather persuade mediocre minds not to argue too stubbornly on such matters.[17]

The apparent subject matter was free will, but Erasmus was concerned with a more general agenda, which, to him, was probably more important. Erasmus used the issue of free will as a springboard to show Church officials that he stood with the Roman Church against Luther in the controversy that was by then raging. After criticizing Luther's view of free will he went on to imply Luther's error on the more critical doctrinal issues such as justification by faith alone. But such doctrines Erasmus could not attack from a scriptural standpoint. Erasmus wrote:

> Men were not wont to intrude upon these concealed, even superfluous questions with irreligious curiosity, namely whether God's foreknowledge is contingent; whether our will can contribute anything to our eternal salvation, or whether it simply undergoes the action of operative grace; whether everything we do, good or evil, is done out of mere necessity, or whether we are rather in a state of passive acceptance.[18]

Erasmus sets the stage with the issue of free will, and then goes further to subtly infer that Luther was wrong in his entire position against the Church.

Were I certain—which is not the case—that confession, as we have it now, was neither instituted by Christ, nor could ever have been invented by man, and consequently nobody could require it, and that furthermore no satisfaction is needed for offenses committed, I would nonetheless fear to publicize such an opinion, because, from what I can see, most men are prone to moral turpitude. Now, obligatory confession restrains or at least moderates this propensity. …The truth may be spoken but it does not serve everyone at all times and under all circumstances. If I were certain that a wrong decision or definition had been reached at a synod, it would be permissible but not expedient to speak the truth concerning it.[19]

Erasmus was here attacking Luther's view of the confessional (to a priest) and the subsequent requirement of "satisfaction." Luther had taught that the Church confessional and the subsequent requirement of "satisfaction,"—the practice of which had led to the evil use of indulgences—was not based in Scripture. From what Erasmus wrote here, we further learn of his humanistic understanding of human nature. *Most* men are not *prone* to moral turpitude; *all* men are *guilty* of moral turpitude. Luther had attempted to show his peers that the Church was leading sinners astray with the human instituted practice of the confessional. The requirement of indulgences led the sinner to falsely believe an outward act was sufficient for removal of sin. Luther understood that such teaching had the danger of abuse because it linked the act of forgiveness to a *sovereign* act of human volition. Luther wanted Christians to understand that the matter of confession of sin was an inner transaction between the sinner and God. Luther sought to show that an outward confession of sin to only a man and subsequent human imparted satisfaction, was not effective for the removal of that sin. Luther taught that one's sins were only properly dealt with when one confessed and repented to God—trusting Jesus Christ to justify him before God in spite of that sin.

Concerning the issue of free will Erasmus stated his position as follows:

In my opinion the implications of the freedom of the will in Holy Scripture are as follows: if we are on the road to piety, we should continue to improve eagerly and forget what lies behind us; if we have become involved in sin, we should make every effort to extricate ourselves, to accept the remedy of penance, and to solicit the mercy of the Lord, without which neither the human will nor its striving is effective; for all evil let us consider ourselves responsible, but let us ascribe all good to Divine Benevolence alone, for to It we owe even what we are; and in all things must we believe that whatever delightful or sad happens to us during life, God has caused it for our salvation, and that no injustice can come from Him who is by nature just, even if something should befall us which we deem undeserved; nobody should despair of forgiveness by a God who is by nature most merciful. In my opinion, it used to be sufficient for Christian piety to cling to these truths.[20]

Erasmus furthermore claimed that to teach predestination would cause those struggling to live a moral life to simply give up the fight and the end result would be one of further moral decay.

Luther gave reply to Erasmus' *De libero arbitrio* in his *The Bondage of the Will (De servo arbitrio)* where he first praised Erasmus for his "literary prowess and intellectuality." But Luther claimed that on the subject of free will Erasmus brought nothing new to repudiate his position. Luther's choice of words in his reply to Erasmus show just how seriously he took this attack. Luther wrote: "Your book is, in my opinion, so contemptible and worthless that I feel great pity for you for having defiled your beautiful and skilled manner of speaking with such vile dirt."[21] To Erasmus' claim that for one "to assert" was unpleasant for him, Luther stated that if one were to take away assertions then Christianity itself would disappear.

Luther's response to Erasmus' statement of the problem of free will was one of amazement. Luther claimed that Erasmus' synopsis of the problem (quoted above) was filled with contradictions. He stated that "any Jew or Gentile utterly ignorant of Christ could easily draw up the same," because Christ was not once mentioned.[22] Luther went on to say,

You plainly assert that the will is effective in things pertaining to eternal salvation, when you speak of its striving. And again you assert that it is passive, when saying that without the mercy of God it is ineffective. ... It is not irreligious, curious or superfluous, but extremely wholesome and necessary for a Christian to know whether or not his will has anything to do in matters pertaining to salvation. ... It is necessary to distinguish most clearly between the power of God and our own, between God's works and ours, if we are to live a godly life.[23]

The disagreement between Luther and Erasmus was rooted in their respective understandings of human nature. Luther's view was based in a scriptural understanding of human depravity while Erasmus' view was rooted in the humanism of Scholastic thinking. It is clear from Erasmus' arguments that he did not possess a complete understanding of the extent to which sin has affected human nature.

As reviewed in Chapter 2, Isaiah proclaimed that one's own righteousness is "like a filthy garment,"[24] and Jeremiah said "that a man's way is not in himself; nor is it in a man who walks to direct his steps."[25] Luther used this reference from Jeremiah in his *Assertions*—in addition to many others—to show that Scripture supports the fact that man, outside of the grace of God, does not have the capacity to choose the moral good.

To this assertion, Erasmus responded:

> This [Jeremiah 10:23] pertains to the occurrence of happy and unhappy circumstances, rather than the possibility of a free will. Frequently man plunges profoundly into misfortune, when he is very careful to avoid it. This does not eliminate the freedom of the will—neither among those hit by misfortune, because they did not forsee [*sic*] its coming, nor among those causing it, because they don't humiliate the enemy with the same intention as does God, namely by castigating. If one nonetheless forces these words to apply to the freedom of the will, everyone would have to admit that without the grace of God nobody can keep the right course in life.[26]

However, the discerning spirit should identify Jeremiah's words as pertaining to the capability of the natural human will. Matthew Henry, the noted commentator of old, stated in regards to this passage:

> The prophet here acknowledges the sovereignty and dominion of the divine Providence, that by it, and not by their own will and wisdom, the affairs both of nations and particular persons are directed and determined ... for *it is not in man that walketh to direct his steps*, though he seem in his walking to be perfectly at liberty and to choose his own way.[27]

Erasmus appears to here admit that outside the grace of God, no man—solely in the power of his own will—can keep the right course in life, which is of course to admit that the natural man, who is void of God's grace, does not have the capacity to direct his life towards that which is truly good.

When one asserts that the human will has power, of its own accord, to choose the true good, he has essentially moved himself into a humanistic position. If man, in his natural condition, possessed true freedom to will the true moral good, the sovereignty of human personality would be mandated. A human nature with that power would possess the ability, of its own accord, to know and to do the will of God. But as it has been shown in Chapter 2, Scripture is plain in its contention that human nature, apart from a supernatural enabling, is void of this power. One who holds such a view of human nature has essentially discarded the truth of Genesis 8:21 and Psalm 14:1, to name but two of many such references.

Humanistic philosophy, whether it be a secular humanism or one disguised in a form of religion, always views human personality to possess a sovereignty that it cannot possess. Augustine had effectively confronted that humanistic view of human nature in the early Christian church. The Pelagians had taught that all were born untainted by sin and were thus born morally neutral. According to Pelagius each person chose for himself his moral destiny. Augustine showed that Pelagius' teaching was contrary to Scripture, because one does not choose good or evil from a neutral position. Evil is present naturally at birth. Only One possessed the capability of choosing the moral good from within the power of his nature, and that one, of course, was Jesus Christ.

Luther came to understand the depths to which Adam's sin has taken human nature. He came to the understanding that the initiative to salvation must always be with God, and as such, salvation must—in its purest sense—exclude the *free* will of man. Again, the word *free* is here emphasized because human volition is obviously not totally excluded in the process of salvation. But Jesus made it clear to his audience, that "No one can come to Me, unless the Father who sent Me draws him."[28] Jesus here asserted that human volition must be a responsive one and not a determinate one. Luther developed a keen understanding of human nature from his study of Scripture. He came to realize that human nature could not be changed through human will to uphold God's moral law. Luther knew that human nature could only be changed through one's faith in the revealed truth of God, which was culminated in the revelation of Jesus Christ. Luther so correctly wrote:

> Satan and man, being fallen and abandoned by God, cannot will good, i.e., things which please God or which God wills, but are ever turned in the direction of their own desires, so that they cannot but seek out their own.[29]

Before considering John Calvin's role in the Reformation, the consideration of an excerpt written by Luther in the heat of this confrontation with Erasmus gives a better overall perspective of the debate. While an understanding of the complex relationship between human will and God's will is important, Luther was more concerned with the apostasy that was yet rampant within the Church and with establishing the fact that the certainty of one's salvation was attainable only through the authority of Scripture. Luther wrote:

It is said the Papists profess Christ's Gospel, and deny that their doctrine is of the devil. Yes, they *profess*; but the tree is known by its fruits. They cry, "The Church, the Church!" and by the Church they mean a body presumed to have divine authority, while the members of it lead impious and wicked lives. Erasmus must think as they do of the Church, for he says he will submit to what the Church shall decide. If the Church is what they say, where is the use of Scripture? Why do we risk our lives for what we believe to be Truth when we may be all saved compendiously in a single ship by receiving what the Papists teach? What will you do with pious souls who take Scripture as the Word of God, and cannot believe what contradicts Scripture? Will you say, "We want peace, and therefore you must submit to the Pope"? or, "The Pope has not decided on this point or that and therefore opinion is free"? A man who fears God, who seeks life eternal, and fears eternal death, cannot rest on undecided or dubious doctrines. In my work on "The Bondage of the Will" I condemned the scepticism [*sic*] of Erasmian theology. Christians require certainty, definite dogmas, a sure Word of God which they can trust to live and die by. For such certainty Erasmus cares not. The Papists do not teach it. They cannot teach what they cannot understand. Therefore we can have no agreement with them. No Church can stand without the anchor of faith, and faith stands on the Word of God.[30]

While the polemics between Erasmus and Luther would soon subside, the issues that Luther raised concerning the error of the Catholic Church lived on and remain alive to this day. It is certainly enlightening to review the position of the modern Catholic Church on the issues of indulgences. One finds that little has changed in regards to the essence of those same issues which Luther and Erasmus debated. After Luther's excommunication, he married and spent the remaining years of his life writing, translating the Scriptures into his native German language and positively affecting both governmental and the newly formed Protestant ecclesiastical bodies for truth and righteousness.

Calvin

Apart from Luther, the greatest contribution to the Reformation came from John Calvin. His leadership provided structure and organization to the infant movement, without which it perhaps faced a misfocused and diluted mission, if not extinction altogether. Calvin formulated into a unified systematic theology much of which Luther had emphasized in a non-systematic way. His most important and enduring work, the *Institutes of the Christian Religion*, is usually simply referred to as the *Institutes*. This work was conceived as an organized coherent interpretation of Scripture and as such, served with Scripture (although certainly in a secondary role to Scripture) as a foundation for the young and vibrant Protestant movement. McGrath has characterized the work as "essentially pedagogical in content and style, conceived with educating and informing its reader."[31]

Calvin was born in 1509 in Picardy, France, and was thus only 12 years old when Luther defended his teachings at the Diet of Worms. It is uncertain when he began composing the *Institutes*, but the first version was published in 1536. It is noteworthy that such a prolific and profound writing could have been conceived in such a young mind. It is generally believed that he studied at the University of Paris in both the *Collège de la Marche* and the *Collège de Montaigu*. Both schools, quite famous and prestigious, were steeped in the humanistic learning traditions of that day and they would have well equipped him for study of the Scriptures in their original languages.

McGrath[32] claims that there is uncertainty as to the details of his university education. McGrath's questioning of Calvin's university education stems from the lack of existing documentation to prove the traditional biographical claims. As McGrath tells us, the French authorities were pursuing Luther's followers with a fury and Calvin was forced to flee Paris out of fear for his safety. In that scurry he left behind personal belongings that would have probably provided a concrete record to many biographical details of his Paris days. However, there should be no reason to believe that Calvin would have let this part of his biography stand if he had not in fact attended these schools.

McGrath[33] also addressed some of the circumstances that shifted Calvin from his humanistic identity to the "Reformer" identity for which, of course, he is best noted. Certainly associated with this shift is the change in the spirit of his writing. Before the *Institutes* were published, Calvin wrote a commentary on Seneca's *De clementia*. That work, published in 1532, is humanistic in character. We know from Calvin's own commentary, that prior to leaving the Roman Church, he was a thoroughly committed Catholic and that his conversion from Catholicism had evidently been quite a sudden one. In the preface to his *Commentary on The Book of Psalms*, Calvin stated:

> And first, since I was too obstinately devoted to the superstitions of Popery to be easily extricated from so profound an abyss of mire, God by a sudden conversion subdued and brought my mind to a teachable frame, which was more hardened in such matters than might have been expected from one at my early period of life. Having thus received some taste and knowledge of true godliness, I was immediately inflamed with so intense a desire to make progress therein, that although I did not altogether leave off other studies, I yet pursued them with less ardour. I was quite surprised to find that before a year had elapsed, all who had any desire after purer doctrine were continually coming to me to learn although I myself was as yet but a mere novice and tyro.[34]

It is likely that Calvin's conversion occurred very soon after he published *De clementia,* since most sources give 1533 as the year for which he left the Roman Catholic Church. One general reference states that while he left the Church in 1533, his persuasion to Luther's views occurred over a long period of time.[35] However, since the first version of the *Institutes* appeared in 1536 this statement cannot carry too much weight. Likewise, McGrath puts more weight on Ganoczy's[36] contention that Calvin did not undergo a "sudden conversion" than on Calvin's own words, quoted above, which seem to indicate otherwise. Nonetheless, whatever the time frame may have been, it is certain, judged by the content of the *Institutes*, that Calvin left the Roman Church as a result of the truths that he had discovered from his own study of Scripture.

It was Calvin's understanding of human nature, and the relationship of that nature to the nature of God, that identified him with thought processes that are dramatically opposed to those found in both the humanism of the ancient Greek philosophers and the humanism that one sometimes finds buried within even nominal forms of Christianity. The Roman Catholicism of Calvin's day certainly fit into the latter category. When Erasmus opposed Luther's efforts to bring the light of scriptural truth to the practices and doctrines of the Roman Church, that Church renewed her commitment to, and therefore became further entrenched in, the humanism which was ultimately the product of Scholasticism. The marks of that chosen path remain to this day. It is precisely on the views of human nature and the relationship of that nature to the God of Scripture that is yet a primary source of the Protestant-Catholic dichotomy. Unfortunately, as we will see in Part Two of this work, modern Protestant thinking is yet being influenced by these same humanistic ideas, which are centered in the belief that man has within the power of his personality to first determine, through his powers of reason, the nature of the moral good and, from his power of volition, to move himself to that good.

The Reformers returned to Christianity the understanding that human nature was so radically changed as a result of Adam's disobedience, that the capacity to truly know God, solely within the power of human nature, was lost. Calvin's understanding of "original sin" was distinguished from the understanding that was then prevalent (and yet is) within the Roman Church. In regards to original sin Calvin said that it

> appears to be an hereditary pravity and corruption of our nature, diffused through all the parts of the soul, rendering us obnoxious to the Divine wrath, and producing in us those works which the Scripture calls "works of the flesh."(Gal. 5:19) And this is indeed what Paul frequently denominates *sin*. The works which proceed thence, such as adulteries, fornications, thefts, hatreds, murders, revellings, he calls in the same manner "fruits of sin;" although they are also called "sins" in many passages of Scripture, and even by himself. These two things therefore should be distinctly observed: first, that our nature being so totally vitiated and depraved, we are, on account of this very corruption, considered as convicted and justly condemned in the sight of God, to whom nothing is acceptable but righteousness, innocence, and purity. And this liableness to punishment arises not from the delinquency of another; for when it is said that the sin of Adam renders us obnoxious to the Divine judgment, it is not to be understood as if we, though innocent, were undeservedly loaded with the guilt of his sin; but because we are all subject to a curse, in consequence of his transgression, he is therefore said to have involved us in guilt. Nevertheless we derive from him, not only the punishment, but also the pollution to which the punishment is justly due. Wherefore Augustine, though he frequently calls it the sin of another, the more clearly to indicate its transmission to us by propagation, yet, at the same time, also asserts it properly to belong to every individual. And the Apostle himself expressly declares, that "death has therefore passed

upon all men, for that all have sinned;"(Rom. 5:12) that is, have been involved in original sin, and defiled with its blemishes. And therefore infants themselves, as they bring their condemnation into the world with them, are rendered obnoxious to punishment by their own sinfulness, not by the sinfulness of another. For though they have not yet produced the fruits of their iniquity, yet they have the seed of it within them; even their whole nature is as it were a seed of sin, and therefore cannot but be odious and abominable to God. Whence it follows, that it is properly accounted sin in the sight of God, because there could be no guilt without crime. The other thing to be remarked is, that this depravity never ceases in us, but is perpetually producing new fruits, those works of the flesh, which we have before described, like the emission of flame and sparks from a heated furnace, or like the streams of water from a never failing spring. Wherefore those who have defined original sin as a privation of the original righteousness, which we ought to possess, though they comprise the whole of the subject, yet have not used language sufficiently expressive of its operation and influence. For our nature is not only destitute of all good, but is so fertile in all evils that it cannot remain inactive.[37]

With this reemphasis of the devastating consequences on human nature of Adam's fall, the concept of "original sin" was put back into its scriptural perspective, a perspective that had been lost in the years between Augustine and Luther.

Two main points that are often overlooked should here be noted regarding Calvin's views of human depravity. First, Calvin did not deny the existence of good *qualities* in the natural man. Some erroneously believe that Calvin's view of human moral depravity, as outlined above, excluded the possibility of first perceiving and then acknowledging the good qualities frequently discovered in men of all creeds. He wrote regarding this:

> Whenever, therefore, we meet with heathen writers, let us learn from that light of truth which is admirably displayed in their works, that the human mind, fallen as it is, and corrupted from its integrity, is yet invested and adorned by God with excellent talents. ... Now, shall we deny the light of truth to the ancient lawyers, who have delivered such just principles of civil order and

polity? … Shall we say that those, who by the art of logic have taught us to speak in a manner consistent with reason, were destitute of understanding themselves? Shall we accuse those of insanity, who by the study of medicine have been exercising their industry for our advantage? … Let us learn from such examples, how many good qualities the Lord has left to the nature of man, since it has been despoiled of what is truly good.[38]

Secondly, Calvin did not believe that the knowledge of God's *existence* was hidden from man because of Adam's fall. He eloquently taught from his *Institutes* that God has endowed every person with the knowledge of his existence, and pointed out that even the great Roman poet Cicero observed that "there is no nation so barbarous, no race so savage, as not to be firmly persuaded of the being of a God."[39] Calvin, therefore, did not bring human reason into play to prove the existence of God. He correctly viewed God's existence as self-evident.

Of course, in spite of man's innate sense of God's existence, humanistic thinking has always produced, in all civilizations, those who have denied that existence. In regard to these, Calvin wrote:

while the stupid insensibility which the wicked wish to acquire, to promote their contempt of God, preys upon their minds, yet the sense of a Deity, which they ardently desire to extinguish is still strong, and frequently discovers itself.[40]

Calvin therefore believed that even atheists reach points in their lives when they become cognizant of God's existence. In the chapters that follow we discuss some of the thought processes that have led to a preponderance of atheistic thinking in modern Western civilization. Modern atheism, spawned primarily by the teachings of Darwin, Nietzsche, Freud and Marx, substitutes mechanisms of nature to account for all reality, including human nature. Secular humanism arises in all cultures because it is the philosophy that one must resort to when one foolishly says in his heart that there is no God. Many years before Darwin, Calvin wrote:

How detestable is this frenzy, that man, discovering in his body and soul a hundred vestiges of God, should make this very excellence a pretext for the denial of his being! They will not say they are distinguished from the brutes by chance; but they ascribe it to nature, which they consider as the author of all things, and remove God out of sight.[41]

With the Reformed rediscovery of a scriptural view of human depravity came a substantial departure from Aquinas' belief that man possessed a natural inclination to goodness, or a natural inclination to *want* to come to a true knowledge of God. Calvin did not believe that the mere knowledge of God's existence created in man the desire to know, in a true sense, that God. He wrote, "Some perhaps grow vain in their own superstitions, while others revolt from God with intentional wickedness; *but all* [italics added] degenerate from the true knowledge of him."[42] The natural tendency in human nature is to believe about God what one *wants* to believe about God, and not what God says about himself in Scripture. Pantheistic and humanistic philosophies have sprung from man's futile attempt to understand, on his own terms, the God he intuitively knows to exist. Regarding pantheism, Calvin cautioned his reader against those who taught that a secret inspiration and universal mind animates and actuates the world. These do so, according to Calvin, "to set up a shadowy deity, and to banish all ideas of the true God, the proper object of fear and worship."[43] Calvin concluded in this regard:

> Wherefore we are justly excluded from all excuse for our uncertain and extravagant deviations, since all things conspire to show us the right way. But, however men are chargeable with sinfully corrupting the seeds of divine knowledge, which, by the wonderful operation of nature, are sown in their hearts, so that they produce no good and fair crop, yet it is beyond a doubt, that the simple testimony magnificently borne by the creatures to the glory of God, is very insufficient for our instruction. For as soon as a survey of the world has just shown us a deity, neglecting the true God, we set up in his stead the dreams and phantasms of our own brains; and confer on them the praise of righteousness, wisdom, goodness, and power, due to him.[44]

Unfortunately, this phenomenon of believing about God what one wants to believe is also readily apparent in the works of modern humanists who operate under the guise of religion. These, as we will see in Chapter 10, continue to put forth their own brand of God, and they also should be considered Calvin's target.

> Pride and vanity are discovered, when miserable men, in seeking after God, rise not, as they ought, above their own level, but judge of him according to their carnal stupidity, and leave the proper path of investigation in pursuit of speculations as vain as they are curious. Their conceptions

of him are formed, not according to the representation he gives of himself, but by the inventions of their own presumptuous imaginations.[45]

Calvin thus emphasized the scriptural truth which teaches, that while man may intuitively be convinced of God's existence, the desire for a *true* knowledge of God is not an inherent trait of human nature. Calvin was not merely pulling his arguments out of his own reasoning but was expounding scriptural teachings on the subject. Scripture is very clear regarding the consequences of Adam's sin on human nature. In addition to the Hebrew Scripture discussed in Chapter 2 affirming this fact, the Apostle Paul was clear in this teaching. In his letter to the Romans he stated. "For even though they knew God, they did not honor Him as God, or give thanks; but they became futile in their speculations, and their foolish heart was darkened."[46]

The human inability to come unaided to a true knowledge of God because of an inherited nature that is in rebellion against Him has resulted in the humanism that ascribes to human personality a sovereignty that it cannot possess. Calvin implied that the misunderstanding of man's fallen state was the basis for the error in the philosopher's thinking. Calvin claimed that from this misunderstanding "proceeded the darkness" that controlled the minds of the philosophers because they sought for an "edifice among ruins, and for beautiful order in the midst of confusion."[47] The philosophers did not understand the extent to which human nature had become corrupt with the fall of Adam. It is interesting to note that Calvin directly analyzed the philosopher's position to show it as one holding to the sovereignty of human personality. Calvin treated all aspects of human personality in his analysis. He wrote:

> The philosophers, indeed, with general consent, pretend, that in the mind presides Reason, which like a lamp illuminates with its counsels, and like a queen governs the will; for that it is so irradiated with Divine light as to be able to give the best counsels, and endued with such vigour as to be qualified to govern in the most excellent manner; that Sense, on the contrary, is torpid and afflicted with weakness of sight, so that it always creeps on the ground, and is absorbed in the grossest objects, nor ever elevates itself to a view of the truth; that Appetite, if it can submit to the obedience of reason, and resist the attractions of sense, is inclined to the practice of virtues, travels the path of rectitude, and is formed into will; but that, if it be devoted to the servitude of sense, it is thereby so corrupted and depraved as to degenerate into lust. And as,

according to their opinion, there reside in the soul those faculties which I have before mentioned, understanding, sense, and appetite, or will,—which appellation is now more commonly used,—they assert that the understanding is endued with reason, that most excellent guide to a good and a happy life, provided it only maintains itself in its own excellence, and exerts it innate power; but that the inferior affection of the soul, which is called *sense*, and by which it is seduced into error, is of such a nature that it may be tamed and gradually conquered by the rod of reason. They place the will in the middle station between reason and sense, as perfectly at liberty, whether it choose to obey reason, or submit to the violence of sense.[48]

Here Calvin showed his reader that the philosophers mistakenly believed that human personality was so sovereign as to have the proper knowledge and wisdom to choose, in and of its own power, the moral good and in the same manner to refuse evil. The humanistic mind always views human personality to have command over the human moral predicament, and, unfortunately, Aquinas' teaching, as the defender of Aristotle, had put Roman Catholic views of the subject into the same philosophical camp.

Calvin's view of the inefficacy of human reason to discover a true knowledge of God was, therefore, contrary to the teaching of Aquinas. Regarding human ability, based purely on reason, to know God and to understand the depth of his love for his creation, Calvin stated that even "the most sagacious of mankind are blinder than moles."[49] He readily admitted that within some of the philosopher's writings one could sometimes find truth that is consistent with the truth of Scripture. However, Calvin viewed this as evidence that God has provided his creation with sufficient evidence of himself "that they might not be able to plead ignorance as an excuse for impiety."[50] And certainly, one can never find in the philosopher's writing, according to Calvin, any indication of God's love for his creatures, the knowledge of which is dependent for salvation. Calvin insisted that the lack of such knowledge led to the confusion often found in the philosopher's works, such as "that frigid dogma of Aristotle" which destroys the "immortality of the soul." This erroneous dogma is one that teaches "the soul to be so united to the body as to be incapable of subsisting without it." Calvin reminded his reader that the "powers of the soul are far from being limited to functions subservient to the body."[51] He concluded that "human reason, then, neither approaches, nor tends, nor directs its views towards ... [understanding] the true God, or in what character he will manifest himself to us."[52]

Just as man's depraved condition has incapacitated the power of his reason to come to a true understanding of God's character, so Calvin taught that man's will, solely in the power of that will, was likewise incapacitated to move one to the true moral good. Calvin emphasized that human will was initially free, but when Adam chose to disobey God, its freedom, in the truest sense, was lost. Calvin's view of the human will was, therefore, essentially in agreement with the view initially espoused by Luther. It is the Reformed view of the human will that goes far in removing it from any vestige of humanistic philosophy, both the humanism of the Renaissance and even modern-day humanism. Calvin conceded that the term "free will" was semantically a problem because in a sense man does possess free will. His possession of free will is not in the sense that he has the capability to choose the moral good without a true knowledge of the God of Scripture, "but because he does evil voluntarily, and not by constraint."[53] However, the use of the term "free will" was regarded by Calvin to be dangerous because of the error in perception it usually induced. Calvin stated:

> How few are there, pray, who, when they hear free will attributed to man, do not immediately conceive, that he has sovereignty over his own mind and will, and is able by his innate power to incline himself to whatever he pleases?[54]

Regarding Augustine's view of free will, Calvin sought to clarify some common misunderstandings. As we discussed in Chapter 3, because of Augustine's early writing, he is sometime represented as a proponent of free will. However, Calvin emphasized that when Augustine spoke of free will, he was speaking of how it was originally created (See Chapter 3). Calvin tells us that Augustine

> hesitates not to call the will a slave. He expresses his displeasure in one place against those who deny free will; but he declares the principal reason for it, when he says, "Only let no man dare so to deny the freedom of the will, as to desire to excuse sin." Elsewhere he plainly confesses, that the human will is not free without the Spirit, since it is subject to its lusts, by which it is conquered and bound. Again: that when the will was overcome by the sin into which it fell, nature began to be destitute of liberty. Again: that man, having made a wrong use of his free will, lost both it and himself. Again: that free will is in a state of captivity, so that it can do nothing towards righteousness. Again: that the will cannot be free, which has not been liberated by Divine grace. Again: that the Divine justice is

not fulfilled, while the law commands, and man acts from his own strength; but when the Spirit assists, and the human will obeys, not as being free, but as liberated by God. And he briefly assigns the cause of all this, when, in another place, he tells us, that man at his creation received great strength of free will, but lost it by sin.[55]

As pointed out in the introduction to this work, the Reformer's teaching of the inefficacy of the human will has created divisions within Protestant Christianity, particularly since the advent of Arminian and Wesleyan theologies. But when the extent of man's depravity is acknowledged, that division is often mitigated, because the true source of conflict between a Christianity compatible with humanism with one that is not, lies in understanding the extent to which Adam's sin affected human nature. On this point, Scripture, when studied objectively, is quite clear. Some have difficulty with Calvin's teaching on the will because they assume he discounts the complete role of human will in the affairs of man. But such thinking is not correct. For example in his preface to *Commentary on the Book of the Psalms*, Calvin, when informing his reader why he chose to comply with certain requests that this particular work be completed, stated:

> One reason which made me comply with their solicitations, and which also had from the commencement induced me to make this first attempt, was an apprehension that at some future period what had been taken down from my lectures, might be published to the world contrary to my wishes, or at least without my knowledge. I can truly say, that I was drawn to execute this work rather from such an apprehension, than led to it from *my own free will*. [italics added][56]

Calvin certainly did not thus discount his own "free will" as it applied to non-moral issues. And Calvin did not view human volition as having *no* role in the salvation process. Man is created in the image of God and, as such, has a personality of which volition is a characteristic part. One must exercise that volition to turn from his sin and follow Christ. The question goes back to where the sovereignty of will lies. One who comes to a true knowledge of the one and only true God has relinquished his will to the will of that God; his will has become a *responsive* one. When one's will is completely submitted to the will of God, that submitted will can no longer be perceived as a sovereign entity. A will that has become submitted to God is the result of a true knowledge of God that produces a fear and reverence … to instruct us to implore all good at his hand, and to render him the praise of all that we receive. For how can you entertain a thought of God without immediately reflecting, that, being a creature of his formation, you must, by right of creation, be subject to his authority? that [*sic*] you are indebted to him for your life, and that all your actions should be done with reference to him? If this be true, it certainly follows that your life is miserably corrupt, unless it be regulated by a desire to obeying him, since his will ought to be the rule of our conduct.[57]

When human will operates in accordance with truth it always operates in a sense of obedience to the will of God. Or in other words, human will when operating in accordance with truth functions as a *responsive* will to the sovereign will of God. This is why, Calvin put more emphasis on knowing the character of God and subsequently to knowing "what is agreeable to his nature" rather than on the "disquisitions on the essence of God."[58]

Calvin made it clear that one bears responsibility for his sin since God has provided to every person sufficient light of Himself through His creation so as to make all without excuse. That the one outside of Christ is responsible for his damnation and yet cannot come to God unless God first enables his will, through an enlightenment of his reason, is an apparent dichotomy that can only be understood by realizing the extent to which man is incapacitated because of Adam's sin. But this teaching which Calvin emphasized is clearly one born from knowledge of Scripture. In the book of Romans, the Apostle Paul directly addressed the issue of which we are speaking. The Apostle writes in regards to the salvation of Jacob but the damnation of Esau:

> Rebekah also, when she had conceived twins by one man, our father Isaac; for though the twins were not yet born, and had not done anything good or bad, in order that God's purpose according to His choice might stand, not because of works, but because of Him who calls, it was said to her, "The older will serve the younger." Just as it is written, "Jacob I loved, but Esau I hated." What shall we say then? There is no injustice with God, is there?" May it never be! For He says to Moses, "I will have mercy on whom I have mercy, and I will have compassion on whom I have compassion." So then it does not depend on the man who wills or the man who runs, but on God who has mercy. For the Scripture says to Pharaoh, "For this very

purpose I raised you up, to demonstrate My power in you, and that My name might be proclaimed throughout the whole earth." So then He has mercy on whom He desires, and He hardens whom He desires. You will say to me then, "Why does He still find fault? For who resists His will?" On the contrary, who are you, O man, who answers back to God: The thing molded will not say to the molder, "Why did you make me like this," will it?[59]

Exaltation of the necessity and efficacy of Scripture for the attainment of a true knowledge of God stands out in Calvin's *Institutes*. The inability to arrive at a true knowledge of God through the process of human reason necessitates the testimony of Scripture. Calvin wrote concerning the confidence given to the Hebrew patriarchs that they conveyed God's very word:

> It is beyond a doubt that their minds were impressed with a firm assurance of the doctrine, so that they were persuaded and convinced that the information they had received came from God. For God always secured to his word an undoubted credit, superior to all human opinion.[60]

And as to the necessity of God's word in an authoritative written form, Calvin states:

> For, if we consider the mutability of the human mind,—how easy its lapse into forgetfulness of God; how great its propensity to errors of every kind; how violent its rage for the perpetual fabrication of false religions,—it will be easy to perceive the necessity of the heavenly doctrine being thus committed to writing, that it might not be lost in oblivion, or evaporate in error, or be corrupted by the presumption of men.[61]

The Roman Catholic Church did not view Scripture as having ultimate authority in matters of doctrine and church practice. Calvin, as did Luther, understood how such tradition had allowed the church to be corrupted by the influence of humanistic thinking. He emphasized the absolute authority of Scripture and taught that Scripture should judge the church and not vice-versa. Calvin wrote in this regard:

> There has very generally prevailed a most pernicious error, that the Scriptures have only so much weight as is conceded to them by the suffrages of the Church; as though the eternal and inviolable truth of God depended on the arbitrary will of men. For thus, with great contempt of the Holy Spirit, they inquire, Who can assure us that God is the author of them? Who can with certainty affirm, that

they have been preserved safe and uncorrupted to the present age? Who can persuade us that this book ought to be received with reverence, and that expunged from the sacred number, unless all these things were regulated by the decision of the Church? It depends, therefore, (say they,) on the determination of the Church, to decide both what reverence is due to the Scripture, and what books are to be comprised in its canon. Thus sacrilegious men, while they wish to introduce an unlimited tyranny, under the name of the Church, are totally unconcerned with what absurdities they embarrass themselves and others, provided they can extort from the ignorant this one admission, that the Church can do every thing. … It is a very false notion, therefore, that the power of judging of the Scripture belongs to the Church, so as to make the certainty of it dependent on the Church's will. Wherefore, when the Church receives it, and seals it with her suffrage, she does not authenticate a thing otherwise dubious or controvertible; but, knowing it to be the truth of her God, performs a duty of piety, by treating it with immediate veneration.[62]

In conclusion, we see that the work of Luther and Calvin was important in the history of Christianity because both churchmen played key roles in the birth of a Christianity that stood apart from one that had, and still has, the philosophical underpinnings of Greek humanism. Their work provided a sharp line of demarcation between a Christianity that had been infested with humanistic ideas and one that held to a view of human nature consistent with the one presented in Scripture. While the former viewpoint, which assumes human personality to possess sovereignty over human nature, is sometimes openly expressed, more often than not it is silently implied. As we outlined in Chapter 4, the Renaissance humanist Petrarch was highly influenced by Cicero. Calvin reminded us that Cicero in the person of Cotta asserted

> that, since every man acquires virtue for himself, none of the wise men have ever thanked God for it. "For," says he, "we are praised for virtue, and in virtue we glory; which would not be the case, if it were a gift from God, and did not originate from ourselves."[63]

If true moral virtue is ever attained, it is always a gift from God, and as a gift, it is always attained by God's grace which, by definition, is unmerited favor. Therefore, as the Apostle Paul proclaimed to the Ephesians, one is saved alone by grace through faith, and it is never because of what one has done or how one has lived, so that no one can boast.[64] These philosophical differences that were present in Luther's and Calvin's era are yet present today. Unfortunately, as we will see in Chapter 10, there are those today who are attempting to put back into Christianity a system of thought that again attempts to elevate human personality to a sovereign position.

6

Historical Humanism: The Enlightenment

Thou believest that there is one God; thou doest well: the devils also believe, and tremble. James 2:19 [KJV]

The Enlightenment is generally considered to span the 17th and 18th centuries. Like the Renaissance, it is a difficult period to fully characterize due to the diversity of ideas in those who shaped its character. It is an important period to this work because many of the ideas that originated then have a bearing on both the secular and non-secular humanism that prevails in our own era. While most Renaissance humanists gave at least political allegiance to the Christianity of their era, the humanists of the Enlightenment sought to remove from the human consciousness all vestiges of the concept of God that had been established early in the history of Christianity from the precepts of Scripture. A deistic philosophy which acknowledged the existence of a supreme being, but which was ultimately based on humanistic ideas, became popular with the most influential thinkers of the Enlightenment.

This era is also known as the Age of Reason because herein the birth of modern science was realized. The humanists of the Enlightenment, because of the phenomenal successes in science, came to believe that science could, and would, provide any necessary knowledge for human advancement. Furthermore, the perception that reason could enable moral living once again became dominant. Certainly the content of Scripture, in the minds of the era's most notable thinkers, was not regarded as a reliable source for gaining a proper understanding of reality.

Before discussing some of the philosophical ideas associated with the Enlightenment, we will briefly discuss some of those pioneering individuals who introduced into Western civilization the methods of modern science. Of these, Isaac Newton is one of the great scientists of history and must be considered a product of the Reformation. In the years following the Reformation, the quantity and quality of knowledge generated in mathematics and the physical sciences was inimitable, and this new knowledge spawned a fresh way of looking at the phenomenological world. We shall also look at how this new knowledge clashed with the Roman Catholic Church and how it responded to this perceived threat. In the sense that scientific achievement rose to unprecedented heights, the era is properly named; but, in the sense that deistic concepts of ultimate reality were thereby fueled, the period could perhaps be better named the "Endarkenment."

The Post-Reformation Astronomers

The revolution in astronomy began quietly during the era of Luther with the work of Nicholas Copernicus. The Polish-born astronomer was well educated, having studied both law and medicine before settling into mathematics and astronomy. Copernicus revolutionized man's perception of the universe by proposing that the earth revolved around the sun instead of vice versa, the commonly held belief of that time. The erroneous belief that the earth was centered in the universe had been based on the writings of both Aristotle and Ptolemy. Copernicus published his ideas near the end of his life and they were, for the most part, immediately rejected. The Church's rejection of the Reformers' message had forced it back into medieval thinking, not only on subjects of theology, but also on scientific topics. Since Aquinas had set up Aristotle as an authority in all matters of knowledge, the Roman Church, to maintain a philosophical consistency, was forced to reject the Copernican theory. If the Church had admitted to Aristotle's error in this area, Aquinas' views on human nature and theology could have also been challenged.

Johanne Kepler, Galileo Galilei, and Isaac Newton were the pioneering giants in astronomy and physics whose works directly triggered the modern scientific revolution. The German Kepler was born in 1571, about 25 years after the death of Luther. Primarily a mathematician, he was interested in making sense of the astronomical observations reported by Copernicus a few years earlier. Kepler's fame came from the formulation of three laws that accurately predicted the planetary motion around the sun. He was the first to show that planets travel around the sun in elliptical paths at non-uniform rates of speed.

In 1609, Galileo constructed a telescope and discovered firsthand new astronomical phenomenon such as the rings of Saturn and the satellites of Jupiter. He also discovered the laws of physics describing falling bodies and was the first to conclude that all bodies fall at constant acceleration despite any differences in mass. This discovery was also contrary to Aristotle's contention that bodies fall at speeds proportional to their weight.

As a Protestant, Kepler's teaching did not immediately draw the attention of the Roman Church. It was when the Roman Catholic Galileo began to espouse his views in favor of the Copernican theory that the Church moved to squelch his voice. Galileo knew that his discoveries, which further verified Copernicus' main ideas and again proved Aristotle to be in error, would bring him trouble. He wrote to Kepler:

> I have not dared to make [it] known, as I have been deterred by the fate of our teacher Copernicus. He, it is true, won undying fame amongst some few, but amongst the multitude (there are so many fools in the world) he was only an object of scorn and laughter.[1]

However, in 1632, Galileo finally made his observations known in the work, *Dialogo sopra i due massimi sistemi del mondo, tolemaico e copernicano, (Dialogue on the Two Principal World Systems, Ptolemaic and Copernican)* which he dedicated to the Pope. Instead of pleasing the Pope, however, the book, which challenged the Aristotelian interpretation of the universe, set in motion a movement that sought to silence the pioneering Galileo. Galileo was called to Rome where he faced charges of heresy. In Rome he was sentenced to life imprisonment, but the sentence was subsequently reduced to house arrest where he remained until his death in 1642. In addition, his book was ordered burned.

It was Isaac Newton who synthesized the works of Kepler and Galileo, along with his own observations, into a consistent theory of gravity. Newton was born only about ten years after the Catholic Church had condemned the writings of Galileo. Newton's contributions to science are even today considered revolutionary. His discoveries are the foundation of classical mechanics where even the modern student of physics begins his study. Newton's three laws of motion and his discovery of the universal law of gravitation form the basis of our understanding of how forces act on bodies. These laws, of course, are just as valid today as they were then,[2] and it is this knowledge that has enabled man to explore the vastness of his universe including his achievement of walking on the earth's moon. When the American astronauts were being launched into space, on their way to the moon, mission control radioed the ship to ask who was driving it. The answer that came back to Houston was "Isaac Newton."

Consistent with Calvin's teaching reviewed in the previous chapter, Newton insisted that the evidence of nature was sufficient to convince the rational mind of an intelligent creator. He wrote in his *Opticks*:

How came the bodies of animals to be contrived with so much art, and for what ends were their several parts? Was the eye contrived without skill in optics and the ear without knowledge of sounds? How do the motions of the body follow from the will, and whence is the instinct in animals?[3]

Gay stated that Newton "would have despised the deists, who turned God into a master mechanic, and would have been outraged by the atheists, who denied Him altogether."[4] However, Newton not only believed in God's existence, but he also sought—through his intense study of Scripture—a personal relationship with the God of whom he spoke.

Michael White, a modern biographer of Newton, unfortunately portrays Newton as a confused alchemist who probably experimented in the occult instead of one who possessed a mind that was consumed to know both scientific and biblical truth.[5] White maintains that Newton was Arian in his beliefs, i.e., Newton believed that Jesus was a created being, and thus, was not fully God. But based on White's presentation of the evidence, to call Newton an Arian appears to be too bold an accusation. While Newton's study led him to examine Scripture's teaching of the triune nature of God, White's revisionist account does not seem to support the assignment of this label. Newton's association of the doctrine of the Trinity with Catholicism, no doubt led him to question its scriptural basis. But merely his questioning of the doctrine—which appears to have occurred primarily in his early thirties—does not necessarily qualify him for a lifetime label of Arianism. The intellectual temperament of Newton's era was still mainly influenced by the major European universities which were yet under Catholic control. Newton understood how Catholic Scholasticism had negatively influenced scientific thinking. Subsequently, when James II came to power in England and sought to bring Cambridge University (Newton's university association) under Catholic control, Newton intensely fought that effort. He knew that a humanistic papal influence at Cambridge would be detrimental to the new developing scientific methodology. White's biographical account of Newton's theology, therefore, seems to be based too much on conjecture.

That Newton recognized the power and exclusivity of Scripture for specific revelation of the mind of God is readily apparent in his work entitled *Observations upon the Prophecies of Daniel and the Apocalypse of St. John.* White, not surprisingly, labels this work as "shambolic." However, it is extremely doubtful that the following words were conceived from a mind immersed in the evil practices of the occult.

In the infancy of the nation of *Israel*, when God had given them a Law, and made a covenant with them to be their God if they would keep his commandments, he sent Prophets to reclaim them, as often as they revolted to the worship of other Gods: and upon their returning to him, they sometimes renewed the covenant which they had broken. These Prophets he continued to send till the days of *Ezra*: but after their Prophecies were read in the Synagogues, those Prophecies were thought sufficient. For if the people would not hear *Moses* and the old Prophets, they would hear no new ones, no not *tho* [*sic*] *they should rise from the dead.* At length when a new truth was to be preached to the *Gentiles*, namely, *that Jesus was the Christ*, God sent new Prophets and Teachers: but after their writings were also received and read in the Synagogues of the Christians, Prophecy ceased a second time. We have *Moses*, the Prophets, and Apostles, and the words of Christ himself; and if we will not hear them, we shall be more inexcusable than the *Jews*. For the Prophets and Apostles have foretold, that as *Israel* often revolted and brake the covenant, and upon repentance renewed it; so there should be a falling away among the Christians, soon after the days of the Apostles; and that in the latter days God would destroy the impenitent revolters, and make a new covenant with his people. And the giving ear to the Prophets is a fundamental character of the true Church. For God has so ordered the Prophecies, that in the latter days *the wise may understand, but the wicked shall do wickedly, and none of the wicked shall understand.* Dan. xii 9,10.[6]

The assertion of Newton's heresy has probably risen because it fits into a humanistic agenda which seeks to divorce significant scientific achievement from those who hold to a Christian worldview. But the Christian's desire to know absolute truth was, and still is, conducive to the success of science. Of course, the two systems of knowledge do not operate in the same framework (contrary to what some Scholastics taught), but genuine Christianity produces a mind-set that is conducive to the pursuit of truth whether that truth is physical or metaphysical. Humanists often want to forget the fact that many of the world's foremost scientific discoveries are products of Christian minds. And in the attempt to bolster their case for such thinking, secular humanists often resort to Rome's treatment of its own Galileo, who, as we have just discussed, was vilified for having sided with Copernicus against the writings of Ptolemy and Aristotle. However, as was pointed out in the previous two chapters, the Catholic Church had already adopted an interpretation of reality that had the philosophical underpinnings of humanism. So to attribute this gross lack of judgment to Christianity *per se*, and not to a faltering Catholic Church, is likewise an error in judgment.

Newton was consumed with a drive to know truth, but he understood that the mechanisms for understanding the physical truths of the universe differ from those necessary to understand the truth of Scripture. He did not attempt to link the two systems of knowledge. The knowledge required for moral salvation comes only through a supernaturally acquired faith, which enables one to realize the supernatural character of Scripture. Human reason alone cannot decipher its truth. The fact that Newton possessed one of the greatest scientific minds in the history of humanity is proof, however, that reason and Christianity are compatible.

Newton's work eventually forced a change in the intellectual temperament of his era because he proved that human reason could decipher the physical laws by which the universe operated. However, the discovery of these seemingly immutable laws of physics fueled deistic ideas. The deists divorced the God of Scripture from their view of reality because the mechanistic workings of the universe could be accounted for by human reasoning. Their viewpoint soon dominated the intellectual climate of the Enlightenment and thus enabled science to stand apart from any concept of God. And from a practical, scientific point of view, that outlook is preferred to one that merges the two systems as did Aquinas. But a deistic viewpoint automatically discounts the workings of God in human personality, and that cannot be done since, at that point in the overall scheme of reality, God still intervenes in nature.

Voltaire

The beginning of the Enlightenment in Europe, particularly in France, is closely linked to the life and works of Voltaire. Voltaire was born in Paris in 1694, under the name Francois-Marie Arouet. He changed his name to Voltaire at about the age of 23. Raised Catholic, Voltaire received his education at the hands of the Jesuits and the influence of that education is evident in his writings even though he eventually became a rather harsh critic of Christianity. Nonetheless, Voltaire did not divorce himself completely from the Roman Catholic establishment (i.e., he was never excommunicated as a result of his criticisms of the Church). Understanding Catholicism's influence on Voltaire is pertinent to understanding his thought processes and how he was influential in the development of the Enlightenment and its subsequent impact on modern Western humanism.

Like Erasmus, who lived more than 200 years before him, Voltaire was a man of letters. The similarities between Erasmus and Voltaire, apart from their common love of literature, are somewhat striking. Although Voltaire was not "a religious," as was Erasmus, both were Roman Catholics who viewed Scholastic philosophy with disdain. Both had preferences for moving in the social circles of the rich and famous, and both were well-known for their sarcastic wit. Each also had a propensity for criticizing those in power whose behavior they perceived to be less than desirable. Voltaire actually served two brief prison sentences in the Bastille for his writings against authority. Furthermore, both Erasmus and Voltaire lived as aliens in England for a significant period of time. As a result of Voltaire's second incarceration, he was banished to England for about two and a half years where he learned the English culture and its language.

In England Voltaire received firsthand knowledge of the advancements in science that were then occurring and thereby gained a great respect for Isaac Newton. Even then, the educated populace had perceived the far-reaching ramifications of Newton's work. In response to an unnamed person stating that Newton was the greatest man that had ever lived, Voltaire, in a short essay entitled *On Bacon and Newton*, penned the following words:

> This man was certainly in the right; for if true greatness consists in having received from heaven the advantage of a superior genius, with the talent of applying it for the interest of the possessor and of mankind, a man like Newton—and such a one is hardly to be met with in ten centuries—is surely by much the greatest; and those statesmen and conquerors which no age has ever been without, are commonly but so many illustrious villains. It is the man who sways our minds by the prevalence of reason and the native force of truth, not they who reduce mankind to a state of slavery by brutish force and downright violence; the man who by the vigor of his mind, is able to penetrate into the hidden secrets of nature, and whose capricious soul can contain the vast frame of the universe, not those who lay nature waste, and desolate the face of the earth, that claims our reverence and admiration.[7]

The Catholic Church's hindrance of scientific advancement no doubt played a role in Voltaire's cynical criticism of Christianity. In the face of the Protestant advance, the Roman Church had unabashedly retreated to the Scholasticism of Aquinas. Voltaire was vehemently opposed to the teachings of the Schoolmen because he correctly perceived the negative influence that their teachings had had on scientific progress. In the same essay quoted above, Voltaire reminisced about certain inventions that had occurred in the Middle Ages. When he referred to that era, he called it an age of "scholastic barbarity." He then went on to sarcastically claim that, in that era, "a man that was capable to maintain a thesis on the 'Categories of Aristotle,' the *universale a parte rei*, or such-like nonsense, was considered as a prodigy."[8] His association of Scholastic philosophy with "nonsense" showed just how much disdain he had for the Scholastic influence that then still existed. And later in the same essay, when speaking of the accomplishments of Descartes, he stated that Descartes "left France purely to go in search of truth, which was then persecuted by the wretched philosophy of the Schools."[9]

Because of his intense dislike for the Scholasticism that had so shaped French thought, Voltaire attributed Newton's success to the absence of that influence in Newton's world. Voltaire wrote:

> It was his [Newton's] peculiar felicity not only to be born in a country of liberty, but in an age when all Scholastic impertinencies were banished from the world. Reason alone was cultivated, and mankind could only be his pupil, not his enemy.[10]

With knowledge of how the Catholic Church's allegiance to Scholasticism had hindered scientific advancement, Voltaire became one of the Church's greatest critics. Unfortunately, his criticisms were aimed, as were Erasmus' two centuries before him, at the symptoms of the Church's failure and not at its theological root causes.

While Voltaire retained belief in the existence of a supreme being throughout his life, his concept of God was clearly divorced from the God of Scripture. The belief in God's existence is often congruous with humanistic thinking. Consistent with Calvin's teachings, Voltaire's belief in the existence of God was based on the fact that God's existence is self-evident. No doubt, Voltaire was aware of Newton's faith and this may have influenced his ideas regarding the compatibility between reason and belief in a supreme being. Voltaire stated: "It is perfectly evident to my mind that there exists a necessary, eternal, supreme, and intelligent being. This is no matter of faith, but of reason."[11] On another occasion Voltaire wrote:

> Tonight I was in a meditative mood. I was absorbed in
> the contemplation of nature; I admired the immensity,
> the movements, the harmony of those infinite globes
> which the vulgar do not know how to admire. I admired
> still more the intelligence which directs these vast forces.
> I said to myself: "One must be blind not to be dazzled by
> this spectacle; one must be stupid not to recognize the
> author of it; one must be mad not to worship Him. What
> tribute of worship should I render Him?"[12]

And in a letter written to Frederick William, Prince of Prussia, during the
latter part of his life, Voltaire again made plain his views on the existence of
God. Here he stated that "all nature cries aloud that He does exist: that
there *is* a supreme intelligence, an immense power, an admirable order, and
everything teaches us our own dependence on it."[13]

Although Voltaire clearly believed in God's existence, knowledge of God's
existence is not synonymous with a true knowledge of God. The ultimate
dividing line between a humanistic system of philosophy and a system based
in the truth of Christianity is not contingent on what one believes about
God's existence, but upon what one believes about the God that is revealed
in Scripture. Voltaire wrote, obviously in response to a question about the
existence of the human soul, "It is not proved that this faculty [the soul]
survives our death … The safest course is to do nothing against one's conscience. With this secret, we can enjoy life and have nothing to fear from
death."[14] Voltaire did not thus regard the teaching of Scripture as trustworthy. Despite his belief in God's existence, he had no understanding that one
could know that God personally and as a result of that knowledge be saved
from the depravity of one's sin. Voltaire believed that speculation on the
nature of God always resulted in the creation of sects, whose belief systems,
in his opinion, were always open to debate. Voltaire wrote:

> Every sect, of every kind, is a rallying-point for doubt
> and error. Scotist, Thomist, Realist, Nominalist, Papist,
> Calvinist, Molinist, and Jansenist are only pseudonyms.
> There are no sects in geometry. One does not speak of a
> Euclidean, an Archimedean. When the truth is evident,
> it is impossible for parties and factions to arise. …Well,
> to what dogma do all minds agree? To the worship of a
> God, and to honesty. All the philosophers of the world
> who have had a religion have said in all ages: "There is a
> God, and one must be just."[15]

The Enlightenment humanists could not understand that Scripture is mankind's only authoritative source for knowing the truth about God. To those who think that this presupposition is irrational, an element of faith is admittedly involved. But if one can accept the fact that nature itself teaches the reality of a supreme being, as Voltaire rightfully did, then it should not be too great a leap to believe that such a God could and would provide an absolute source of knowledge of Himself. The Christian knows Scripture to be God's word because of its affect on the human spirit. He knows the truth of the new birth spoken of by Jesus in John 3, because he has experienced it. He knows that the nature with which he was born indeed becomes reborn through the exercise of faith. Factions involving religion have risen either because of the rejection of the absolute authority of Scripture or, if such Scriptural authority is acknowledged, because of the inability of its reader through a supernatural enabling—by God's Spirit—to discern its critical message.

Unfortunately, Voltaire did not have the privilege of being steeped in a Christianity that taught the absolute authority of Scripture. During Voltaire's era, the French government had harshly persecuted her Protestant population. Protestants in the vein of Luther and Calvin, were, of course, those who primarily viewed Scripture as having absolute authority in matters of Christian doctrine. (It should be noted that Voltaire often came to the defense of persecuted Protestants, not because he agreed with their views, but because he understood the necessity of a separated Church and state if truth were ever to triumph.) When speculating on the reason that Christianity had sometimes caused painful confrontations and factions, Voltaire actually suggested that scriptural error was likely responsible. Voltaire related, in story form, an imaginary "vision" he experienced in dialogue with various philosophical figures who had impacted Western history, i.e., Socrates, Jesus, etc. The dialogue included a discussion about those who had lost their lives in the name of religion. In the dialogue Voltaire asked the imaginary Christ, "Did you not say once that you were come not to bring peace, but a sword?" Voltaire has Jesus replying to this question, "It is a copyist's error. I told them that I brought peace and not a sword. I never wrote anything; what I said may have been changed without evil intention."[16] This error of Voltaire was the direct result of his failure to understand Scripture's specific role in the revelation of the mind of God, in whom he claimed to believe. Those who refuse to accept the authority of Scripture and its supernatural character will invariably be offended by its message because scriptural revelation shines light on the nature of man and reveals the desperate state of human nature outside of saving faith in Jesus Christ. The Apostle John wrote concerning this:

> And this is the judgment, that the light is come into the
> world, and men loved the darkness rather than the light;
> for their deeds were evil. For everyone who does evil hates
> the light, and does not come to the light, lest his deeds
> should be exposed. But he who practices the truth comes
> to the light, that his deeds may be manifested as having
> been wrought in God.[17]

It is the offensive nature of this light that has caused genuine Christians to be persecuted, even to the point of death. Stephen was stoned to death during the very early days of the Christian church[18] because of the offense that the gospel generated in the hearts of those who threw the stones. Even today, as these words are written, Christians are dying at the hands of those who are offended by the message of Christ because that message causes light to shine on their own dark, evil natures.[19]

Voltaire's error was similar to that of the Presocratic philosophers discussed in Chapter 1. The rejection of God's revealed truth always leads to a false perception that the only reality of importance is the sum of that which is perceived phenomenologically. It was these perceptions that gave rise to the deism of the Enlightenment, which in turn gave rise to the atheism of modernity (discussed in the next chapter). It is only physical truth, which dictates the reality of the phenomenological, that science is equipped to reveal. The revolutionary breakthroughs that were occurring in scientific knowledge were chiefly responsible for reviving, on a major scale, the deceiving perceptions of reason's power to decipher the totality of reality.

With the emphasis that Enlightenment thinking had placed on human reason, as in the era of classical Greek philosophy, the rational faculties of man, along with the dictates of conscience, again became the only standard by which all morality was judged. Voltaire's humanism emphasized the power of human reason and conscience without allowing the freedom of human will that classical Greek humanism and the humanism of the Scholastics had included in their systems of thought. Voltaire's position on the role of human will stands apart from the usual humanistic view, probably because of both his intense dislike of Scholastic philosophy and the movement towards a scientific determinism which is inherent in deistic thought. John Locke, whose philosophy was influenced by a Calvinistic background, apparently influenced Voltaire's view of human volition. Concerning free will Voltaire wrote:

> Ever since men have been able to reason, philosophers have
> obscured the question of free will; but the theologians have
> rendered it unintelligible by absurd subtleties about grace.
> Locke was perhaps the first man to find a thread in the

labyrinth, for he was the first who, instead of arrogantly setting out from a general principle, examined human nature by analysis. … In the *Essay on the Human Understanding*, Locke shows that the question is fundamentally absurd, and that liberty can no more belong to the will than can color and movement.[20]

As mentioned in the introduction, the important outcome of what one believes about the will's freedom is where it puts the beholder on the subject of man's basic moral nature resulting from Adam's rebellion against God. Voltaire said of Augustine:

St. Augustine was the first who brought this strange notion [original sin] into credit: a notion worthy of the warm and romantic brain of an African debauchee and penitent, a Manichaean and Christian, tolerant and a persecutor—who passed his life in perpetual self contradiction.[21]

Therefore, in Voltaire's thinking, one observes a denial of free will without the acknowledgment of man's natural moral depravity. But it is man's separation from the God of Scripture, because of his sin, which prevents him from sovereignly choosing the moral good. Voltaire mocked the theologians who brought the "absurd subtleties about grace" into the argument. However, those subtleties about grace are so important to the issue because outside of God's grace one has no power to escape the nature that condemns him. While Voltaire understood the impossibility of escaping one's nature in the power of one's own will he did not understand the source of that inadequacy. He wrote in his *Philosophical Dictionary*:

Can one change one's character? Yes, if one changes one's body. It is possible for a man to be born a mischief-maker of tough and violent character, and, as a result of being stricken with apoplexy in his old age, to become a foolish, tearful child, timid and peaceable. His body has changed. But as long as his nerves, his blood and his morrow remain the same, his nature will not change any more than will a wolf's and a marten's instinct. Our character is composed of our ideas and our feelings: and, since it has been proved that we give ourselves neither feelings nor ideas, our character does not depend on us. … If one does not reflect, one thinks oneself master of everything; but when one does reflect, one realizes that one is master of nothing. … Religion, morality put a brake on a nature's

strength; they cannot destroy it. The drunkard in a clois-
ter, reduced to a half-setier of cider at each meal, will no
longer get drunk, but he will always like wine.[22]

With only phenomenological reality as a reference point for his view of
reality, Voltaire, as well as his fellow Enlightenment philosophers, could not
understand the scriptural teaching of supernatural regeneration, which serves
to thoroughly change human nature. The whole aim of all Scripture is the
revelation of salvation to a condemned human race, through a supernatural
regeneration (or rebirth) of human nature. When the alcoholic, who first
realizes that he has no power over that nature which is propelling him towards his downward spiral, turns to Jesus the Christ, in repentance for moral
cleansing, his character—or his nature—*is* truly changed. Such one truly
becomes a new creation[23] in Christ. The humanist does not understand
that the nature all are born with is propelling the entire human race towards
that same destruction. One who is limited to interpreting reality strictly
through the methods of science will never have a correct view of reality,
because he cannot understand how the supernatural yet affects human nature.

While Voltaire accused Augustine of philosophical contradictions, it
was his views that were, in reality, contradictory. Voltaire incorrectly stated
that the purpose of religion was "to make men merit the goodness of God by
their virtue."[24] No man can merit the goodness of God in the power of his
own will by anything he does, no matter how good it might appear. Man
simply does not have the power within himself to change his nature such
that he can merit God's favor. Voltaire's philosophical inconsistencies stemmed
from his inability to understand the relationship between God and the human race that the fall of Adam dictated. We will now turn our attention to
Immanuel Kant, who, as we shall see, based his ideas of morality on the
workings of conscience and thereby placed himself squarely in the humanist
tradition.

Kant

Immanuel Kant, born in 1724 about 3 years before Newton's death,
was a native of Königsberg, Prussia (now Kaliningrad, Russia), and there
received his entire education. He obtained his doctorate in the natural sciences, studying both physics and mathematics. Kant spent most of his life as
a professor at the same university where he had formerly been a student. As
his career progressed he became increasingly interested in philosophy and
ended up as a professor of logic and metaphysics.

Kant was raised in a Protestant Christian environment and that heritage is reflected in his work. But while the framework of his philosophy is grounded in Christianity, his thinking is ultimately incongruous with a genuine Christian interpretation of reality. Kant's philosophy was rooted firmly in a view of personality's sovereignty, and as such, his work is thoroughly humanistic in character.

In 1784, Kant sought to define the Enlightenment in a short essay entitled *What is Enlightenment?* The essay began with the following sentences:

> Enlightenment is a man's release from his self-incurred tutelage. Tutelage is a man's inability to make use of his understanding without direction from another. Self-incurred is this tutelage when its cause lies not in lack of reason but in lack of resolution and courage to use it without direction from another. *Sapere aude!* "Have courage to use your own reason!"—that is the motto of enlightenment.[25]

This thought captures well the spirit of the Enlightenment and its exultation to self reliance. Kant attempted to capitalize on the successes of human reason in the sciences by extending those successes into the arena of moral knowledge. As such, he is usually regarded as one of the more significant philosophers of the Enlightenment.

As did most Enlightenment thinkers, Kant believed in the existence of God, but he believed that the means to moral living was centered in the rational functioning of volition. According to Kant, the rational faculties, working in conjunction with those of volition, serve to bring one to moral salvation through a proper functioning of conscience. Kant's ideas later gave rise to the atheistic philosophy of Schopenhauer who exalted volition over reason. As we will see in the next chapter Nietzsche subsequently picked up on that theme and his ideas remain a powerful force in modern secular humanism.

Kant stated in the first sentence of his *Fundamental Principles of the Metaphysic of Ethics*, "Nothing can possibly be conceived in the world, or even out of it, which can be called good without qualification, except a Good Will."[26] In Kant's thinking, a "Good Will" was intrinsic with ultimate moral value.

Kant wrote:

> A good will is good not because of what it performs or effects, not by its aptness for the attainment of some proposed end, but simply by virtue of the volition, that is, it is good in itself, and considered by itself is to be esteemed

much higher than all that can be brought about by it in favour of any inclination, nay, even of the sum total of all inclinations.[27]

Kant taught that reason's purpose was not to guide the will, but was to "produce a *will*, not merely good as a *means* to something else, but *good in itself*."[28] According to Kant, "Good Will" or moral worth was found in one's sense of duty. Furthermore,

> an action done from duty derives its moral worth, *not from the purpose* which is to be attained by it, but from the maxim by which it is determined, and therefore does not depend on the realization of the object of the action, but merely on the *principle of volition* by which the action has taken place, without regard to any object of desire.[29]

The reader should note that Kant's idea of morality is not *seemingly* far removed from that which was defined in Chapter 2 when we stated that it was God's will which is the source of absolute morality. In the sense that God's will is obviously the only truly "Good" will, it might first appear that Kant has his philosophy on solid ground. However, a careful perusal of Kant's work shows that the "Good Will" of which he speaks cannot be identified with the will of the God of Scripture, the will of which we spoke of in Chapter 2, when we defined *that* will as the ultimate source of morality. Kant writes:

> Amongst the *rational* principles of morality, the ontological conception of *perfection*, notwithstanding its defects, is better than the theological conception which derives morality from a Divine absolutely perfect will. The former is, no doubt, empty and indefinite, and consequently useless for finding in the boundless field of possible reality the greatest amount suitable for us; moreover, in attempting to distinguish specifically the reality of which we are now speaking from every other, it inevitably tends to turn in a circle, and cannot avoid tacitly presupposing the morality which it is to explain; it is nevertheless preferable to the theological view, first, because we have no intuition of the Divine perfection, and can only deduce it from our own conceptions, the most important of which is that of morality, and our explanation would thus be involved in a gross circle; and, in the next place, if we avoid this, the only notion of the Divine will remaining to us is a conception made up of the attributes

of desire of glory and dominion, combined with the awful conceptions of might and vengeance, and any system of morals erected on this foundation would be directly opposed to morality.[30]

It should be apparent to the reader that Kant has discounted Scripture's power to convey the knowledge of God's perfection since he states that it can only be deduced "from our own conceptions."

Kant taught that for any action to have moral worth it had to be done from duty and not inclination. He wrote:

> *Duty is the necessity of acting from respect for the law.* I may have *inclination* for an object as the effect of my proposed action, but I cannot have *respect* of it, just for this reason, that it is an effect and not an energy of will.[31]

Again, at first glance, it might appear that Kant's arguments might represent an orthodox Christian point of view when he defines duty as a "necessity of acting from respect for the law." If Kant was here referring to the law of God, his thinking would be somewhat in line with our discussion in Chapter 2 of the law of God in the context of morality. An absolute standard of morality is simply that which is congruous with the will of God. And since law is that which is given to make known the will of the one who wills, God gave his law to help man understand the absolute nature of morality.[32] But Kant is not referring to the law of God. He is referring to his *categorical imperative* which is the maxim he proposed to define a basis of absolute morality. That imperative states, "I am never to act otherwise than so *that I could also will that my maxim should become a universal law.*"[33] With this imperative Kant essentially set up human conscience and reason as a moral absolute.

One might be tempted to come to Kant's defense by noting that the law of God was negated with the coming of Christ, and, therefore, Kant's formulation of an absolute law based on human reason and conscience is a valid one. But in response to that argument one should be reminded of Christ's own words. Jesus told those who were confused about God's law:

> Do not think that I came to abolish the Law or the Prophets; I did not come to abolish, but to fulfill. For truly I say to you, until heaven and earth pass away, not the smallest letter or stroke shall pass away from the Law, until all is accomplished. Whoever then annuls one of the least of these commandments, and so teaches others, shall be called least in the kingdom of heaven; but whoever keeps and teaches them, he shall be called great in the kingdom of heaven.[34]

Furthermore, in conjunction with these words from Matthew are the words that Jesus used to clarify how God's law should today be regarded:

> And one of them, a lawyer, asked Him a question, testing Him, "Teacher, which is the great commandment in the Law?" And He said to him, "You shall love the Lord your God with all your heart, and with all your soul, and with all your mind. This is the great and foremost commandment. And a second is like it, You shall love your neighbor as yourself. On these two commandments depend the whole Law and the Prophets."[35]

Kant's *categorical imperative* may take into account the latter law, but, without doubt, he failed to include into his system of morality the first and the greatest law to which Jesus referred.

Kant understood human nature sufficiently to know that the "Good Will" of which he spoke could not, in reality, be attained. Any action of the human will, no matter how moral it might appear, Kant asserted, would always have behind it "some secret impulse of self-love, under the false appearance of duty."[36] Thus, Kant insisted that morality could not be known through experience or example but had to be grasped through reason based on *à priori* principles. He wrote:

> This being so [the fact that behind all human action is a tendency to self-love], nothing can secure us from falling away altogether from our ideas of duty, or maintain in the soul a well-grounded respect for its law, but the clear conviction that although there should never have been actions which really sprang from such pure sources, yet whether this or that takes place is not at all the question; but that reason of itself, independent on all experience, ordains what ought to take place, that accordingly actions of which perhaps the world has hitherto never given an example, the feasibility even of which might be very much doubted by one who founds everything on experience, are nevertheless inflexibly commanded by reason; that, *ex. gr.* even though there might never yet have been a sincere friend, yet not a whit the less is pure sincerity in friendship required of every man, because, prior to all experience, this duty is involved as duty in the idea of a reason determining the will by *à priori* principles.[37]

Kant's ideas here appear to be somewhat compatible with the Reformation realization of moral depravity. However, as I will show momentarily, Kant did not hold to a scriptural view of human nature. While Kant may be making a good case for the workings of human conscience, he was wrong in attempting to extract from the functioning of man's rational faculties a system of absolute morality. Absolute moral knowledge cannot be based in human reason. To base one's moral system in human reason sets up human personality as a sovereign entity. Absolute morality must be based in God's word and that word for modern man is complete in Scripture.

To convince his reader that example was useless in deriving morality, Kant took an example from the words of Jesus in his attempt to show that one cannot use example to gain moral knowledge. Kant wrote:

> Even the Holy One of the Gospels [Jesus] must first be compared with our ideal of moral perfection before we can recognize Him as such; and so He says of Himself, "Why call ye Me (whom you see) good; none is good (the model of good) but God only (whom ye do not see)?" But whence have we the conception of God as the supreme good? Simply from the *idea* of moral perfection, which reason frames *à priori*, and connects inseparably with the notion of a free-will.[38]

Kant misused this portion of Scripture because he did not understand its meaning. This response of Jesus was to the rich young man in the 10th chapter of Mark's Gospel.[39] As the Apostle relates, the young rich man asked Jesus, "Good teacher, what shall I do that I may inherit eternal life?" To this question Jesus gave the answer to which Kant refers. Jesus went on to tell him, "You know the commandments, 'Do not commit adultery,' 'Do not murder,' 'Do not steal,' 'Do not bear false witness,' 'Do not defraud,' 'Honor your father and your mother.'" This young man was one who, on the surface, was concerned with living a moral life. He was one who likely would have agreed with Kant's idea of the moral absolute as set it forth in Kant's *categorical imperative*. He believed that he was in sufficient moral standing to inherit eternal life. He told Jesus that he had kept the commandments since childhood. However, the moral "good" from which this man was operating was a faulty one and Jesus, of course, knew this. Jesus responded to his question with the intent to make him understand the true meaning of moral good.

The very illustration that Kant chose to show that morality cannot be learned from example is, in fact, an example given to teach the meaning of true morality. The purpose of Jesus' answer "Why do you call Me good? No one is good but One, that is, God," was to help the young man understand why he was indeed good. Jesus is a perfect example of the moral good because he was God. Jesus was in effect saying, "You are calling me good for the wrong reason since what you think is good is not good: my goodness lies in my divinity, the source of the moral absolute." If the young man could have understood that he was talking to God, he would have been calling him good for the right reason, and further, he then would have understood his short-coming. It is interesting to contemplate Jesus' next words. He knew that the young man had not kept the law. Human nature, outside of redeeming faith, is not enabled to do so. But Jesus, likely out of his great compassion, did not call him on that truth. Jesus, as God, was in a position to directly express His will to the young man. God's will, as expressed in His word, is always the source of absolute morality. The rich young man had God's word directly spoken to him, but we know how he responded to those words. The words, "Go your way, sell whatever you have and give to the poor and come follow me" were God's words to that unnamed young man because He was God. This man could have taken hold of eternal life at that very moment if he had, in faith, responded to that Word.

While Kant regarded the nature of man to be afflicted by evil, his philosophy required that he deviate in a major way from a scriptural understanding of man's fallen nature. Although Kant rejected the position which teaches that man, as a species, is slowly striving towards moral perfection, he sought middle ground between the idea of human depravity and a philosophy that holds to man's innate goodness. In a sympathetic statement towards the latter viewpoint, Kant wrote:

> We may note that since we take for granted that man is by nature sound of body (as at birth he usually is), no reason appears why, by nature, his soul should not be deemed similarly healthy and free from evil. Is not nature herself, then, inclined to lend her aid to developing in us this moral predisposition to goodness?[40]

According to Kant, evil was not evil unless the conscious was aware of the specifics of the moral law. Kant wrote that "nature is not to bear the blame (if it is evil) or take the credit (if it is good), but that man himself is its author."[41] Kant's thinking was firmly established in a position that held to the sovereignty of human personality in the determination of one's moral standing. Kant further stated:

> Man *himself* must make or have made himself into whatever, in a moral sense, whether good or evil, he is or is to become. Either condition must be an effect of his free choice. … Granted that some supernatural cooperation may be necessary to his becoming good, or to his becoming better, yet, whether this cooperation consists merely in the abatement of hindrances or indeed in positive assistance, man must first make himself worthy to receive

it, and must *lay hold* of this aid (which is not a small matter)—that is, he must adopt this positive increase of power into this maxim, for only thus can good be imputed to him and he be known as a good man.)[42]

Kant's teaching here is diametrically opposed to the teaching of Scripture. Man does not have the ability to make himself into a morally good being. Kant's philosophy is humanism thinly disguised in a Christian framework and is an outstanding example of why a proper understanding of human volition is important. A misunderstanding of will's power is always rooted in a view of human nature that is inconsistent with the truth of Scripture. It is clear that Kant viewed moral salvation to be within the capability of human nature. Kant wrote:

> But in the moral religion (and of all the public religions which have ever existed, the Christian alone is moral) it is a basic principle that each must do as much as lies in his power to become a better man, and that only when he has not buried his inborn talent (Luke XIX, 12-16) but has made use of his original predisposition to good in order to become a better man, can he hope that what is not within his power will be supplied through cooperation from above. Nor is it absolutely necessary for a man to know where this cooperation consists; indeed, it is perhaps inevitable that, were the way it occurs revealed at a given time, different people would at some other time form different conceptions of it, and that with entire sincerity. Even here the principle is valid: "It is not essential, and hence not necessary, for every one to know what God does or has done for his salvation;" but it is essential to know *what man himself must do* in order to become worthy of this assistance.[43]

Kant's work is an outstanding example of why understanding the relationship between human personality and the personality of God, no matter what one might believe about the existence of God, is important if one's philosophy is to remain free from the damning effects of humanism. While Kant was not a deist, his philosophy was conducive to the deistic ideas which gained prominence in the Enlightenment. Kant's thinking perpetuated the idea that man could be reconciled to God through the mechanisms of human personality and conscience alone. He did not emphasize Jesus' own statement regarding himself when he proclaimed, "I am the way, and the truth, and the life; no one comes to the Father, but through Me."[44] We shall now consider the thought processes of some American forefathers who were highly influenced by the philosophies of the Enlightenment.

The American Enlightenment

The European Enlightenment ran concurrent with America's cultural and philosophical beginnings. The American counterpart of the European Enlightenment exerted its primary influence through the leadership of Thomas Jefferson and Benjamin Franklin. When Christian leaders exhort their fellow Christians to return to the spiritual roots of America's founding fathers, they often forget that certain of those "forefathers" had their values firmly established in humanism. While it is true that some of America's early leaders were fervent in their Christian faith—Washington, for example—others plainly embraced the humanistic philosophy of deism. The American Constitution was not conceived to establish Christianity as a state religion but was drafted to allow all citizens the freedom to believe as they wish without hindrance or fear of any state sanction.[45]

Before considering the humanism of Jefferson and Franklin, we will first briefly consider that of Thomas Paine. Paine was born in England in 1737, and immigrated to America at about the age of 37. He is, of course, best known for *Common Sense,* the revolutionary document influential in America's resolve to become independent from Britain. Paine's writings possessed a unique power that stirred the American spirit towards independence, shown in the following two excerpts from two of his most popular writings:

> O ye that love mankind! Ye that dare oppose not only the tyranny but the tyrant, stand forth! Every spot of the old world is overrun with oppression. Freedom hath been hunted round the globe. Asia and Africa have long expelled her. Europe regards her like a stranger, and England hath given her warning to depart. O receive the fugitive, and prepare in time an asylum for mankind.[46]

> The heart that feels not now is dead; the blood of his children will curse his cowardice, who shrinks back at a time when a little might have saved the whole, and made *them* happy. I love the man that can smile in trouble, that can gather strength from distress, and grow brave by reflection. 'Tis the business of little minds to shrink; but he whose heart is firm, and whose conscience approves his conduct, will pursue his principles unto death.[47]

But while Paine's patriotic zeal was heralded, his zeal for the God of Scripture certainly cannot be thought of in like fashion. Given the fact that he often appealed to moral principle, some may find this surprising. Paine's philosophy was classic deism. Review of his thought processes is instructive because they so well show the humanistic thinking that influenced much of America's early history. Many years after the revolution, in 1794, Paine wrote a small treatise called *The Age of Reason* where he succinctly laid out his deistic views. Paine wrote:

> THE WORD OF GOD IS THE CREATION WE BE-HOLD; and it is in *this* word, which no human invention can counterfeit or alter. ... It is only in the CRE-ATION that all our ideas and conceptions of a *word of God* can unite. ... It preaches to all nations and to all worlds; and this *word of God* reveals to man all that is necessary for man to know of God. Do we want to contemplate his power? We see it in the immensity of the creation. Do we want to contemplate his wisdom? We see it in the unchangeable order by which the incomprehensible whole is governed. Do we want to contemplate his munificence? We see it in the abundance with which he fills the earth. Do we want to contemplate his mercy? We see it in his not withholding that abundance even from the unthankful. In fine, do we want to know what God is? Search not the book called the Scripture, which any human hand might make, but the scripture called the Creation.[48]

Paine did not view Scripture as coming from the mind of God. The humanism in his deistic philosophy is again succinctly expressed in the same work. Paine wrote:

> I do not believe in the creed professed by the Jewish church, by the Roman church, by the Greek church, by the Turkish church, by the Protestant church, nor by any church that I know of. My own mind is my own church.[49]

Paine did not understand that the God of creation is a sovereign God who never yields his sovereignty to any man. It is apparent that he had a misplaced confidence in the power of his own mind and did not subscribe to a scriptural view of human nature. The humanist always fails to understand the desperation that sin has perpetrated on the human race. The prophet Isaiah, speaking the very mind of God, wrote:

Let the wicked forsake his way, And the unrighteous man his thoughts; And let him return to the Lord, And He will have compassion on him; And to our God, For He will abundantly pardon. "For My thoughts are not your thoughts, Neither are your ways My ways," declares the Lord. "For as the heavens are higher than the earth, So are My ways higher than your ways, And My thoughts than your thoughts.[50]

The non-secular humanist always believes that he can know the God of creation on his own terms. But it is evident from these inspired words of Isaiah that any attempt to understand the ways of God, in the power of one's own reason, is folly.

Thomas Jefferson's name is nearly synonymous with the American version of the European Enlightenment. He was born in 1743 to a somewhat wealthy Virginia family where he was afforded the opportunity of a quality education. That education spurred his interest in a wide range of subjects including the intellectual and cultural changes the Enlightenment was producing in Europe. As one of America's foremost early statesmen, Jefferson essentially authored the Declaration of Independence. Thereafter, he became a Virginian legislator and then Virginia's governor. He was the Secretary of State under Washington and was elected the third President of the United States in 1800.

Jefferson believed that only the free use of reason and inquiry could lead to a proper functioning government, and, therefore, he insisted that a state-sponsored religion would be detrimental to society. In Jefferson's opinion, the rights of one's conscience should never be submitted to the powers of the state. And for his view of government, Jefferson can rightfully be admired. Jefferson had keen insight into the destructive influences that state sponsored religions, as a consequence of their inherent civil power, would perpetrate on any society.

But Jefferson wrongly attributed the rise of Christianity to the workings of human institutions. Jefferson wrote, "Had not the Roman government permitted free inquiry, Christianity could never have been introduced. Had not free inquiry been indulged, at the aera [*sic*] of the reformation, the corruptions of Christianity could not have been purged away."[51] The fact is, and it is somewhat surprising that Jefferson was ignorant of it, Christianity became established in Europe in spite of the fact that many Roman governments sought diligently to eradicate it. Furthermore, Luther found out early on in his protest that he did not have the privilege of free inquiry. He would have been burned alive were it not for a network of friends that aided his escape. Christianity has survived in cultures where its practice was forbidden even under the penalty of death.

Jefferson's efforts to establish a government that did not coerce allegiance to any philosophical or religious viewpoint were certainly conducive to the growth of biblical Christianity in early America. Americans are privileged to have inherited a philosophy of government that respects the rights of people to believe as they wish although, unfortunately, modern secular humanists pervert Jefferson's view of the separation of church and state to the point of being opposed to any expression of religion within government. This clearly was not Jefferson's intent.

The philosophy of Jefferson is an excellent example of the humanistic thinking that often blossoms in periods of transition where the influence of humanism goes from a less important role to a dominant one. Before the Revolutionary war, enough of those in America's leadership and general populace identified themselves with Christianity such that the nation at that time in her history could best be classified as Christian. However, with the philosophy of the Enlightenment, a way of thinking far removed from a philosophy compatible with Scripture—even though a concept of deity remained—began to emerge. It is informative to read what Jefferson thought of the Christ of Scripture. The following excerpt is from a letter Jefferson wrote to Benjamin Rush, and it is interesting that Jefferson more or less urged Rush to keep the thoughts conveyed therein private.

> The doctrines which he [Jesus] really delivered were defective as a whole, and fragments only of what he did deliver have come to us mutilated, misstated, and often unintelligible. They have been still more disfigured by the corruptions of schismatizing followers, who have found an interest in sophisticating and perverting the simple doctrines he taught, by engrafting on them the mysticisms of a Grecian sophist, frittering them into subtleties, and obscuring them with jargon, until they have caused good men to reject the whole in disgust, and to view Jesus himself as an imposter. ... The question of his being a member of the Godhead, or in direct communication with it, claimed for him by some of his followers, and denied by others, is foreign to the present view, which is merely an estimate of the intrinsic merit of his doctrines.[52]

Similar thinking can be seen in the philosophy of Benjamin Franklin. Franklin, of course, is one of the stalwarts of early American history. Franklin was essentially a self-educated man having acquired much of his education through the printing skills he learned at an early age. The editorial suaveness he acquired in the publishing business aided the development of his critical thinking skills. Those skills he later used to form the discussion group called the *Jutno*. (That organization later became the American Philosophical Society.) Although Franklin never served as an American President, he was an influential statesman, having been a primary player in the drafting of the Declaration of Independence. He was also one of the original framers of the U.S. Constitution.

In addition to his many political and diplomatic skills, Franklin was gifted in the art of scientific inquiry, which at that time was still in its early stages. He was awarded honorary degrees from both Oxford and the University of St. Andrews for his scientific achievements. He became a fellow of the Royal Society of London and won its coveted Copley Medal for his contributions to the study of electricity. His scientific interests brought him into contact with the chemist Joseph Priestley, best known today for his discovery of oxygen. Priestley was born in England in 1733, the son of a minister, and later immigrated to America. By noting some of the details of his friendship with Priestley, we gain insight into both the fascination that Franklin had with the sciences and his more general philosophical views.

Priestley wrote in a letter to a Dr. Horsley, that early in his life he "was very sincere and zealous" in his "belief of the doctrine of the trinity." But at "about the age of twenty", he "saw reason to change" his opinion, and became one who denied the deity of Christ.[53] In that same letter Priestley wrote:

> Being now fully persuaded that Christ was a man like ourselves, and consequently that his pre-existence, as well as that of other men, was a notion that had no foundation in reason or in the scriptures, and having been gradually led (in consequence of wishing to trace the principle corruptions of christianity) to give particular attention to ecclesiastical history, I could not help thinking but that (since the doctrine of the pre-existence of Christ was not the doctrine of the scriptures, and therefore could not have been taught by the apostles) there must be some traces of the rise and progress of the doctrine of the trinity, and some historical evidence that unitarianism was the general faith of christians in the apostolical age, independent of the evidence which arose from its being the doctrine of the scriptures.[54]

Evidently Priestley had not studied the Scripture as well as he had studied chemistry. As the Apostle John tells us in his letter, Jesus plainly spoke of his preexistence to the Jews who opposed him. The Apostle John gave us the dialogue:

> *Jesus*: Your father Abraham rejoiced to see My day; and he saw it, and was glad.
> *The Jews*: You are not yet fifty years old, and have You seen Abraham?
> *Jesus*: Truly, truly, I say to you, before Abraham was born, I AM.[55]

That the Jews then picked up stones to kill him, after this bold assertion as to his preexistence, indicates they knew that Jesus was claiming to be co-eternal with the Father. It was on the erroneous views of Christ's deity that Priestly founded American Unitarianism, and today Unitarianism is a leading entity of non-secular humanistic philosophy in America. That Priestley had a strong influence on Franklin is evident in a letter written from Franklin to Priestley in 1780. The letter read, in part, as follows:

> I always rejoice to hear of your being still employed in experimental researches into nature, and of the Success you meet with. The rapid Progress *true* Science now makes, occasions my regretting sometimes that I was born so soon. It is impossible to imagine the height to which may be carried, in a thousand years, the power of man over matter. We may perhaps learn to deprive large masses of their gravity, and give them absolute levity, for the sake of easy transport. Agriculture may diminish its labor and double its produce; all diseases may by sure means be prevented or cured, not excepting even that of old age, and our lives lengthened at pleasure even beyond the antediluvian standard. O that moral science were in as fair a way of improvement, that men would cease to be wolves to one another, and that human beings would at length learn what they now improperly call humanity![56]

While Franklin's foresight into scientific endeavor is admirable, he knew that its potential to change man's moral dilemma would be a challenging feat. The scientific method used to understand nature is always insufficient to understand human nature because science is incapable of dealing with the supernatural. It is only a supernatural power that can change the natural human heart. That natural human heart is set against the God of Scripture. Only a supernatural faith in the God of Scripture can yield the power to change human nature from its humanistic bent—a bent that causes one to trust in the power of his own personality—to one that trusts in the God of

Scripture for the moral cleansing necessary for salvation. It is important to understand that it is *the God of Scripture* to which the natural heart is opposed. All the authors discussed in this chapter whole-heartedly acknowledged the existence of God. But none of these Enlightenment thinkers embraced *the God of Scripture*. In response to an inquiry of his views of Christianity from Erza Stiles, the then president of Yale College, Ben Franklin wrote the following:

> As to Jesus of Nazareth, my opinion of whom you particularly desire, I think the system of morals and his religion, as he left them to us, the best the world ever saw or is likely to see; but I apprehend it has received various corrupting changes, and I have, with most of the present dissenters in England, some doubts as to his divinity; tho' it is a question I do not dogmatize upon, having never studied it, and think it needless to busy myself with it now, when I expect soon an opportunity of knowing the truth with less trouble.[57]

If one cannot comprehend the divinity of Christ one cannot understand how God has counteracted the devastating effects of human rebellion to change the course of human nature. One then necessarily remains ensnared in humanism because the only mechanism that one is left with to conquer the challenges of life is his own personality, i.e., his own will and reason which he will always use in accordance with a self-derived morality to pursue his own emotional contentment.

7

Historical Humanism: Secular Humanism

> *By night an atheist half believes a God.*
> *Edward Young (1683-1765)*

Western humanism presupposes that human personality can determine for itself, independent from a true knowledge of Scripture, what the moral good is and subsequently act upon that determination. This outlook leads to the false perception that human destiny lies completely within the power of human personality. I recently came upon a particularly poignant example that demonstrates the extent to which this philosophy has permeated modern American culture. The use of day-planners is encouraged by many American corporations to help their employees manage time and one popular brand features for its users a "monthly focus." The monthly focus for one particular month was *"Choices-The power to choose always gives you the final say."*[1] That slogan originates with the belief that within human personality is a sovereign power over human destiny. However, as we have emphasized throughout this work, *true* sovereignty over one's nature is not attainable through any aspect of one's own being. Human nature, as a created entity, is not of an absolute character; human nature is not self-sufficient. Adam's sin resulted in the loss of a natural knowledge of the God whose will defines true morality. Human nature cannot sovereignly choose (i.e., to choose entirely of its own accord) the true moral good.

When one's view of reality is constructed outside the framework of Scripture, or outside a proper understanding of Scripture, that view will be based on ideas that are philosophically consistent with humanism. The humanistic ideas that we have considered thus far—apart from those of the Greek Sophists—have included in them a concept of supreme being. But knowledge of God's *existence* does not produce a true knowledge of God. Knowledge of ultimate reality is only available to the one who has, in faith, submitted himself to the God of Scripture, and it is this knowledge which, in struggle with the Western humanism of which this work deals, has shaped modern Western culture.

Over time all humanism leads to either the denial of God's existence, or if that existence is acknowledged, to either an overt or covert disavowal of His will. Non-secular humanism, the latter case, has the same ultimate outcome on one's world-view as the former case (i.e., atheism), and in some respects is more destructive because it usually leaves its proponent in a web of false security. If human personality were indeed a sovereign entity, it would of necessity be absolute in its nature, and the possibility of any effective supernatural power ruling over it would be excluded. The secular humanism spawned by atheistic thinking is, therefore, the philosophical end to which all humanism aims.

Western perceptions of reality, particularly in the last two hundred years, have become increasingly independent of a genuine knowledge of the God of Scripture. Western thinking is increasingly reverting to the secular humanism similar to that of the ancient Greek Sophists where man was proclaimed "the measure of all things." Here was a system where each person determined for himself the standards of morality. In that system (see chapters 1 and 2), man's sense of well being (i.e., his emotional state) was controlled more by volition than by intellect. In this chapter we shall see how this emphasis is once again becoming important with movement to the philosophy of Friedrich Nietzsche.

With the consideration of *secular* humanism, we have arrived at that humanism which is usually conceived of when the term "humanism" is mentally processed. The thought processes that are today described as "humanistic" are almost always linked to its secular connotation, and since secularism is the end to which all humanism aims, that general association, although not entirely correct, is an understandable one. In this chapter we will deal with the humanism that has been built on presumptions of atheism. The philosophical foundations of our current modern era, based in secular humanism, were established in the 19th century. These transitional years between the Enlightenment and the 20th century produced the foundation of modern thought. We will here consider some aspects of the lives and works of Darwin, Nietzsche, Freud and Marx, four significant designers of modern thought whose influence on modern Western civilization, with perhaps the exception of Marx, continues to grow.

Darwin

Regardless of one's education level, nearly all know of Charles Darwin's influence on Western civilization. Darwin's name is synonymous with the subject of biological evolution. Evolutionary theory has existed since the ancient Greek philosophers, but Darwin propelled these age-old ideas into new light because he attempted to prove the mechanism by which that evolution occurred. Darwin attempted to put the subject into the arena of scientific respectability and, of course, humanists maintain that he succeeded. In the years following Darwin, much research was initiated on the presupposition that Darwin's conclusions were based in fact. That research remains strong to this day. Modern proponents of evolution continue to force educators to accept Darwin's basic ideas of natural selection as irrefutable scientific fact. Western scientists active in the biological sciences have been browbeaten into paying lip service to the validity of Darwin's claims, even though the inadequacies of many of his evolutionary conclusions have been proven.

That modern secular humanism is reverting to Sophistic-type thinking is apparent from what is happening in the field of Western education. Evolutionary theories are taught not as fact on the basis of knowledge; the average school board does not have the expertise to decide upon that basis. Decisions to teach evolution as fact are based more on emotion—"feelings" for which side is "perceived" as right—than on genuine knowledge. This is Sophistic-type decision making in its purest form. Are we to believe that those who decide educational curriculum have actually investigated the facts like Dr. Jack Cuozzo has done? Cuozzo has proven the fraud upon which the "facts" surrounding *Neanderthal Man* are built.[2] If educational systems were serious about basing their beliefs on scientific fact, they would not exclude the research of scientists like Cuozzo.

The main ideas behind evolutionary thought more correctly fall into the arena of philosophy instead of science. Disciplines that are best suited to yield the certainty of knowledge required by rigorous scientific theory are those which can be studied through the methods of reproducible experimentation. Evolutionary science does not meet that criterion, because here the scientist is attempting to reconstruct historical events—much like the modern forensic scientist does today. Forensic science is far from irrefutable, as witnessed by the fact that it sometimes imprisons the innocent and fails to imprison the guilty.

Darwin's ideas further contributed to the perception of a false sovereignty within the power of human nature. Man can only be sovereign over his own nature if there is no sovereign entity above him. Darwin's work was instrumental in setting in place the mechanisms that provided the veil of imagined legitimacy to those who today think in a secular humanistic vein. As Beer tells us (when comparing the ideas of Wallace[3] to Darwin's), in her introduction to Darwin's *The Origin of Species*,

> It was Wallace who uncoupled the human from all other species development so as to preserve a place for the soul, and Darwin who, more radically, faced the complete integration of the human into the natural order. In this story no simple contraries survive.[4]

Darwin was born in Shrewsbury, England in the year 1809 to a physician father and to the daughter of a wealthy businessman. His paternal grandfather, Erasmus Darwin, was also a physician who had already achieved a degree of notoriety from his own theories of evolution. Charles was encouraged to follow the family tradition to a career in medicine. In 1825 he enrolled in the University of Edinburgh to study medicine; however, the young Darwin, not too academically inclined at this point, dropped those studies after only about two years. He entered Cambridge with the intent of studying theology. In his autobiography Darwin stated in regards to this period:

> Having spent two sessions in Edinburgh, my father perceived or he heard from my sisters, that I did not like the thought of being a physician, so he proposed that I should become a clergyman. He was very properly vehement against my turning an idle sporting man, which then seemed my probable destination. I asked for some time to consider, as from what little I had heard and thought on the subject I had scruples about declaring my belief in all the dogmas of the Church of England; though otherwise I liked the thought of being a country clergyman. Accordingly I read with care *Pearson on the Creed* and a few other books on divinity; and as I did not then in the least doubt the strict and literal truth of every word in the Bible, I soon persuaded myself that our Creed must be fully accepted. It never struck me how illogical it was to say that I believed in what I could not understand and what is in fact unintelligible. I might have said with entire truth that I had no wish to dispute any dogma; but I never was such a fool as to feel and say "credo quia incredibile".[5]

It is interesting to note here a peculiar circumstance regarding the young Darwin's decision to pursue theological studies. Darwin credited his father with instilling in him the desire to study theology, and yet Darwin specifically stated that his father was not a believer.[6] It should thus not be too surprising that Darwin's studies in theology fizzled as did his studies in medicine. As stressed throughout this work, within the sole power of one's will, one cannot understand the meaning of Scripture. Scripture is clear in its contention that the natural man cannot receive the things of God.[7] For one to understand Scripture one must be supernaturally enabled.

Giving up on theology, Darwin dabbled in the classics, elementary mathematics, and moral philosophy. He became attracted to geology and botany through the influence of Cambridge professor John Stevens Henslow. After Darwin received his B.A. degree, Henslow arranged for him to serve as the resident naturalist on the *HMS Beagle*, a naval survey ship whose mission was to chart the partial coastline of South America. The *Beagle* sailed from the latter part of 1831 to the latter part of 1836 and essentially transported Darwin around the entire world. The ship sailed to South America, to the Galapagos Islands, then to Australia, Africa and many other small islands in-between. On this massive voyage, Darwin recorded the observations that would serve as the basis for his ideas on natural selection, the concept which became the cornerstone of his *Origin of Species,* published some twenty-three years later.

The development of Darwin's philosophical thought processes are instructive to study because they represent an outstanding example of a nonsecular humanism evolving into secular humanism. Darwin wrote in his autobiography that, at the time of his voyage, he was yet "quite orthodox" in his religious beliefs. His claim to orthodoxy was based on the fact, as noted in the preceding quote, that he then did not "in the least doubt the strict and literal truth of every word in the Bible." Darwin obviously had assumed Scripture's veracity on the basis of a culturally-based conviction as opposed to true knowledge of its content based on supernatural enabling. Nonetheless, it is apparent that at this point in his life, he genuinely believed in the existence of a supreme being, even to the point of referring to that being as the creator. This is deduced from his concluding remarks to his *Origin of Species* where he wrote:

> Analogy would lead me one step further, namely, to the belief that all animals and plants have descended from some one prototype. But analogy may be a deceitful guide. Nevertheless all living things have much in common, in their chemical composition, their germinal vesicles, their cellular structure, and their laws of growth and reproduction. We see this even in so trifling a circumstance as that the same poison often similarly affects plants and animals; or that the poison secreted by the gall-fly produces monstrous growths on the wild rose or oak-tree. Therefore I should infer from analogy that probably all the organic beings

which have ever lived on this earth have descended from
some one primordial form, *into which life was first breathed
by the Creator* [italics added].[8]

These thoughts identify, at least in some points, with the modern designation of theistic evolution. However, Darwin's theological views became far
removed from any semblance of orthodoxy before his *Beagle* voyage ended.
Darwin further wrote concerning this period:

But I had gradually come, by this time, to see that the Old
Testament from its manifestly false history of the world,
with the Tower of Babel, the rainbow as a sign, etc., etc.,
and from its attributing to God the feelings of a revenge-
ful tyrant, was no more to be trusted than the sacred books
of the Hindoos [*sic*], or the beliefs of any barbarian.[9]

As stated in the introduction to Chapter 2, orthodox Christianity has always held to the integrity of the Old Testament. Both Jesus and his Apostles
validated the Old Testament's accuracy on the subject of Noah.[10] Furthermore, after reflecting on Christianity during this period, Darwin came to
also reject any possibility that Christianity could be true. He later wrote:

By further reflecting that the clearest evidence would be
requisite to make any sane man believe in the miracles by
which Christianity is supported,—that the more we know
of the fixed laws of nature the more incredible do miracles
become,—that the men at that time were ignorant and
credulous to a degree almost incomprehensible by us,—
that the Gospels cannot be proved to have been written
simultaneously with the events,—that they differ in many
important details, far too important as it seemed to me to
be admitted as the usual inaccuracies of eye witnesses;—
by such reflections as these, which I give not as having the
least novelty or value, but as they influenced me, I gradually came to disbelieve in Christianity as a divine revelation.[11]

While Darwin first began aboard the *Beagle* to question the truth of
both the Old and New Testaments, that questioning progressed to altogether discounting the God of Scripture, although, based on his writings in
the *Origin,* it is clear that he had not at this point dismissed in his thinking
the *existence* of a supreme being.

Darwin's chief objection to a scriptural view of God was its clear teaching that, in its natural state, all humanity is damned. Humanists always fail
to understand the gravity of sin and the fact that every man, outside of
God's plan for his salvation, as clearly taught in Scripture, is condemned to
an eternal death. Every man has inherited from the first man Adam a nature

that is set against the God of Scripture. As the Authorized Version reads, the one who does not believe *"is condemned already,"* i.e., is already judged guilty [italics added].[12] On this point Darwin wrote:

> I can indeed hardly see how anyone ought to wish Christianity to be true; for if so the plain language of the text seems to show that the men who do not believe, and this would include my Father, Brother and almost all my best friends, will be everlastingly punished. And this is a damnable doctrine.[13]

It was in his later years that Darwin began to altogether doubt the existence of a creator–supreme being. In his *Autobiography* Darwin outlined some of the thought processes that led him to those conclusions. The processes that led him to this agnosticism (or probably atheism) were simply a continuation of those processes mentioned above that had caused him to reject Christianity. One often struggles with how a God who is described as a sovereign loving God can allow human pain. It was this problem that evidently caused Darwin to entirely deny the God of Scripture, and this issue, even today, frequently surfaces in humanistic perceptions of ultimate reality. I touched briefly in Chapter 2 on the subject when reviewing the American PBS television series *Genesis*. The humanist's failure to properly understand the moral predicament of humanity is always apparent when this subject is discussed because human pain cannot be understood outside a proper understanding of moral philosophy. Secular humanists often argue against the existence of God because of the incessant suffering they observe in human affairs. The reasoning goes as follows. If there exists a magnanimous God, as Christian doctrine clearly claims, then such a God could never have created a world where catastrophes of nature would snuff out thousands of people in one fell swoop (as for example, in the great earthquake in India in January of 2001). Therefore, the humanist reasons, since such tragedies occur on a somewhat regular basis, the "good," omniscient, and omnipotent God of the Christian cannot exist. Many humanists, therefore, reject the scriptural representation of the Hebrew/Christian God based on such reasoning, and Darwin likewise found the logic in this argument particularly appealing. Darwin wrote:

> This very old argument from the existence of suffering against the existence of an intelligent first cause seems to me a strong one; whereas, as just remarked, the presence of much suffering agrees well with the view that all organic beings have been developed through variation and natural selection.[14]

C. S. Lewis addressed the issue of human suffering especially well in his work, *The Problem of Pain*. Lewis taught that for one to have a proper perspective of human pain, one must first understand the nature of God in relationship to the nature of man. Lewis expressed sympathy with the argument in question, stating that he, too, as an atheist before his conversion, struggled with the issue. Lewis then stressed the fact that love may cause pain to its object when "that object needs alteration to become fully lovable." Lewis wrote:

> The problem of reconciling human suffering with the existence of a God who loves, is only insoluble so long as we attach a trivial meaning to the word "love," and look on things as if man were the centre of them. *Man is not the centre* [italics added]. God does not exist for the sake of man. Man does not exist for his own sake. "Thou has created all things, and for thy pleasure they are and were created (Rev. iv, 11)." … To ask that God's love should be content with us as we are is to ask that God should cease to be God: because He is what He is, His love must, in the nature of things, be impeded and repelled by certain stains in our present character, and because He already loves us He must labor to make us lovable.[15]

Lewis was driving his reader to grasp first the fact that human personality is not sovereign in the overall scheme of reality and, secondly, to grasp the severity of the separation between God and man because of human sin. Lewis attributed modern man's loss of consciousness of the severity of his sinful nature to two factors. The first was the fact that "we have so concentrated on one of the virtues—'kindness' or mercy—that most of us do not feel anything except kindness to be really good or anything but cruelty to be really bad." Lewis here made an astute observation regarding the psychology of modern man. Modern man often derives a sense of moral justification from treating one's acquaintances with "kindness," even though if the truth were known, as Lewis puts it, many who feel so justified have "never made the slightest sacrifice for a fellow creature."[16]

The second cause Lewis ascribed to the modern notion that "the sense of Shame is a dangerous and mischievous thing."[17] Lewis stated that we have sought "to overcome that sense of shrinking, that desire to conceal, which either Nature herself or the tradition of almost all mankind has attached to cowardice, unchastity, falsehood, and envy."[18] But it is only when one "feels real guilt—moments too rare in our lives"[19] that the anger towards God, usually triggered by a perception of unjust pain (which is often responsible for one's denial of his existence), can be dissipated. Stated Lewis,

"When we merely *say* that we are bad, the 'wrath' of God seems a barbarous doctrine; as soon as we *perceive* our badness, it appears inevitable, a mere corollary from God's goodness."[20]

Lewis dug to the root cause of all humanism when he reminded his reader of Augustine's teaching that sin was "the result of Pride, of the movement whereby a creature (that is, *an essentially dependent being whose principle of existence lies not in itself but in another) tries to set up on its own, to exist for itself* [italics added]."[21] It is in man's attempt to "set up on its own, to exist for itself" that the false perception of one's sovereignty is eventually conceived, and so, as Lewis put it, "the gravitation away from God, the journey homeward toward habitual self," must characterize fallen man. Instead of man inclining to good (as Aquinas wrongly taught), Lewis tells us that man is "all day long, and all the days of [his] life … sliding, slipping, falling away—as if God were … a smooth inclined plane on which there is no resting."[22]

Lewis identified the will as the root source of the vast separation between God and man. Lewis wrote that the act of self-will on the part of the creature, which constitutes an utter falseness to its true creaturely position, is the sin that can be conceived as the fall. Therefore, according to Lewis, human pain is often an instrument God uses to call one's attention to a will that has turned to its own way and, thereby, to its own destruction. Lewis poignantly reminded his reader that the human spirit will not even begin to try to surrender self-will as long as all seems to be well with it. So although Lewis had difficulties with the semantics of Calvin's declaration of "total depravity" and man's subsequent loss of "free will," his thinking was yet ultimately compatible with a scriptural view of human nature. Lewis acknowledged the depravity of human nature when he stated that, "we behave like vermin … because we are vermin,"[23] and further, "when the saints say that they—even they—are vile, they are recording truth with scientific accuracy."[24] Thus, Lewis viewed the human condition as a consequence of being "members of a spoiled species."[25]

The pain of which we have been speaking was not foreign to Darwin. In 1851 he experienced the loss of his oldest daughter, ten-year-old Anne. The pain of that loss—the absolute dread of every parent—was particularly difficult for Darwin because of the special relationship they shared. She was extremely dear to his heart. In their biography of Darwin, Desmond and Moore recorded the intense suffering Darwin experienced as a result of that tragedy. In describing the scene immediately following Anne's passing, the authors penned the following selected words:

Charles kissed the shrunken little face one last time and hid himself by the window. It was raining now, pouring. The sodden landscape, a graveyard of extinct life, made a mockery of his bitter tears. …This was the end of the road, the crucifixion of his hopes. He could not believe the way Emma[26] believed—nor *what* she believed. There was no straw to clutch, no promised resurrection. Christian faith was futile. Dragging himself to his room, he lay agonized in bed for hours, his stomach churning. He stopped crying long enough to see Dr [*sic*] Gully, who gave the cause of death as "Bilious Fever with typhoid character." … Towards six o'clock Fanny went in and found Charles still crying bitterly. … Annie's cruel death destroyed Charles's tatters of belief in a moral, just universe. Later he would say that this period chimed the final death-knell for his Christianity, even if it had been a long, drawn-out process of decay. … Charles now took his stand as an unbeliever.[27]

Darwin's reaction to that tragedy was, as C. S. Lewis called those like it, a "final and unrepented rebellion."[28] It is important to note that Darwin had not yet at that point in time published his *Origins*, the publication that would eventually equip the Western world with its pseudo-philosophic basis for a complete rejection of the God of Scripture.

One can readily understand the ends, in this regard, to which Darwinistic thought has taken modern man by reflecting on the work of modern philosophers such as Daniel C. Dennett. Dennett's views of reality are totally grounded in the ideas of Darwin. His views of ultimate reality have essentially come full circle to a philosophy similar to that of the Greek Sophists where ultimate reality was perceived as contained only within the material of the cosmos. Dennett wrote:

How did the Tree of Life get started? Skeptics have thought a stroke of Special Creation—a skyhook—must be needed to get the evolutionary process going. There is a Darwinian answer to this challenge, however, which exhibits the power of Darwin's universal acid to work its way down through the lowest levels of the Cosmic Pyramid, showing how even the laws of physics might emerge from chaos or nothingness without recourse to a Special Creator, or even a Lawgiver.[29]

And so it becomes apparent that modern secular humanism is well grounded in the life and work of Charles Darwin. For the secular humanist "no simple contraries survive."[4] We will now turn our attention to the life and works of

Friedrich Nietzsche who, although not fully accepting Darwin's ideas of natural selection, was the most influential humanist to seriously build, in a philosophical way, on the basic implications of Darwin's ideas.

Nietzsche

Friedrich Nietzsche was born in 1844 in Röchen, Prussia (near Leipzig), the son of a Lutheran minister. His father's death when he was only four years of age left him at home with his mother, grandmother, a sister, and two aunts, and one can only wonder if that situation was somehow conducive to the misogynic character that many biographers attribute to him. From about 1858 to 1866, he attended Pforta School, one of Germany's most prestigious preparatory schools. From there he went to Bonn and Leipzig Universities where he studied classical philology. Even though he never formally completed a degree, he was given a professorship at the University of Basle at the mere age of 24. The university position was short-lived because he was not well adjusted to its rigors. He left Basle at about the age of 35, and his best known writings came from that post-university period. Some biographers believe he contracted syphilis, leading to a general condition of poor health. By the time he was 45, both his physical and mental capacities were in a severe state of decline. Before his death at age 56, he had completely lost touch with reality.

Nietzsche's early thinking was influenced by the philosophy of Authur Schopenhauer. Some knowledge of Schopenhauer is, therefore, needed to understand Nietzsche. When Schopenhauer died, Nietzsche was about 16 years of age, so they were essentially of successive generations. Schopenhauer's philosophy is popularly described as an atheistic pessimism where he perceived the universe to be a product of an irrational blind force.[30] Schopenhauer taught that will was the driving force behind all reality and, particularly, the driving force behind human personality. Schopenhauer wrote:

> All *willing* arises from want, therefore from deficiency, and therefore from suffering. The satisfaction of a wish ends it; yet for one wish that is satisfied there remain at least ten which are denied. Further, the desire lasts long, the demands are infinite; the satisfaction is short and scantily measured out. But even the final satisfaction is itself only apparent; every satisfied wish at once makes room for a new one; both are illusions; the one is known to be so, the other not yet. No attained object of desire can give lasting satisfaction, but merely a fleeting gratification; it is like

the alms thrown to the beggar, that keeps him alive to-day that his misery may be prolonged till the morrow. Therefore, so long as our consciousness is filled by our will, so long as we are given up to the throng of desires with their constant hopes and fears, so long as we are the subject of willing, we can never have lasting happiness nor peace.[31]

Schopenhauer's words have a certain element of truth, as is common, of course, in the works of most of the world's renowned philosophers. Man can never truly be satisfied outside of a true knowledge of the God of Scripture. As Augustine so succinctly stated in the opening remarks to his *Confessions*, "Thou movest us to delight in praising Thee; for Thou hast formed us for Thyself, and our hearts are restless till they find rest in Thee."[32] Schopenhauer's pessimism ultimately stemmed from a perception of evil which was a unique inclusion into the secular Western scheme of philosophy. His philosophy captured certain aspects of depraved human will, and furthermore, showed the extent of its penetration into the human condition. But, unfortunately, Schopenhauer taught that human salvation could only be found in a state of Nirvana (absence of desire), an idea he borrowed from Hinduism. However, man must *want* to be saved before he can be saved, but he must also realize that that salvation cannot be attained solely in the power of his own will.

Even though Nietzsche eventually rejected much of Schopenhauer's thought, including the aforementioned solution, he retained Schopenhauer's emphasis on the supremacy of the human will. Nietzsche believed that "might made right" within all human societies. True morality was simply what the ideal man willed it to be. (Note how this philosophy fits into the Sophistic ideas discussed in Chapter 1.) According to Nietzsche, the advanced society was chiefly a product of human will. In speaking of that society's (i.e., the aristocratic or advanced society) origin, Nietzsche wrote:

> Let us admit to ourselves unflinchingly how every higher culture on earth has hitherto *begun*! Men of a still natural nature, barbarians in every fearful sense of the word, men of prey still in possession of an unbroken strength of will and lust for power, threw themselves upon weaker, more civilized, more peaceful, perhaps trading or cattle-raising races, or upon old mellow cultures, the last vital forces in which were even then flickering out in a glittering fire-work display of spirit and corruption. The noble caste was in the beginning always the barbarian caste: their superiority lay, not in their physical strength, but primarily in

their psychical—they were *more complete* human beings (which, on every level, also means as much as "more complete beasts"—).[33]

Nietzsche believed that those with the stronger wills should, from the inherent power of that will, take control of humanity. He viewed the strong-willed as superior creatures, who should (and perhaps someday would) dominate those who fell to their prey. Nietzsche wrote:

A good and healthy aristocracy ... accepts with a good conscience the sacrifice of innumerable men who *for its sake* have to be suppressed and reduced to imperfect men, to slaves and instruments. Its fundamental faith must be that society should *not* exist for the sake of society but only as foundation and scaffolding upon which a select species of being is able to raise itself to its higher task and in general to a higher *existence*.[34]

This natural separation in classes, according to Nietzsche, led to two distinct moralities, the master morality and the slave morality. The master morality derived from the noble, strong willed, ruling class. In this view the concept of morality stemmed solely and unabashedly from a secular humanistic perspective, which was rooted purely in the will, with reason and conscience as will's subject. Nietzsche wrote:

The noble type of man feels *himself* to be the determiner of values, he does not need to be approved of, he judges "what harms me is harmful in itself," he knows himself to be that which in general first accords honour to things, he *creates values*. Everything he knows to be part of himself, he honours: such a morality is self-glorification.[35]

That Nietzsche here attempted to place the moral absolute into the sovereignty of human will should be apparent to the reader. The slave morality, on the other hand, according to Nietzsche was founded upon the desire of those who were in subjugation to the strong. In describing the slave morality Nietzsche stated:

Suppose the abused, oppressed, suffering, unfree, those uncertain of themselves and weary should moralize: what would their moral evaluations have in common? Probably a pessimistic mistrust of the entire situation of man will find expression, perhaps a condemnation of man together with his situation.[36]

Nietzsche maintained that the slave morality was synonymous with Judeo-Christian virtues. He viewed both Judaism and Christianity as systems of weakness to be despised. Nietzsche believed that only within slave morality did "pity, the kind and helping hand, the warm heart, patience, industriousness, humility, friendliness come into honour."[37]

Nietzsche's philosophy represented a shift in Western humanism in that it implied that the controlling aspect of human personality should be centered in the will instead of the intellect. His philosophy is the epitome of modern humanistic thought because its extreme secular nature created a de-emphasis in reason and this, in turn, has brought humanism full circle to a philosophy that has similarities to that of the ancient Greek Sophists. Nietzsche challenged the roots of Western humanism which, as discussed in Chapter 1, put emphasis on the powers of human reason to decipher the moral good. Wrote Nietzsche in his attack on Socratic thought: "I seek to understand out of what idiosyncrasy that Socratic equation reason = virtue = happiness derives: that bizarrest of equations and one which has in particular all the instincts of the older Hellenes [i.e., the Sophists] against it."[38] In his response to Darwin's theory of natural selection, Nietzsche clearly revealed the de-emphasis that he sought to give to the powers of reason. Nietzsche wrote:

> Species do *not* grow more perfect: the weaker dominate the strong again and again—the reason being they are the great majority, and they are also *cleverer*. ... Darwin forgot the mind (—that is English!): *the weak possess more mind*. ... To acquire mind one must need mind—one loses it when one no longer needs it. He who possesses strength divests himself of mind.[39]

While it would be wrong to claim that Western secular humanism today consciously operates with a greater emphasis on the influence of the will over that of the intellect, Nietzsche's works continue to have influence in shaping the modern secular Western man. Certainly as time progresses, society seems to be headed more in the direction of Nietzsche's thinking. Although the modern humanist is still influenced by Enlightenment thinking, the emphasis that the Enlightenment placed on the rational faculties of man often today falls prey to lip-service when Nietzsche's "will to power" becomes the focus of living. Nietzsche's philosophy was a direct response to the Darwinistic ideas which had set the stage for promoting a perception of life with no meaning. Nietzsche taught that meaningful life was only reached when the supernatural was excluded from one's perception of reality and when the will was permitted to reign sovereign over one's nature.

Nietzsche's *The Anti-Christ*, written in 1888 towards the end of his productive years, furthermore reflects his vituperative spirit against anything associated with Christianity. In its opening lines Nietzsche rhetorically asks, "What is more harmful than any vice?" and promptly answers his own question: [it is] "Active sympathy for the ill-constituted and weak—Christianity."[40] In Nietzsche's mind, Christianity was the epitome of weakness. While Nietzsche wrongly perceived a sovereignty in human will, the Christian knows that the God of his faith is sovereign over creation, of which he (the Christian) is merely a part. From that realization, the Christian indeed perceives a weakness inherent in that subordinate relationship. The ironic aspect of this perception is that when the Christian submits in acknowledgment of that inherent weakness, he is thereby empowered to strength. This is the meaning of the Apostle Paul's statement, "For when I am weak, then I am strong."[41] Nietzsche's entire life was lived under the delusion of a falsely perceived personal strength. He died in utter weakness of both mind and body, and the tragic end of his life was a testimony to the depravity of the philosophy that he so religiously espoused. And certainly the final outcome of Nietzsche's life is consistent with the truth of Scripture. In his letter to the Corinthian Christians of ancient Greece, the Apostle Paul reminded them that "God has chosen the weak things of the world to shame the things which are strong."[42] Those who realize and confess their weakness in relationship to the God of the universe will ultimately frustrate those who in their own estimation are strong in themselves. It is only those who submit to the God of Scripture who gain the strength that the ungodly man thinks he has, but in reality is that for which he hopes.

Nietzsche's error, as is the error of all philosophers whose teachings are incompatible with Scripture, was his failure to comprehend the reality of God's direct communication with man. Nietzsche, of course, did not regard Scripture as coming from the mind of God; he openly ridiculed it. Regarding Israel's special revelation of God's Word, Nietzsche wrote:

> The entire *history* of Israel was useless: away with it!—
> These priests perpetrated that miracle of falsification the
> documentation of which lies before us in a good part of
> the Bible: with unparalleled disdain of every tradition, every historical reality, they translated their own national
> past *into religious terms*, that is to say they made of it a
> stupid salvation-mechanism of guilt towards Yaweh and
> punishment, piety towards Yaweh and reward.[43]

Nietzsche exhibited the same distrust of the New Testament. Although Nietzsche did accept the fact of a historical Jesus, he did not accept Jesus' claim to deity. He especially held the Apostle Paul in contempt, believing him to be an impostor and supreme deceiver. Nietzsche wrote:

> In Paul was embodied the antithetical type to the "bringer of glad tidings", the genius of hatred, of the vision of hatred, of the inexorable logic of hatred. *What* did this dysangelist not sacrifice to his hatred! ... The life, the example, the teaching, the death, the meaning and the right of the entire Gospel—nothing was left once this hate-obsessed false-coiner had grasped what alone he could make use of.[44]

Nietzsche so opposed the God of Scripture that he sought to destroy even the moral guidance system of the human conscience. Nietzsche's attempt to negate the function of conscience continues to have a devastating influence in Western culture. Throughout this work, we have emphasized the natural role of human conscience. However important the role of conscience, one cannot derive from it an absolute standard of morality because it is not absolute in its ability to decipher the true moral good. Within the course of proper action, one man's conscience may rightfully permit him to do something that another man's conscience, which likewise in the course of proper action, might not allow him to do. There is a certain degree of relativity in the function of human conscience. Nonetheless when the conscience is functioning properly, it will always condemn the universally immoral, i.e., it will always condemn that which God does not will for humanity. And of course, if it is repeatedly violated, it will completely cease to function. As we discussed in the previous chapter, Kant's moral philosophy was one based on conscience. Because of the link between conscience and God's imprint on human nature, Nietzsche attacked Kant with a vengeance. In refuting Kant, he was essentially saying, "Do what *you* decide is moral; what *you will* to do, with only relative consideration of reason or conscience." Nietzsche wrote against Kant:

> A word against Kant as *moralist*. A virtue has to be *our* invention, *our* most personal defense and necessity: in any other sense it is merely a danger. What does not condition our life *harms* it: a virtue merely from a feeling of respect for the concept "virtue", as Kant desired it, is harmful. "Virtue", "duty", "good in itself", impersonal and universal—phantoms ... The profoundest laws of preservation and growth demand the reverse of this: that each one of us should devise *his own* virtue, *his own* categorical impera-

tive. A people perishes if it mistakes *its own* duty for the concept of duty in general. Nothing works more profound ruin than any "impersonal" duty, any sacrifice to the Moloch of abstraction.—Kant's categorical imperative should have been felt as *mortally dangerous*! … The theologian instinct alone took it under its protection![45]

Humanistic philosophy never comprehends the effect that evil has perpetrated on the human condition. When Nietzsche's philosophy is taken seriously, as it was with Germany's Hitler, its inherent evil nature becomes especially apparent. In Chapter 2 of this work, when discussing the philology of Genesis 3:15, we noted that enmity occurred between the serpent (that evil-one responsible for the human fall) and the "seed of the woman" who was the promised Christ of Israel. Nietzsche's philosophy was a particularly evil one because he specifically targeted the Christian as both his enemy and the enemy of the ideal society. Of course, as we have seen in the previous chapter, ideas from the Enlightenment had sufficed to bring humanistic ideas again to the forefront and served to suppress the influence of genuine Christianity. Nietzsche was operating from knowledge of the superficial Christianity which had once again taken hold in Europe. By Nietzsche's day the widespread positive effects of the Reformation had largely subsided. The existing residual Christianity had little influence in European society. However, the ultimate cause behind the dichotomy between Christianity and humanism derives from the spirit world. True morality has its derivation in the God of Scripture, and we know that "God is spirit; and those who worship Him must worship in spirit and in truth."[46] Likewise the philosophies that oppose the morality of the God of Scripture also ultimately have their origin in the spirit world. Jesus made it clear to those nonsecular humanistic Pharisees who were seeking his destruction that the ultimate source of their unbelief was in the unseen spirit world. Jesus told them bluntly:

> Why do you not understand what I am saying? It is because you cannot hear My word. You are of your father the devil, and you want to do the desires of your father. He was a murderer from the beginning, and does not stand in the truth, because there is no truth in him. Whenever he speaks a lie, he speaks from his own nature; for he is a liar, and the father of lies. But because I speak the truth, you do not believe Me.[47]

As was the Pharisees' thinking of Jesus' day, so too was Nietzsche's thought grounded in the falsehood of that great deceiver of all men's souls. And just as the Pharisees' teachings were armed with just enough truth to lure into their web those too blind to understand spiritual truth, so too was Nietzsche's. Contrary to what Nietzsche taught, the greatest and noblest societies have their origins in some type of Godly influence. Even Japan's post-war recovery to her prosperous state cannot be divorced form America's compassion for her suffering in the aftermath of those two terrible explosions. Had America, at that time in her history, been steeped in Nietzsche's philosophy, neither Japan nor Germany would today be in the enviable economic states that they both today find themselves. Nietzsche's philosophy was simply, but tragically, wrong.

Freud

The consideration of Charles Darwin and Sigmund Freud as major contributors to the secular humanism of Western culture stands apart from that of Nietzsche in that neither of them were philosophers *per se*. While Nietzsche's formal education was in the humanities, both Darwin and Freud were educated in the natural sciences. Nonetheless, they all played a significant role in steering Western humanism away from its non-secular moorings into the realm of pure secular humanism. That Freud's ideas were the offspring of Darwinian teaching is usually acknowledged by even his most ardent supporters. In an introduction to a brief review of Freud's work, one professor of psychology wrote:

> The same year that the three-year-old Freud was taken by his family to Vienna saw the publication of Charles Darwin's *Origin of Species*. This book was destined to revolutionize man's conception of man. Before Darwin, man was set apart from the rest of the animal kingdom by virtue of his having a soul. The evolutionary doctrine made man a part of nature, an animal among other animals. The acceptance of this radical view meant that the study of man could proceed along naturalistic lines. Man became an object of scientific study, no different, save in complexity, from other forms of life. ... Darwin ... had a tremendous impact upon the intellectual development of Freud ... as ... upon so many other young men of that period.[48]

It is in this perspective that the life and works of Freud must be considered.

Freud was born in what is now the Czech Republic in the year 1856. Because of growing anti-Semitism, his family moved to Austria when he was only three years of age. He lived his entire life in Vienna, only leaving for England to flee Nazi persecution in the last few months of his life. Freud originally planned a career in law but instead chose science after contemplating Goethe's poem *On Nature*. He earned his medical degree from the University of Vienna at the age of 25 and remained at the University to immerse himself in neurological research. He preferred research to medical practice but was forced by financial need into private practice. In 1885, he received an appointment to work under the French neurologist Jean Charcot. Charcot in Paris and Joseph Breuer[49] in Vienna were pioneering techniques in hypnosis for the treatment of patients suffering emotional disturbances then referred to as *hysteria*. It was under the tutelage of Charcot that Freud began to put together the ideas that would lead to the discipline of psychoanalysis.

For consideration of Freud's basic ideas we will examine some of his own words taken from a series of lectures delivered at Clark University in 1909. These lectures give us a succinct summary of Freud's thinking up to that point. Freud eventually modified some of his original ideas, but nonetheless these lectures, given when he was 53 years of age, provide a good frame of reference for his general beliefs regarding the human psyche.

The theme of Freud's early ideas revolved around his concept of the unconscious. Freud's observation of Charcot's use of hypnosis in the treatment of "hysteria" induced into his thinking a new concept, which he referred to as the "unconscious" memory. Freud wrote:

> Hystericals and all neurotics behave ... not only in that they remember the painful experiences of the distant past, but because they are strongly affected by them. They cannot escape from the past and neglect present reality in its favor. This fixation of the mental life on the pathogenic traumata is an essential, and practically a most significant characteristic of the neurosis.[50]

Freud maintained that certain traumatic events, usually experienced early in the patient's life, were the cause of the manifested neurotic symptoms: "Hysterical patients suffer from reminiscences. Their symptoms are the remnants and the memory symbols of certain (traumatic) experiences."[51] Freud believed that the neurotic had suppressed these traumatic experiences from the conscious mind into the unconscious mind. The traumatic event, according to Freud, was remembered in the unconscious mind but not in the conscious mind. Freud referred to this process as "repression." The psychoanalytic cure consisted of moving the "traumatic" memory from the unconscious mind into the conscious mind. Only when these memories were brought into consciousness could the neurosis be resolved and a cure be effected.

Charcot and Breuer had used hypnosis to bring to their patient's con-science mind the significant instances of the forgotten past. While the tech-niques of hypnosis were sometimes successful at relieving the symptoms of *hysteria,* Freud found that he could not, on a regular basis, successfully hyp-notize his patients and, therefore, he believed that hypnosis was unreliable for probing the unconscious. As a substitute to hypnosis, Freud pioneered the technique of *free association* where the analyst encouraged the patient to audibly speak the first impression to enter the patient's mind when stimu-lated by the analyst's suggestion.

Freud noted that his efforts to bring the events which he thought might be responsible for the patient's neuroses into consciousness through this new technique were often met with resistance. Freud referred to that resistance as "some sort of a force"[52] and attributed it to a wish which had been aroused that was "in sharp opposition to the other desires of the individual, and not capable of being reconciled with the ethical, aesthetic and personal preten-sions of the patient's personality."[53] Freud came to believe that these wishes were sexual in nature and concluded that the human psyche was based in sexuality. He believed that the malfunctioning behaviors of the neurotic were rooted in the patient's sexual wishes:

> Psycho-analytic investigations trace back the symptoms of
> disease with really surprising regularity to impressions from
> the sexual life, [and] show us that the pathogenic wishes
> are of the nature of erotic impulse-components
> (*Triebkomponente*), and necessitate the assumption that to
> disturbances of the erotic sphere must be ascribed the great-
> est significance among the aetiological factors of the dis-
> ease. This holds of both sexes.[54]

Freud admitted that in many cases of emotional disturbance the problem could be traced to a traumatic experience that did not have its apparent root in sexuality. But Freud claimed that if one were to sufficiently investigate and analyze the personality, the cause of any emotional difficulty would go back to the early childhood or adolescence of the patient where incompat-ible repressed sexual wishes were responsible for the symptoms.[55]

In recent years, the entire work of Freud has come under strong criti-cism from both a cultural and scientific standpoint.[56] And while much of that criticism is justified, it is important to differentiate between the points in Freud's teaching where such criticism is warranted and those points where it is not. Although Freud's thinking was certainly thoroughly humanistic, to debunk his *entire* work on either scientific or philosophical grounds is incor-rect. Some of Freud's insights have shed light on the complexities of the human psyche. For example, certain aspects of his work have probably contributed to the modern awareness of the destructiveness of the sexual abuse of children. While Freud's work might be responsible for some false accusations perpetrated on alleged offenders, the problem of sexual molestation is a very real one. In recent years that subject has gone from one that, in earlier days, was often "swept under the rug" to one that has been exposed for the destructive force that it perpetrates on its victims. The works of Freud have thus perhaps saved many potential children of victimization by, if nothing else, producing in the Western consciousness a heightened awareness of its existence. Recent punishments for such offenses, at least in the United States, are generally more severe and forthcoming than perhaps they have ever been in the nation's history. Certainly, the child who has been sexually preyed upon will attempt to suppress such memories from his consciousness and that repression, if not dealt with, will most certainly lead to neurotic behaviors.

Criticism of Freud's work must be based on the fact that he derived his most bizarre ideas from a boggled attempt to create a system whereby a natural cause and effect scenario could account for the very real problem of human guilt. In attempting to understand human behavior from purely a natural, scientific perspective, Freud generated many ideas that were a figment of his imagination so as to rationalize the origin of the powerful emotion of guilt. While he correctly identified guilt as the source of the emotional instability which he probably witnessed on nearly a daily basis in the course of his clinical work, he did not understand the true source of its origin. As an example of the extremes that his rationalizations took him, he taught that infantile sexuality produced the practice of thumb sucking and viewed the practice as sexual in nature because of its association with pleasure. Freud further falsely claimed that since the child did not differentiate between the sexes "every child ... [had in him] ... a bit of the homosexual disposition." According to Freud, in the healthy person this infantile sexuality resolved itself in two general directions, one of which was the movement towards the "service of procreation" and the other towards "object-choice" where "all components of the sexual impulse are satisfied in the loved person."[57] Freud maintained that when the sexual function failed to develop properly, sexual perversion could result. He stated that the "equal value of both sexes as sexual objects, [found naturally in childhood] may be maintained and an inclination to homosexual activities in adult life ... which, under suitable conditions, [could rise] to the level of exclusive homosexuality."[58] These erroneous thoughts led to perhaps his most controversial view (and rightly so) of human sexuality which revolved around his claim that all children see in a parent a sexual "object-choice."

> The child takes both parents, and especially one, as an object of his erotic wishes. Usually he follows in this the stimulus given by his parents, whose tenderness has very clearly the character of a sex manifestation, though inhibited so far as its goal is concerned. As a rule, the father prefers the daughter, the mother the son; the child reacts to this situation, since, as a son, he wishes himself in the place of his father, as daughter, in the place of the mother. … We must express the opinion that this with its ramifications presents the *nuclear complex* of every neurosis, and so we are prepared to meet with it in a not less effectual way in the other fields of mental life. The myth of King Oedipus, who kills his father and wins his mother as a wife is only the slightly altered presentation of the infantile wish, rejected later by the opposing barriers of incest.[59]

Freud referred to this as the Oedipus complex and the ramifications of that invention became central to his system of psychoanalysis. Freud essentially derived this bizarre idea from the analysis of his own mind. While it might reflect his own abnormal psychology, the universal application of the Oedipus complex to all humanity was certainly an erroneous, if not idiotic, conclusion.

Freud observed in the human psyche a tendency towards an aggression which fought against the formation of a law-abiding society. This perception is evidence of Freud's knowledge of human depravity, a not surprising discovery in light of the fact that Freud worked incessantly with emotionally troubled individuals and all such difficulties are ultimately connected to man's fallen nature. It is evident that Freud was aware of the flawed nature of humanity, but he was unable to associate that defect with its true cause. Freud did not, of course, view human depravity as a consequence of man's rebellion against God. Freud wrote:

> The tendency to aggression is an innate, independent, instinctual deposition in man, and … constitutes a most powerful obstacle to culture. … The natural instinct of aggressiveness in man, the hostility of each one against all and of all against each one, opposes this program of civilization. …[the evolution of which] may be simply described as the struggle of the human species for existence.[60]

This "tendency to aggression" is a product of man's selfish will, a result of man's separation from the God of Scripture. The problem of human guilt (as discussed in Chapter 2), is a universal problem of human existence, and is ultimately the result of man's rebellion against his Creator. Adam's rebellion against God created in all his progeny a nature bent on evil. The natural human drive to seek one's own will, or to depart from God's will, predisposes him to wrong doing. Morally wrong actions are responsible for the guilt that cripples personality. As modern Western man turns increasingly away from the God of Scripture to self-determined standards of behavior, his character becomes increasingly prone to this aggression of which Freud wrote. I will show in the succeeding paragraphs how Freud fit this aspect of human nature into his model of human personality.

While Freud had little respect for religion in general, his criticisms on the subject were largely aimed at Christianity because it was this force, from a philosophical standpoint, which most powerfully moved against his system of thought. Freud knew enough of Christianity to know that it offered answers to his most profound questions. However, since he rejected Scripture as the source of ultimate truth, he was forced to rely on his own power of observation to devise his own philosophy of human nature. Only Scripture is equipped to address the source of human guilt, and therefore, only there can one find the ultimate resources for emotional healing. Freud, of course, sought healing for his patients, but the farce, of at least some, of his proclaimed cures through his methods of psychoanalyses are now well documented.[61] Freud's own self-analysis suggests that he was in as much need of a cure for his own troubles as those for whom he sought treatment. Many of his most bizarre and controversial ideas, such as his inception of the Oedipus complex, likely have their origin in his own neuroses. He wrongly sought to universalize to human nature the characteristics which were unique to his own being. Thus, Freud's attacks on Christianity, although subtle, were nonetheless potent ones. While Freud demonstrated a knowledge of Christianity, that knowledge was of a shallow textbook variety, yielding no true understanding of its purpose and function. Concerning religion, Freud wrote:

> The religions of humanity, too, must be classified as mass-delusions ... Needless to say, no one who shares a delusion recognizes it as such. ...There are, as we have said, many paths by which the happiness attainable for man can be reached, but none which is certain to take him to it. Nor can religion keep her promises either. When the faithful find themselves reduced in the end to speaking of God's *inscrutable decree*, they thereby avow that all that is left to them in their sufferings is unconditional submission as a last-remaining consolation and source of happiness. And if man is willing to come to this, he could probably have arrived there by a shorter road.[62]

Of course, the Christian would agree with the first statement of this quote. The religions of humanity are indeed mass-delusions and those so deceived do not recognize it as such. But the God of Scripture has no origin in man. Man has his origin in Him.

In his later years Freud attempted to develop a comprehensive theory of personality. That theory revolved around a three component system consisting of the id, the ego and the super-ego. While Freud's model is not perfectly in-line with the traditional Western model, it nonetheless has strong parallels to it. The traditional Western model of personality consists of three primary components, as noted in Chapter 1, to which even Plato subscribed. These components consist of the intellectual, the emotional and the volitional aspects of human nature. The functioning of these components is unique to the individual, just as one's fingerprints are, and that uniqueness is the basis for the uniqueness of individual personality. The Western ideal of individual value derives from this uniqueness and the Western understanding of personality is usually based on this traditional model. Even Ludwig Feuerbach, the humanistic German philosopher nearly contemporary with Freud, whose ideas contributed to the inception of atheistic communism with his emphasis on the materialistic, astutely described "human essence as the unity of understanding, willing, and feeling."[63] Humanistic philosophy implies that either the intellectual (the Socratic Greek ideal) or the volitional aspect of human nature (the Sophistic ideal of Nietzsche) equips human personality with sovereignty over its own nature.

The id, the ego and the superego can be loosely identified with the emotional, rational, and volitional aspects of human nature, respectively. According to Freud:

> The ego has the task of bringing the influence of the external world to bear upon the id and its tendencies, and endeavors to substitute the reality-principle for the pleasure-principle which reigns supreme in the id. In the ego, perception plays the part which in the id devolves upon instinct. The ego represents what we call reason and sanity, in contrast to the id which contains the passions. All this falls into line with popular distinctions which we are all familiar with; at the same time however, it is only to be regarded as holding good in an average or "ideal case."[64]

Since the malfunctioning personality has as its primary symptom the disturbance of the emotional aspect of personality, Freud regarded the id as the foundation upon which the personality was built. He regarded the id as the true psychic reality. According to Freud, the id is driven by one consideration only, to obtain satisfaction for instinctual needs in accordance with the pleasure principle. The primary aim of the pleasure principle is to avoid pain. This is in-line with our discussion in Chapter 1, where we emphasized that man, in his basest state, will make decisions based on his desire to satisfy, in the easiest manner possible, his desire for emotional contentment. While the id can primarily be identified with the emotional aspect of personality, it is moved upon by two distinct elements of volition. One of these elements is of a primitive nature, associated with the fulfillment of instinctual needs, such as food and sex, etc. This element of volition remains distinct from the one connected to the super-ego.

Freud taught that the super-ego originated from an internalization of the inherent aggressiveness of human nature (see ref. 60). The super-ego, according to Freud, became the ego's opponent in the form of the conscience where it manifested its aggressiveness against the ego. This tension between the super-ego and the subordinate ego gave rise to the sense of guilt. Freud thus believed that guilt derived from the function of the super-ego. Here we observe Freud's scheme for destroying the validity of a Christian based morality. Christian morality is driven from a conscience that is ultimately formed from the precepts of Scripture. Freud devised a scheme that could provide a natural cause for the existence of guilt. The universal guilt of the human race cannot be divorced from the universal condition of fallen human nature. Since Freud could not acknowledge the true source of guilt, he was forced to devise his own system to explain it.

In Freud's system, the volitional aspect of human nature is associated with the movement of the ego on the id, which is derived from the super-ego. As before mentioned, one aspect of human volition moves upon the id by instinct, and this movement, of course, is the same level of volition that is found in the animal kingdom. But Freud put the aspect of will that is unique to human nature in the super-ego, the function of which is driven by the conscience and the moral convictions of the individual. It is imperative to understand the role that Freud placed on the super-ego to understand how his ideas have had adverse effects on Western culture. It is out of the super-ego (or ego-ideal as Freud sometimes referred to it) that the religious and moral nature of man, according to Freud, has its origin. Freud wrote:

> It is easy to show that the ego-ideal answers in every way to what is expected of the higher nature of man. In so far as it is a substitute for the longing for a father, it contains the germ from which all religions have evolved. The self-judgment which declares that the ego falls short of its ideal produces the sense of worthlessness with which the religious believer attests his longing.[65]

With his conception of the super-ego, Freud was forced to reveal, in a particularly keen way, his moral philosophy. In Freud's model of personality, the super-ego, as the primary motivator of the aspect of will involving morality, played a primary role in his view of the origin of human guilt. To further understand Freud's view of the origin of guilt, consider his words that follow:

> When one asks how a sense of guilt arises in anyone, one is told something one cannot dispute: people feel guilty (pious people call it "sinful") when thy have done something they know to be *bad*. But then one sees how little this answer tells one. Perhaps, after some hesitation, one will add that a person who has not actually committed a bad act, but has merely become aware of the intention to do so, can also hold himself guilty; and then one will ask why in this case the intention is counted as equivalent to the deed. In both cases, however, one is presupposing that wickedness has already been recognized as reprehensible, as something that ought not to be put into execution. How is this judgment arrived at? One may reject the suggestion of an original—as one might say, natural—capacity for discriminating between good and evil. Evil is often not at all that which would injure or endanger the ego; on the contrary, it can also be something that it desires, that would give it pleasure. An extraneous influence is evidently at work; it is this that decides what is to be called good and bad. Since their own feelings would not have led men along the same path, they must have had a motive for obeying this extraneous influence. It is easy to discover this motive in man's helplessness and dependence upon others, it can best be designated the *dread of losing love*. If he loses the love of others on whom he is dependent, he will forfeit also their protection against many dangers, and above all he runs the risk that this stronger person will show his superiority in the form of punishing him. What is bad is, therefore, to begin with, whatever causes one to be threatened with a loss of love; because of the dread of this loss, one must desist from it. This is why it makes little difference whether one has already committed the bad deed or only intends to do so; in either case the danger begins only when the authority has found it out, and the latter would behave in the same way in both cases.[66]

In dealing with the origin of guilt, Freud distinctly revealed his moral philosophy. Freud's sense of morality was established in the humanism with which this work is concerned. From the preceding quote, Freud believed that one's sense of right and wrong was ultimately formed from "the dread of losing love." Of course, by that expression Freud was referring to human love or human friendship. If by this declaration Freud had meant the love of the God of Scripture, the Christian could perhaps understand that statement. The love of the God of Scripture is the very essence of true love since God *is* love.[67] The moral philosophy of one who knows the God of Scripture is indeed shaped from that relationship. While Freud sought a naturalistic explanation of guilt with great diligence, guilt is yet, ultimately the result of man's rebellion against his Creator. Freud's solution to the problem of human guilt was to ignore both the pangs of conscience and the God who designed that conscience as a natural guide to morality. Freud taught that the id should only be moved on by the instinctual desires outside of the super-ego. This was his way of saying "if the sexual urge strikes then do not be concerned with your conscience. Go ahead and satisfy the urge." Freud stated:

> A certain part of the suppressed libidinous excitation has a right to direct satisfaction and ought to find it in life. The claims of our civilization make life too hard for the greater part of humanity, and so further the aversion to reality and the origin of neuroses, without producing an excess of cultural gain by this excess of sexual repression. We ought not to go so far as to fully neglect the original animal part of our nature; we ought not to forget that the happiness of individuals cannot be dispensed with as one of the aims of our culture.[68]

But despite Freud's teaching, human sexual activity is best suited to the confines of a monogamous, heterosexual and loving marriage. The solution to the diseases of the human psyche which are often manifested in human sexuality can only be found in the pages of Scripture. Unfortunately, the solution Freud outlined in the preceding quote, as we will discuss in Chapter 8, has become the direction to which modern man, in his efforts to satisfy his craving for significance and meaning, has turned.

Marx

In concluding Part One of this work, we will briefly consider the contributions to Western humanism of Karl Marx and his colleague Friedrich Engels. The socialism spawned by their theories can perhaps be regarded as the epitome of secular humanism. Humanism often leads to some form of socialism, if not communism, when it is followed to its purest philosophical conclusions. With the collapse of the Soviet Union in the latter part of the 20th century, the influence of Marxism has become mostly concentrated in Eastern cultures. However, communism is yet primarily a Western institution since the ideas behind its conception was a product of Western thinking. The fact that Marxism directly influenced millions of people for over a span of almost 100 years, and even today remains a factor in world politics, certainly commands acknowledgment of its success, at least to a certain degree. And that success was not a happenstance. As Smelser stated in his introduction to a brief collection of Marx's writings, "There is a Marxist contribution to, indeed a Marxist explanation for, almost every aspect of individual and social life that one could imagine—human nature, economics, religion, politics, philosophy, social stratification to name only a few."[69] But while Marx's humanistic understanding of human nature demonstrated some aspects of prudence, ultimately communism's failure must be—or will be in the situations where it still exists—assigned to Marx's misunderstanding of that nature.

Marx was born in 1818 at Trier, a small Prussian city located about 40 kilometers east of Luxembourg. Both his parents were descendants of a long line of Jewish rabbis, but his immediate family converted to Christianity sometime in the vicinity of his early childhood.[70] Many biographers state that the motive behind that conversion was simply for social convenience, since even then Jewish persecution was prevalent in certain German communities. However, it is difficult to say with certainty that his parents were not genuine in their Christian faith. At the age of 17, Karl began his university studies in law at the University of Bonn. Not unlike many immature young men who first try their hand at higher education, the young Marx was more interested in the pursuit of pleasure than in that of serious academic study. Had his father permitted him to suffer the consequences of that failure the world may never have heard of him. But his father encouraged his transfer to the University of Berlin where he became immersed in the philosophical culture inspired by Hegel. Marx's leftist views can be, at least partially, attributed to Hegel's influence even though he wrongly interpreted Hegel's philosophy as one based in atheism. After Berlin, Marx attended the University of Jena where he received a doctorate in philosophy at the age of 23. Evidently, Marx had wanted a teaching position, but that goal was probably blocked because of his emerging radical tendencies. Shortly after receiving his doctorate, he moved to Cologne where he tried his hand at journalism. At Cologne he edited the *Rheinische Zeitung*, a leftist publication that was soon suppressed by the powers it criticized. After only a year he moved to Paris and there formed his relationship with Frederick Engles. It was also in Paris that his thinking began to gel into communistic philosophy. After a short stay in Belgium, Marx moved his family to England in 1848 and remained there, essentially living in poverty, until the end of his life in 1883.

Engles was the son of a wealthy German textile industrialist and was Marx's junior by two years. He has, by some, been considered Marx's inferior in intellectual ability, but this may be a wrong assumption since Engle's contributions to the theories of communism are probably underestimated. This is evidenced by Engles' own writing, as for example, in the 1844 publication of *The Condition of the Working Class in England.* However, the message of the *Communist Manifesto* was so intimately intertwined from the minds of both authors that it is difficult to properly know where the thoughts of one end and those of the other begin. Engles, like Marx, spent his last years in England and provided a meager income for the destitute Marx family.

While it is not within our scope to analyze the tenets of Marxism, it is necessary to consider briefly the one that most directly bears on Marx's view of human nature. That tenet known as *dialectical materialism* most clearly demonstrates his view of human nature. Marx viewed human nature as a product of the need and desire of material goods. In Marx's thinking, the entire historical development of the human species, including his systems of government and social structures, stemmed solely from the economics that provided those goods. Thus, when it is said that Marx was a materialist, it means he believed that man's material needs and wants were the primary driving forces that formed human nature.

Marx's materialistic thinking in a purely naturalistic sense was based on what might appear as sound philosophical principle. It is the logic behind the concept that has given communism its widespread influence. As noted in Chapter 1, the ancient Greek Sophists—the first Western secular humanists—believed that the pursuit of the "good life" should be the primary goal for living. That goal would then naturally play a significant role in forming the criteria for acceptable human behavior. And furthermore, since man's natural psychic existence—or the basic temperament of his personality— lies mainly in the emotional part of his nature, there is a natural tendency to build one's sense of emotional "well being" on wealth and material possessions.

The dialectical aspect of the term *dialectical materialism* comes from Hegel's influence on Marx. Hegel expounded on the idea of the Greek dialectic whereby discussion and reasoning, in the form of dialog, revolving around any subject with opposing points of view, was believed to be the mechanism which would yield the light of truth to that subject. In the Hegelian sense of the dialectical, any particular philosophy on the history and nature of man (the thesis) would give rise to an anti-thesis which would force a resolution (the synthesis.) Marx believed that communism was the inevitable solution to the inevitable problems produced by capitalism. Marx taught that capitalism always led to economic oppression of the masses (i.e., the workers who produced the goods of capital) by the few who possessed political power through their control of wealth and that all systems of capitalism would inevitably give rise to two classes of people, the haves and the have-nots, or the *bourgeoisie* and the *proletariat* respectively. Therefore, as Marx stated at the very beginning of the *Communist Manifesto*, communism is based in the belief that "the history of all hitherto existing society is the history of class struggles."[71]

Communistic philosophy rose to prominence because of the human depravity of which we first spoke in Chapter 2. Communism is ultimately a man-made system, which attempts to address the problems produced by the inherent selfishness in unredeemed man. If man's primary purpose for living is to attain "the good life," and if the good life is derived through economic gain, human nature in its unredeemed state will then strive to get all the good it can even if it comes at the expense of others. Human selfishness ultimately produced the economic conditions that gave birth to Marx's ideas. Marx's moral system was based on a Darwinian ethic in which "might made right." As such, armed struggle against the prevailing capitalistic systems was justifiable and even encouraged in Marxian thought. The reader should note the parallels between Marx's philosophy and the philosophy of the early Greek secular humanists. Marx believed that under a system of communism, the function of government would eventually cease. This is essentially the same position of the Greek Sophists who held to the ideas of *physis*, whose proponents believed that the positive law of the state was unnatural and unnecessary. Communism is, therefore, based on the false assumption that human nature will change for the better if wealth is properly redistributed.

In a sense, the idea behind communism is a noble one. The very first Christians entered into a communal arrangement in order to expedite and strengthen the very early Christian Church (see Acts 2:44-46). However, that communal sharing did not arise from a belief that the basis of all reality was economic in nature but from the knowledge that man's ultimate reason for living was found in the one and only true God. The early Christians' sharing of their materialistic goods was from their knowledge that any emotional security that might proceed from a trust in monetary wealth was a false security. The one who has given himself to the God of Scripture knows that materialistic possessions are only a means to an end. That end is certainly not to gain any sense of true emotional fulfillment or to seek primarily one's sense of well-being from that wealth. Man's primary purpose in life should be to live to the honor of his Creator. It is only through that relationship that he can become truly emotionally satisfied. Communism's failure is due to its false premise that man's need and desire for materialistic possessions define his purpose for living.

Some of the world's most troubled individuals are those who have great wealth, while some of the most contented people are those who have little wealth, but have a living relationship with the Creator of the universe. Man's ultimate emotional need is to love and to be loved. The ultimate love that anyone can experience is the redeeming love that comes from a proper relationship with Jesus Christ. Only then can one have the peace with God that his conscience desires. That is the peace which comes from knowing that one's sins have been forgiven. No amount of material possessions can give that peace and contentment. Any system that is based on the idea that man is primarily an economic entity ends up being a cold and mechanistic one. Instead of changing the human condition, the ultimate ideological goal of communism, the system ends up exacerbating the very condition that it seeks to reform. In communistic systems, the party members simply evolve into the bourgeoisie. Man's ill-found desire to seek emotional contentment through material means remains unextinguished. Even loving family relationships in such systems become suspect. Thus humanistic thinking that contributes to the destruction of family relationships becomes prevalent within communistic systems. Engles wrote:

> It [monogamy] was the first form of the family to be based, not on natural, but on economic conditions—on the victory of private property over primitive, natural communal property. The Greeks themselves put the matter quite frankly: the sole exclusive aims of monogamous marriage were to make the man supreme in the family and to propagate, as the future heirs to his wealth, children indisputably his own. Otherwise, marriage was a burden, a duty which had to be performed, whether one liked it or not, to gods, state, and one's ancestors. ...Thus when monogamous marriage first makes its appearance in history, it is not as the reconciliation of man and woman, still less as the highest form of such a reconciliation. Quite the contrary. Monogamous marriages comes on the scene as the

subjugation of the one sex by the other; it announces a
struggle between the sexes unknown throughout the whole
previous prehistoric period.[72]

While most Western feminists might reject the economic philosophies of
Marx and Engles, many, because of the commonality of humanism and
socialism, would likely empathize with Engles' analysis of marriage. Communism and the humanistic philosophies that spawned it, cannot provide
answers to man's ultimate need. That need is spiritual birth, which can only
come from faith in the One who unabashedly proclaimed, "You must be
born again," and by whom that new birth comes. Marx despised those words,
as yet do all humanists, because to acknowledge them as truthful, the humanist must first acknowledge the bankruptcy of the self-sufficient philosophy upon which he has built his life.

PART TWO

MODERN

8

The Humanistic Search for a Sense of Personal Fulfillment

There is a strange and mighty race of people called the Americans who are rapidly
becoming the coldest in the world because of this cruel, maneating idol, lucre.
Edward Dahlberg (1900-1977)

In the final chapter of Part One, we saw how Darwin laid the groundwork for the belief in a human existence independent of a creator. Darwin established a perceived legitimacy for the idea that all life is due to a happenstance—a chance-controlled natural process. When that is believed, man must view himself as a sovereign entity. If man is sovereign, moral knowledge cannot be external but must come from within the confines of his own nature. After Darwin came Nietzsche who proclaimed, "If you will it—take it, do it—your will is God." Freud encouraged people to throw off the sexual standards derived from Scripture so as not to further cripple society with guilt. Marx convinced millions that the driving force shaping human nature proceeded from man's consuming drive towards material gain.

In addition to the secular humanism of these thinkers is the humanism that lies buried within modern Judaism and nominal forms of Christianity. The Christianity of Rome yet remains in the clutches of the Greek humanism birthed centuries ago, and even some segments of the Western Christianity produced by the Reformation have since thrown off the scriptural precepts upon which they were founded. Humanistic thinking is beginning to penetrate even the evangelical Christianity once thought immune to those advances (discussed in Chapter 10). Combine all these philosophies and one has a brief snapshot of where Western society is today. Modern Western culture contains such diverse beliefs of what constitutes the moral good that that diversity now nearly equates with its definition. Western culture has become one where most people do what is right in their own eyes and where the genuine Christian presence that yet remains is slowly being whittled away.

In Part Two we briefly discuss where this hodge-podge of ideas has taken modern Western man. The ideas spawned by both secular and non-secular humanism have equipped modern man with either a sense of no purpose or with a sense of purpose that is centered entirely within himself. In this chapter we concentrate on two specific areas to which modern man has primarily turned in his search for emotional contentment. First, Western man is increasingly seeking his sense of purpose and fulfillment through the attainment of wealth. The universal pursuit of wealth has become the glue that is holding Western culture together. Secondly, the pursuit of sexual pleasure outside the confines of loving marriages is increasingly becoming the norm. While the attainment of either goal may contribute to one's sense of short-term well being, neither one, in and of itself, will bring the lasting peace and satisfaction that the pursuer believes that it will yield.

The Western Pursuit of Material Wealth, i.e., the Chase of the Mammon

If one were to randomly poll any social grouping from any part of the world today and ask what single word might be used to describe Western civilization, the reply likely to dominate would be "materialistic." There can be little doubt that the drive for material wealth has become a major defining characteristic of modern Western man. Here I refer to a pursuit of wealth that is somewhat distinct to Western culture (or where it exists in other cultures, it is a result of Western influence). Of course, the pursuit of material goods, to a certain extent, is obviously necessary for life itself and, therefore, that pursuit is a universal, desirable trait of man with no particular Western distinction. However, there is a genuine Western distinction to this trait, due primarily to the shear magnitude of wealth inherent and pervasive within Western culture. While America comprises only about 5% of the world's population, her GNP accounts for more than 25% of the world's total, and this same ratio is similarly skewed for many of the prominent nations of Western Europe.

The aspects of the subject which I address here, therefore, lie beyond the pursuit of life's necessities which all men naturally and justifiably seek. There is, of course, nothing morally wrong with desiring and pursuing a decent standard of living, and it should not be inferred from this discussion that the possession of wealth is necessarily a characteristic of a humanistic mind-set. The humanistic pursuit of wealth discussed in this chapter is one that is the result of a mind-set that has purposefully sought to find in one's economic standing the primary source of emotional fulfillment—that internal peace which all men seek. It is a mind-set that seeks from one's economic resources a sense of self-sufficiency. It is an outlook on life that attaches to itself a fierce sense of independence that stems from the perception that one is in control of one's destiny because of the power that his wealth has enabled.

Because the urge to sovereignly control one's destiny is so powerful, the concept of personal success and self-esteem has become inherently linked to one's degree of material wealth. In modern Western society success is more and more measured not by one's relationship to the God of Scripture but by the size of one's house, the brand of one's wristwatch and the brand name on one's automobile. So pervasive and destructive is the perception that personal worth is directly linked to economic worth that Jesus characterized all as belonging to one of two classes of people with two respective allegiances. One allegiance is the love of a lifestyle associated with riches. The other is associated with a lifestyle that is consistent with a love of the one and only true God. Jesus stated, "No one can serve two masters; for either he will hate the one and love the other, or he will hold to one and despise the other. You cannot serve God and Mammon."[1]

In his well-known and time-proven scriptural commentary, Matthew Henry gave a particularly informative definition of the word mammon. Most readers of Scripture infer that mammon simply means money, but Henry tells us that mammon is a Syriac word that implies any type of worldly gain. Mammon is the gain of the world or whatever is "accounted by us to be" so. The "lust of the flesh, lust of the eye, and the pride of life" constitutes the meaning of mammon.[2] The Western pursuit of wealth is usually linked to these very characteristics. Western corporate cultures often intentionally appeal to these very distinctives to perpetuate the cycle of lust and greed that drives the psychology of extravagant living. The extravagant lifestyle is one where a never-ending desire to possess something bigger and better than one's neighbor abound. That cycle is subtly tied into one's concept of self-worth. The idea that one is more important than another because of the quantity and quality of one's belongings is certainly not exclusive to Western culture, but the problem is particularly rampant in Western culture because of the sheer magnitude of the culture's resources.

It is interesting to peruse the many books on the market that promise to propel one to success and fulfillment. The number of books written in this vein is quite astounding. One such book, the cover of which proclaims the author to be "America's leading life and career coach," promises to teach the reader how to live his "best life" by "getting over" himself "to bring forth" his "deepest wishes in such a way that" he "can't avoid taking action on them." It further promises to teach him "how to determine what needs to stay or go" and reminds him that his "relationships, work, finances, and physical environment must work to nurture" and not to "deplete."[3] The book promises to show the reader "how to create circumstances ... by which great luck can find" him and promises that if he will follow the book's precepts his "extraordinary life will unfold as it is meant to."

The author begins the book by informing her reader how she was at the end of hope, on the brink of being admitted to a psychiatric hospital for treatment of depression and suicidal tendencies. It was under these circumstances that she stated:

> *I decided* to turn my life around. *I decided* to find a way out from behind what I had taken to call the "black curtain." *I decided* [italics added] that I could change, that I did not have to be "a very sick girl," as my family and doctors said I was.[4]

The implication of absolute self-determination is obviously and unabashedly being proclaimed here. In the power of self-will, the author claims to have defeated those dark forces within her that had been responsible for her prior problems. After the bleak description of her failing emotional health, a few paragraphs later, she tells her reader how her career blossomed. She stated,

> I ... went from coaching actors who could barely pay me $50 a month to being "discovered" in a *Money* magazine article, which featured a client whom I had coached to raise her income to $500,000. I soon found myself in a bidding war between two companies who wanted to publish my first book.[5]

She transformed herself. It is remarkable that here, as in nearly all of these humanistic self-help books, one is never directed towards the only true source of emotional fulfillment. Unless one seeks his fulfillment in a genuine relationship with the God of creation he will never know a lasting peace. One simply cannot live his or her "best life" outside of a genuine relationship with God. The authors of this type literature usually assume that the reader is looking to them to find the keys to a success that is defined in terms of economic gain. However, seldom do such authors admit that the ultimate goal of their advice is to generate a feeling of well-being based on financial success.

Recently, a new approach in this genre of books has appeared on the scene. Steven R. Covey has written a series of books that purports to lay out the essential habits of success. Covey's approach is somewhat unique to the secular market because he introduces a spiritual element to the subject. His first major book, *The 7 Habits of Highly Effective People*,[6] made a significant splash in the lucrative self-help/success market by selling millions of copies and, even after its introduction in the early nineties, continues to be in demand. The accolades for Covey's philosophy continue unabated and they come from some of the most powerful and influential people in the Western business world.

In *The 7 Habits of Highly Effective People*, Covey first distinguished between what he called the Personality Ethic and the Character Ethic. The Character Ethic, according to Covey, is that which predominated in the early history of America. (Covey defines the First World War as a demarcation line between the two ethics.) The Character Ethic was based on "things like integrity, humility, fidelity, temperance, courage, justice, patience, industry, simplicity, modesty and the Golden Rule." Benjamin Franklin's autobiography, according to Covey, is a good example of that ethic. But the Character Ethic eventually gave way to the Personality Ethic. Covey characterized the Personality Ethic as essentially a superficial approach to success, which mainly focuses on image, positive mental attitudes, and even sometimes, on manipulation.[7]

Covey rightfully prioritized the Character Ethic over the Personality Ethic, and he correctly made sure not to discount some of the techniques rising from the Personality Ethic. He wrote:

> I am not suggesting that elements of the Personality Ethic—personality growth, communication skill training, and education in the field of influence strategies and positive thinking—are not beneficial, in fact sometimes essential for success. I believe they are. But these are secondary, not primary traits.[8]

While Covey's perception of these two ethics is indeed a particularly keen one, his philosophy, however, is yet a humanistic one that caters to those whose ultimate goal is the mammon of the world. Covey acknowledges that a change in the natural human condition is necessary for true success, but the change he calls for is a man-made change. The change he calls for is yet one perceived from a belief in personality's sovereignty. One reviewer of Covey's work demonstrates this particularly well. He writes: "He [Covey] is neither an optimist nor a pessimist, but a possibilist, who believes that we and we alone can open the door to change within ourselves."[9] Covey simply does not understand that all men are damned because of Adam's sin, and ultimately all ineffectiveness is due to that sin and the subsequent damnation resulting from it. Man alone cannot do anything to negate the effect of that damnation.

Covey called attention to the need for a paradigm shift if one is to understand the necessity for prioritizing the Character Ethic over the Personality Ethic. But Covey's thinking is in further need of a paradigm shift if it is to be distinguished from the thinking of those humanists who supply their audiences with man-made solutions to the problems that stem from fallen human nature.

In critiquing Covey's philosophy, I am not suggesting that the elements of what Covey calls the Character Ethic are unimportant for true success. But unless one understands that the acquisition of moral character is not a sole function of one's will, one will never be able to achieve the success, which comes to those of upright moral character. True moral character only comes to those who use their will to respond to God's will. Furthermore, as we have emphasized throughout this work, it is not just any conception of God's will to which one must respond. True moral character comes to those whose response is to the will of God, which is revealed in Scripture.

It is interesting that Covey specifically made reference to Benjamin Franklin's philosophy as one coming from the Character Ethic. As we reviewed in Chapter 6, the moral philosophy of the Enlightenment was one that was chiefly based in the human conscience. Franklin believed in a concept of God, but his belief was not consistent with the God presented in Scripture. Covey's moral standard is ultimately based on the standard of human conscience. In fact, he bluntly stated as much when he identified it as his standard:

> The principles I am referring to are not esoteric, mysterious, or "religious" ideas. There is not one principle taught in this book that is unique to any specific faith or religion, including my own. These principles are a part of most every major enduring religion, as well as enduring social philosophies and ethical systems. They are self-evident and can easily be validated by any individual. It's almost as if these principles or natural laws are part of the human condition, part of the human consciousness, part of the human conscience. They seem to exist in all human beings, regardless of social conditioning and loyalty to them, even through they might be submerged or numbed by such conditions or disloyalty.[10]

As we have emphasized throughout this work, while the function of conscience is to point one in the right moral direction, conscience cannot be used as an absolute standard to right behavior. Modern man, being influenced by humanistic moral norms (particularly evident in his sexual nature, as we will discuss in the next part of this chapter) is vulnerable to the formation of a conscience that does not always respond in accordance to moral truth.

In his personal note at the end of *The 7 Habits of Highly Effective People*, Covey clearly removed himself from the ranks of secular humanists by expressing his belief in the existence of a transcendent God. However, as we have stressed throughout this work, the belief in the existence of God does not remove one from a humanistic philosophy. Belief in the existence of God does not get one to the truth of God. Covey correctly acknowledges that God is the source of "correct principles," which are the "natural laws" that guide the conscience. However, Covey incorrectly attempts to establish the human conscience as an absolute entity for determining moral principle. Therefore, while he claims that "there are parts to human nature that cannot be reached by either legislation or education, but require the power of God to deal with" he is implying that the power of God is enabled through the workings of human conscience. Covey stated: "I believe that to the degree people live by this inspired conscience, they will grow to fulfill their natures; to the degree that they do not, they will not rise above the animal plane."[11] One should note the similarity of Covey's ideas to Kant's philosophy discussed in Chapter 6. Kant's moral philosophy was essentially grounded entirely in the belief of conscience's power to enable moral choice.

As one might suspect from the title of *The 7 Habits of Highly Effective People*, Covey believes that the development of habits are the driving force for changing human nature. (The reader should note here the similarity to Aristotle's thought which we reviewed in Chapter 1.) There is no doubt that habit plays a role in character development. But that Covey is operating from a humanistic philosophy is further evident when he states that "breaking deeply imbedded habitual tendencies such as procrastination, impatience, criticalness, or selfishness that violate basic principles of human effectiveness involves more than a little willpower and a few minor changes in our lives."[12] Covey teaches that human behavior is entirely in the control of the human will. He would likely agree whole-heartedly with Berman-Fortgang that it was her proactive free will that enabled her to change her nature in a saving way. Again we see that Covey's philosophy has embedded in it an implied position of human sovereignty. Covey basically teaches that one's character is a "composite" of one's habits, and since one's habits are totally in the power of one's will, the power to change the deficiencies that lie within human nature are within the power of one's personality.

If, however, this were a true characteristic of human nature, the prevalence of those who are controlled by drugs, alcohol, illicit sex (discussed in the next section) or any of the many other forms of destructive addictive behavior would not exist. The addict knows that his habit will eventually destroy his prospects for true success yet he is usually powerless to free himself of the destructive path on which he finds himself. Pete Rose, the great Cincinnati infielder, let the sin of greed destroy his baseball career; yet even today, years later, he apparently has no power over that same sin. From an Associated Press clip recently came the following assessment of Rose's involvement in those same activities that destroyed his baseball career decades earlier:

> Rose is still hitting. The casinos, sports books and race-tracks, that is. Rose continues to live like he played—with reckless abandon. Just about everything Rose has picked up since he put down his bat has tned out to be trouble. ... Nothing has changed.[13]

In those instances where one is successful over a destructive habit through his own effort, using sheer determination based on total abstinence, that victory will simply strengthen his resolve towards independence from the one true God and he has thus ultimately put himself in a worse state of affairs than before.

The discontent inherent in human nature that propels one to seek one's satisfaction in wealth is often acknowledged in the self-help books of which we speak. Another one of these books (which has been around for over a quarter century) begins:

> In quiet moments do you sometimes feel you are in a mute search for something that's missing? If so, you are not alone. A great hunger lies across the land. Regardless of age, sex or race, a vague dis-ease—if not outright desperation— pervades. A lot of active seeking with little permanent finding. In our quest most of us chase the rainbows of success, power, prestige or the approval of others. Surely, we reason, what's just beyond will bring peace and a sense of purpose. But once we have what we thought would do the trick, we find the treasure has eluded us.[14]

The reader should note the author's appeal to the universality of the problem. Her description of the human condition rings with truth because it accurately reflects the universal plight of unregenerate man.

But it is the universal moral darkness of man, which we have spoken of throughout Part One of this work, that is responsible for the dread of which she speaks. Scripture is very explicit in its description of the natural human heart for which this malaise is attributed. As evidenced from the very first few chapters in Genesis to the final words of Revelation, the entire theme of Scripture is first to show man the hopelessness of a self-made remedy to the curse of Adam's sin and then to show him that a genuine peace can only be attained through a genuine knowledge of the God of Scripture. The Genesis declaration that "the intent of man's heart is evil from his youth"[15] is universal in scope. It is from that evil that spawns the dis-ease of which Briggs writes. Isaiah declared that "the wicked are like the tossing sea, for it cannot be quiet [i.e., it cannot rest (KJV)] and its waters toss up refuse and mud. 'There is no peace,' says my God, 'for the wicked.'"[16]

While the teachings of the noted humanistic Western thinkers, from the ancient Greek philosophers to Freud, have emphasized in human nature a drive to "the good," the good of which they speak is not the true Good that yields the genuine peace referred to in Scripture. The good of which they speak is found in the false belief that one can move to a state of emotional contentment through the faculties of one's personality. Furthermore, one usually finds in this humanistic concept of "good" a drive to achieve that sense of security through the attainment of wealth. While that pursuit might bring a temporary sense of satisfaction, it is not the ultimate Good that is capable of bringing true peace, i.e., the genuine emotional contentment, which only finds its fulfillment in knowing that one has been reconciled to the God of creation.

The Scripture is plain in its contention that one is only freed from the destructive effects of sin when one first understands that one's problems, no matter to what extent they may be hindering his success, are due to his separation from his creator. All failure is ultimately due to man's alienation from the God of creation. Thus for one to know true success one must have Christ at one's center of existence. Without one's center in Christ, success within one's personality, which yields the true peace for which all men long, is impossible. Christ is the *only* mediator between God and man. It is simply impossible to coach one to true success without first getting the person in need to understand that all personal failure is rooted in one's sinful nature and that the only remedy to that nature is to have it changed by the power of Christ.

Of course, there are numerous examples of those who have apparently enjoyed great success in the power of human strength. To one who grew up in the '60's, the great baseball sluggers—Ted Williams and Mickey Mantle—both immediately come to mind as two who were immensely successful at hitting a baseball apart from any personal Christian faith. However, it must be emphasized that the success that often brings wealth and fame is not the success that man is really seeking. As one retired professional football player said: "How come when I reach all my dreams life isn't the way I thought it would be?"[17] One can have power, fame, and wealth but not be truly successful because true success and happiness are spiritually derived. Human nature has a spiritual dimension that distinguishes it from the rest of God's creation. But because of Adam's sin, the human spirit needs a radical transformation from that which it naturally is. Of course, one can only speculate on what the nature of the human spirit would have been if man had not fallen from God's favor through Adam's act of disobedience. But because that fall did indeed happen, true personal success is only available to the one who understands that he is separated from God because of his sin and from that knowledge turns to God in humble submission for forgiveness. The successes that outstanding athletes enjoy are often not derived from any spiritual aspect but are simply based upon their extraordinary physical abilities. Since the physical aspect of any man is a temporary reality, success in that realm is also a temporary one.[18] It is interesting to compare the lives of Mantle and Williams in their final years of life. In Mantle's final days he acknowledged his need of a savior and accepted the provisions of Christ's atonement for his sin. However, when Williams died, one family member wanted to preserve his remains with cryonics and another wanted a standard cremation. In coming to the defense of the latter family member, a former teammate of Williams was recorded saying, "Ted wanted to be cremated. He was an atheist. He didn't believe in religion."[19] Of Mantle and Williams the one that apparently experienced the only success that matters—in the end—should be obvious to the reader.

Jesus' polarized characterization of the nature of "contentment seeking" rings with truth. If one is not seeking his emotional fulfillment through the salvation that is afforded to one who has first understood his sinful nature and thus turned to Christ, he is in all probability seeking (or has sought) his salvation in the mammon of the world. It's as if Jesus has automatically characterized those who have refrained from coming to Him as those whose purpose in life is the chase of the mammon. If Christ is not master, then something else must be, and that something else will most likely be the wealth of the world.

The one who primarily lives for material gain will never understand the Apostle Paul's advice to Timothy when he cautioned him that he should be content with food and clothing. Paul reminded Timothy that "the love of money is a root of all sorts of evil" and, therefore, he warned Timothy that he should not be greedy for financial gain.[20] The author of a recent best selling book which instructs the reader in how to acquire wealth, and whose teaching is representative of the Western humanistic drive for material gain of which we are here speaking, stated:

> I believe that each of us has a financial genius within us. The problem is, our financial genius lies asleep, waiting to be called upon. It lies asleep because our culture has edu-

cated us into believing that the love of money is the root
of all evil. It has encouraged us to learn a profession so we
can work for money, but failed to teach us how to have
money work for us.[21]

The author is obviously here critiquing the Christian philosophy of riches
based on the Apostle Paul's first letter to Timothy.[22] While the love of money
may not be at the root of *all* evil, it certainly is at the root of *all kinds* of evil.
One who desires to live a moral life should always be cognizant of the deception of riches.[23] It should also be here noted that the Apostle Paul warned
his reader of those who operate under the guise of Christian ministry but
whose real intent is their own financial reward. Those who do that, and they
seem to be growing more and more plentiful with each passing day, are
guilty of even greater evil than those to whom they attempt to minister.

When one puts his faith in Jesus Christ he can rest assured that he will
have the material resources conducive to contentment, joy and peace. Immediately after proclaiming that one cannot both serve God and chase the
mammon, Jesus stated:

Do not be anxious for your life, as to what you shall eat,
or what you shall drink; nor for your body, as to what you
shall put on. Is not life more than food, and the body than
clothing? Look at the birds of the air, that they do not
sow, neither do they reap, nor gather into barns, and yet
your heavenly Father feeds them. Are you not worth much
more than they? And which of you by being anxious can
add a single cubit to his life's span? And why are you anxious about clothing? Observe how the lilies of the field
grow; they do not toil nor do they spin, yet I say to you
that even Solomon in all his glory did not clothe himself
like one of these. But if God so arrays the grass of the
field, which is alive today and tomorrow is thrown into
the furnace, will He not much more do so for you, O men
of little faith? Do not be anxious then, saying, "What shall
we eat?" or "What shall we drink?" or "With what shall
we clothe ourselves?" For all these things the Gentiles eagerly seek; for your heavenly Father knows that you need
all these things. But seek first His Kingdom and His righteousness; and all these things shall be added to you.[24]

As modern Western man becomes more and more removed from the
influence of a biblically based Christianity, he is increasingly prone to seek
his emotional fulfillment through the raw naked pursuit of wealth. Those
who are so inclined will one day find that they have been fatally duped.

The Pursuit of Sexual Pleasure

Next to Western man's inordinate accumulation of wealth in his attempt to obtain a sense of emotional satisfaction, perhaps his most prevalent means for seeking that fulfillment comes from his illegitimate pursuit of sexual pleasure. Modern Western man's obsession with illicit sexual gratification is everywhere apparent. Only a few years ago, if one wanted to view pornographic material, he had to actively seek it out because of its confinement to boroughs of society that were inherently understood to be destructive. With the aggressive progression of the so-called sexual revolution, one need now only turn on his computer or television in the privacy of his home to view about anything the mind can imagine.[25] The only area of the sex trade that most Western legal systems have declared off limits is the participation of children, and even that guideline was recently clouded when the U.S. Supreme Court shockingly ruled that virtual pornography depicting children could not be legally excluded from the marketplace.[26]

The Christian view of human sexuality is often misunderstood. The modern humanist, primarily because of Freud's influence, usually regards Christian-based views of human sexuality as destructively repressive. Much of that misunderstanding stems from the confusion between sexual desire and sexual lust. Understanding the differences between the two is crucial for understanding the scriptural teaching on the proper role of sex in human relationships. The humanist often wrongly equates the two terms. This position is no where more evident than in a viewpoint rendered by John Updike, which one editor entitled: *Lust is Not Immoral.* Updike wrote:

> Originally the word [lust] simply meant pleasure and then was modulated to signify desire and, specifically, sexual desire. How can sexual desire be a sin? Did not God instruct Adam and Eve to be fruitful and to multiply? Did He not say, having created woman from Adam's rib that "therefore shall a man leave his father and his mother, and shall cleave unto his wife: and they shall be one flesh"?[27]

Lust, however, is *not* simply sexual desire. Lust is *unlawful* desire and here we are referring to the law of God which, as we discussed in Chapter 2, is God's explicitly revealed desire for his human creation. Updike identified God's design for human sexuality when he quoted from Scripture. Because Updike presupposed that lust equates with sexual desire, he wrongly argued that lust is not immoral. Lust is immoral, but sexual desire, within the bounds that even Updike quotes from, is not. God did not tell man to leave his father and mother to cleave to as many sexual partners as possible. When one does that—and the one immersed in the sin of sexual lust often does just that—then sexual desire is operating in a mode of lust, and the fruit of that lifestyle always bears witness to its destructiveness.

In that same essay, Updike contrasted Presidential candidate Jimmy Carter's confession to having "committed adultery many times in [his] heart" to the incumbent Ford's response to a reporter's question who asked him how often he had sex. To that question Ford replied, "every chance I get." Updike cast Carter's statement as one that was out of step in modern times while Ford's answer was cast as a healthy post-Freudian response. But in reality, these two statements cannot be contrasted. Updike erred in that attempt because he has clouded the definition between lust and desire. Carter's confession dealt with the former and Ford's deals with the latter. Updike confused the two because, with the fall of Adam, unlawful sexual desire, which arises from lust, joined lawful sexual desire as a naturally occurring process. Both Carter's and Ford's statements demonstrate that naturalness. Carter's confession serves to reinforce the contention that man cannot of himself naturally will the moral good. Of course, the standard of perfection is to be so in love with one's spouse that the thought of adultery would never occur. But man's nature was so changed by Adam's sin that no man, in and of himself, can will that moral perfection. All of humanity is under Adam's curse and that curse is so strong that even those who have experienced the new birth through faith, as we spoke of in Chapter 2, have a tainted will. The Apostle Paul spoke of this in his letter to the Romans when he said, "For that which I am doing, I do not understand; for I am not practicing what I would like to do, but I am doing the very thing I hate."[28] But certainly, the one who has been reborn through the power of Christ's forgiveness gains a freedom of will that the natural man does not have. The one who has accepted God's provision for his sin will be empowered for victory over the temptation of sexual lust. Ford's response cannot be judged morally. If Ford's response would have had a Hugh Hefner mentality behind it, perhaps his response could be deemed immoral. But that is not presumably the case. President Ford appears to have been a man of good character and he likely had his beloved in mind when he responded to that clumsy question, the type for which modern Western reporters are notorious.

Updike attempted to assuage the gravity of his etymological error by linking the Roman Catholic definition of lust to a sexual desire that occurs even within the confines of marriage. Updike pointed out that *The Catholic Encyclopedia* defines even marital relations, which occur for the mere purpose of pleasure, as lustful. However, by this ploy Updike only lends credence to the fact that the medieval Scholastic reasoning from which such conclusions were derived were worthy of the Renaissance rebellion which that reasoning evoked. Whenever anyone attempts to construct morality apart from Scripture it is certain that he will err in those constructs. Scripture does not prohibit sex for pleasure within the confines of marriage. The *Song of Solomon* proves that sexual pleasure in the right context is noble and should therefore, if anything, be encouraged. The fact that one might err to the right instead of the left does not make it any less of an error. As we noted in Chapter 4, the Renaissance humanists were on target when they challenged Scholastic philosophy, but it took the courageous Reformers to finish the task the Renaissance humanists began.

In refusing to acknowledge the supremacy of Scripture, modern humanistic man has no means by which to judge the morality of human sexuality. With that rejection he is left to determine his standards of sexual behavior on the basis of conscience. Because sexual desire is a natural need, the conscience often falsely concludes that sexual desire is no different from hunger. If one is hungry one eats, the reasoning goes. Kant's *categorical imperative* cannot provide sufficient guidance in the area of sexual morality. The conscience is more easily seared in the area of human sexuality than it is in any other. Scripture speaks against sexual lust because it, like any other addictive behavior, destroys the minds, souls and bodies of those it overtakes. Scripture advises people to marry when their sexual desires become unmanageable, but it never condemns anyone simply for sexual desire.[29] However, a properly functioning conscience (i.e., one that is not seared) will always condemn sexual sin. While humanists often attempt to portray the Christian view of sexuality as one in which sexual desire is repressed, a more correct view is found in the knowledge that the new nature imparted by Christian faith results in a repression of harmful sexual lust. It is that transformation in human nature that leads to a societal norm of monogamous marriage, where each partner finds their sexual identity and fulfillment in the love and trust of the partner.

There is no doubt that sexual lust is being fueled by the proliferation of pornography and the extraneous sex trade which its presence always spawns. (This is actually a vicious cycle because it can also be stated with equal accuracy that pornography is fueled by lust.) The sin of pornography, and the wares associated with it, has invaded nearly all major metropolitan areas of Western civilization. Western society has acquiesced to pornography's presence because of humanistic arguments devised to soothe the seared Western conscience. Due to Freud's influence, some propose that pornography can free one of sexual dysfunction caused by irrational guilt. These claim that pornography can actually be beneficial to society. A reader recently wrote to the *Ask Dr.E* "question and answer" feature of *Psychology Today* magazine for advice on how she should respond to her sexually dysfunctional husband who was actively involved in pornography. Dr. E responded with the "reassuring" words from B.F. Skinner who "strongly recommended that pornographic materials be used to keep sexual interest alive."[30] Dr. E's answer obviously reflects the current humanistic standard of morality which shows no regard for the scriptural teaching of sexual purity. Dr. E certainly did not help that couple, since research has shown that pornography actually decreases sexual satisfaction in the intimate relationships of those who indulge in it.[31]

Others equate the freedom of political expression—which Western governments have usually attempted to guarantee—with the freedom to express oneself in anyway one might desire with no regard to moral purity. In the United States such proponents claim that trafficking in pornography is a civil right that falls under the First Amendment to the U.S. Constitution. But despite all of the so-called scientific studies in defense of pornography, a conscience that has not been seared will acknowledge its harmful effects and will avoid its influence. The Apostle Paul, in writing to the Corinthians who were noted for their struggle with sexual sin, mourned over those whose remained in their unrepented sin of "impurity, immorality and sensuality."[32] The legalization of pornography is yet another example of Western civilization's return to Sophistic standards of morality. The reader should recall from the first two chapters that in the Greek system of *nomos*, legislative action deciphered the moral standards by which Greek society functioned. Modern Western legislators have determined that the duty to guarantee its constituents the right to self-expression, no matter how lewd that expression might be, is of a greater importance than any question of morality that is associated with the sexual practices triggered by the pervading presence of pornography.

So what standard of human sexuality has the seared conscience of modern humanistic man established for himself? That standard is given quite succinctly by Seidman:

> A libertarian sexual ethic frames sex as having multiple meanings. Sex may be a medium of pleasure, love or procreation, and sex is said to be legitimate in multiple social settings. Individual choice and consent are considered the guiding norms sanctioning sexual expression. [33]

The modern norm or ethical criteria of the humanistic mind regarding sexual practices has become the willingness of the parties involved. About the only justifiable restraints in the mind of most humanists, are those that involve children.[34]

It is such reasoning that humanists use in their attempt to bring homosexual practice into legitimacy. The practice of homosexuality is another excellent example of why the conscience cannot function as a moral absolute. When human conscience becomes one's standard for the determination of that which is moral, it has little basis on which to condemn homosexuality. The modern humanistic norm, which states, "individual choice and consent are considered the guiding norms sanctioning sexual expression," is hard to refute purely on the basis of the conscience that has been divorced from Scripture. The conscience not influenced by the supernatural revelation of Scripture usually tells its beholder that what two people do in the privacy of their own home is not a moral issue. The one whose conscience is not influenced by Scripture often reasons that if no harm is being done to anyone outside of the freely chosen activity, then that activity is an amoral issue which is no one's business except the parties involved. Homosexuals often use that argument to appeal to the humanistic conscience of those outside of their lifestyle. Their arguments are becoming more and more persuasive to those who have no allegiance to the truth of Scripture. That this is true should be readily apparent to anyone who is following the trends in modern Western public opinion. For example, in a Harris poll of more than 2000 adult Americans conducted in June of 2002, only 34% of those polled opposed Social Security survivor benefits for same-sex couples.[35] That percentage will probably get even smaller in the coming years if America continues its movement towards secular humanism. If that trend continues, most American institutions will soon grant same-sex couples the benefits traditionally afforded to only the traditional family.

In a letter written to the editor of *The Akron Beacon Journal*, a homosexual challenged his readers with the following questions: "Who has the authority to tell me this is wrong? How can anyone be certain that God does not make gay people? Do they know God's Great Plan?"[36] Note how the questioner has cleverly phrased his questions with the words "authority" and "wrong." Anyone who does not subscribe to the truth of Scripture is at a loss to convincingly answer his questions. The writer further stated, "Opposition to recognition of sexual identity is driven by a few words in the Book of Romans." If the author could perceive that "God's Great Plan" can be known through the understanding of Scripture then he would know why his lifestyle is not part of God's plan for his life. However, in rejecting the authority of Scripture, which tells him succinctly in those "few words"[37] how his homosexuality ultimately originated, this author, and those like him, remain separated from their only source of salvation.

To bridge the subject matter of this chapter with the next, we will here consider the life of a particular American whose life by tragic example speaks volumes to the vanity and subsequent destruction which results from building one's philosophy on the humanistic pursuits of which this chapter deals. Furthermore, this example is particularly poignant because it shows firsthand the consequences of living according to Nietzsche's principle of exalting human volition over all else. As Woody Allen stated, "The heart wants what it wants"[38] and when it wants, as Mr. Allen would likely admit, it is more than willing to throw reason aside. While some might claim the following example to be a bizarre oddity, it nonetheless demonstrates what can ultimately become of anyone who seeks his sense of emotional fulfillment from any source, other than in a genuine faith in the God of Scripture.

Thomas Capano, the person of our example, was raised in a home of wealth and first generation position.[39] Thomas' father was the son of a stone mason who came to America as a child from Italy. The Capano family settled in Wilmington, Delaware, and it was there that Thomas was born and raised. His father, a carpenter by trade, worked hard and eventually got his piece of the American dream by making a fortune in real estate and construction. As were many first generation Italian Americans, the Capanos were faithful Catholics. Thomas was sent to a Catholic boys-only prep school where he excelled in both football and track. He was there elected president of the student council and was chosen as a delegate to Boys State. Running on the usual American fast track to success, he enrolled in Boston College and upon graduation attended the same college's law school. Thomas married and began to raise a family while his career as a lawyer began to blossom. As an attorney he eventually became a Delaware State prosecutor. From there he served as a Wilmington's city solicitor and that position was followed by a stint as Wilmington's Chief of Staff. He then he moved to chief counsel to the state's governor. After public service, Capano moved into a private law firm and was earning deep into six figures with total assets valued perhaps in the millions. As a former public servant and prestigious attorney, he was one of Wilmington's most influential people.

However, in spite of his social standing and regular church attendance, all was not well with Mr. Capano. While still married, he started an affair with a young secretary to the governor of Delaware. Without going into the lurid details, Mr. Capano eventually was convicted of her murder, triggered after she attempted to break off the relationship. Capano was so used to exacting his will over others that he could not handle the rejection. While he cleverly attempted to cover his sin, the police and prosecutor were even more clever, dogging the case until they had all the facts needed to successfully prosecute and convict him. Perhaps even more shocking was the discovery, during the course of the trial, of the depths to which Mr. Capano's sexual life had sunk. During the trial the secrets of his many perverted extra-marital sexual escapades became exposed. Furthermore, the extent to which he was willing to destroy the lives of those whom he professed to care about in his attempt to protect himself was flabbergasting. Mr. Capano now awaits execution for his sinful deed. One observing the life of Mr. Capano before his fall may have looked upon the circumstances of his life with envy. Here was what appeared to be a church-going, model citizen who seemed to have it all. He had wealth, position, power and relationships. But Tom Capano, in reality, was bankrupt. He had built his life on the humanistic principles of which this chapter is concerned. He had put his faith in himself and not in the God of Scripture. He was Christian on the outside but on the inside was "full of dead men's bones and of all uncleanness,"[40] and his inner-man became exposed for all to see. Ultimately, as it always does, the humanistic promise of a self-determined sovereign entity had fatally duped him.

It is because of man's will to do as he pleases, or because of his natural desire to make his being sovereign, that he is separated from the God of creation. That separation has resulted in the human drive to achieve a sense of emotional fulfillment along avenues which falsely promise to bring a sense of both security and pleasure without any true regard for God. But the inordinate pursuits of wealth and illicit sexual gratification will never satisfy the deepest desire of the human heart. And so the ultimate question that must be answered is:"Where does one turn to satisfy ones innermost longings if he cannot find it through his pursuit of wealth, position and sexual rela-tionships?" Once again, Augustine's words come screaming back "Thou hast formed us for Thyself, and our hearts are restless till they find rest in Thee." Genuine peace is only found in the knowledge that one has been reconciled to the God of creation, i.e., the God of Scripture and not the God of one's own creation. That reconciliation only comes through faith in the God-Man Jesus, the Son of the Everlasting God of Creation.

9

Modern Humanism and the Family

In matters of truth the fact that you don't want to publish something is, nine times out of ten, a proof that you ought to publish it.

G. K. Chesterton (1874-1936)

In this chapter we consider the influence of Western humanism on the family, that most basic social unit throughout the history of humanity. The best-formed human bonds abide in this social grouping. The phenomena observed in family relationships carry over, more amplified, into society in general. We are here concerned with the immediate nuclear family, defined as a cohabiting, monogamous male-female union and, generally, the offspring of that union.

Ever since the days of *Genesis*, humanism has adversely affected the family. Cain's desire to know God on his own terms constitutes the earliest example of humanism. His attempt to put his will paramount to God's will identified him with the humanistic position. However, Scripture is firm in its contention that God does not trade humanistic desires for His plan of atonement. Cain's desire to establish his own standard of morality cannot be divorced from the contempt he displayed towards his brother Abel.

Humanists always attempt to beat their own path to the moral good. As emphasized throughout this work, Western humanistic concepts of morality are based on the workings of human personality and a conscience divorced from Scripture. While Western humanistic man has traditionally exalted reason as the primary mechanism for arriving at the moral good, he is becoming increasingly prone to follow Nietzsche to the ideals of the ancient Greek Sophists. For the Sophists, man was the measure of all things. They believed in no moral absolutes but taught that every man should live according to only that which was individually perceived as right. However, no matter if reason is exalted over volition or vice versa, all systems of humanism attempt to arrive at the moral good through the dictates of human nature apart from the precepts of God's Word. Today Scripture is little used as a final authority for moral knowledge. But it is only through the supernaturally inspired pages of Scripture that the one and only true God can be known. Those who live divorced from its influence will suffer consequences in their relationships both within and outside of the family.

When Adam sinned his nature was changed such that it no longer communed with God but instead came under God's condemnation. Not only did Adam's sin result in a human race predisposed to run from God, but it also resulted in the predisposition to the human selfishness that even Freud, from his intensive study of human nature, was forced to acknowledge.[1] As Western culture becomes increasingly estranged from the God of Scripture, excessive preoccupation with self is, not surprisingly, becoming a primary characteristic of modern Western man. Self-filled nature estranges man not only from God, but also from his fellow human beings. Unfortunately, even family relationships are adversely affected by the unhealthy love of self so prevalent now within Western culture.

The narcissistic personality is birthed when one's preoccupation with self severely prevents him from effectively relating to others. The *DSM-III* of the American Psychiatric Association states that narcissists are characterized by a "grandiose sense of self-importance. They tend to exaggerate their accomplishments and talents and expect to be noticed as 'special' without appropriate achievement."[2] In regards to interpersonal relationships, the narcissist usually looks at truly successful people with envy and, more importantly for the purposes of our discussion here, he lacks empathy for others. The lack of feeling for others, because of preoccupation with self-image has become a primary characteristic of modern man. Modern Western man has become so concerned with satisfying his need for attention and admiration that he has lost the ability to truly care for others. It is not uncommon in modern relationships to treat one's acquaintances with an outward image of "kindness," while a sense of carelessness operates inwardly, a phenomenon much like C. S. Lewis described in *The Problem of Pain*.[3]

Narcissism and the culture that spawns it are well linked to the topic of the previous chapter. That the narcissistic personality is a product of the materialistic Western culture has been emphasized by Lowen, a psychiatrist specializing in its study.

> On the cultural level, narcissism can be seen in a loss of human values—in a lack of concern for ... one's fellow human beings. A society that sacrifices the natural environment for profit and power betrays its insensitivity to human needs. The proliferation of material things becomes the measure of progress in living, and man is pitted against woman, worker against employer, individual against com-

munity. When wealth occupies a higher position than wisdom, when notoriety is admired more than dignity, when success is more important than self-respect, the culture itself overvalues "image" and must be regarded as narcissistic.[4]

The emphasis in Western culture on achieving meaning and purpose through accumulation of financial gain renders it a breeding ground for the narcissistic personality. Lowen wrote that the narcissist "experiences life as empty and meaningless. It is a desolate state."[5] It is a desolate state because the narcissist finds himself alone when he discovers either the meaninglessness of fame, riches and sexual conquest, or worse, his failure to attain them after falsely perceiving them as his ultimate good.

Lowen's analyses does not come from a Christian perspective, but from his extensive exposure to the narcissistic personality. Lowen has acutely perceived the damning effects on human personality of a society whose moral values are out of kilter. The reader should note how, once again, the Sophistic ideal is portrayed in the emergence of a society dominated by secular humanism. The Sophists were more concerned with image than reality because they falsely believed that image determined reality. Western culture is truly in a backward spiral to the secular humanism from which the "enlightened" Greeks (Socrates, Plato and Aristotle) sought to free it.

An objective psychiatric study of Mr. Capano's personality, a subject of the previous chapter, would probably return a diagnosis of narcissism. Lowen's description appears to perfectly fit some of Capano's most notable character traits. Lowen tells us that the narcissist is

> ruthless, exploitative, sadistic, or destructive to another person because they are insensitive to the other's suffering or feeling. … They live by their wits and are identified with their ability to outsmart or outmaneuver others. That they lie or cheat is unimportant to the goal of winning or their ego image of superiority based on their ability to put one over on another person.[6]

Capano's actions would seem to render him worthy of all those adjectives.

The character trait, however, that is most important to the subject of this chapter, is the narcissist's inability to truly love others. When one cannot love, one cannot build effective human relationships. In the final analysis, this character trait condemned both Capano and Cain. It can be said with certainty that had Cain loved his brother, and likewise, if Mr. Capano had loved his family, neither would have committed the horrible deeds that destroyed their lives. It is modern man's inability to truly love—both God and man—that is a primary cause for the decline of the modern Western family and, therefore, of Western culture in general. A recent edition of *Parade* magazine featured an article by pop psychologist Dr. Joyce Brothers in which she outlined ten powerful guidelines on how to make a family strong.[7] Shockingly, in her ten keys to success the word love was not once mentioned. And yet it is genuine love that is the single most important element that is responsible for a strong and functional family.

On the Nature of Love

If one were to ask any segment of the populace to define love, one might get as many different answers as the number of people polled. Love is a multifaceted and difficult subject. Failure to understand the nature of love has contributed much to human failure and suffering. Some have claimed that love is more action than emotion, but even this clarification, while possessing an element of truth, is an oversimplification.

Genuine love has its origin in the God of Abraham, Isaac and Jacob. The Scripture teaches in I John 4 that God *is* Love. Thus, only those who know that same God can understand the purest form of this emotion. The despair of sin has created in man a void that only God's love can fill, but human sin alienates one from that love.

In his book *The Four Loves*, C. S. Lewis distinguished between two distinct motives for love. The first of these Lewis defined as gift-love. Gift-love motivates one to give of one's time, energy and wealth, i.e., of one's self, to the beloved. This is the love that is most perfectly exemplified in the love that God has manifested for his human creatures. The second motive, Lewis called need-love and stated that it is this love that "is the accurate reflection in consciousness of our actual nature."[8] True love, be it the love of human relationships or the supreme love between God and his creatures, must always be based on this need/give equation.

Until one identifies in his consciousness a need for God, to use the terminology of Lewis, he cannot attain in that consciousness the true reflection of his actual nature. We touched briefly on the humanist's misunderstanding of God's love for his created beings in Chapters 2 and 7. The humanistic mind cannot conceive of a loving God that would permit the destruction of his creation, because it fails to understand the extent to which Adam's sin affected human nature.[9] The condemnation of unredeemed man is a foregone conclusion because of Adam's sin. Adam chose for all his progeny their natural destiny and that choice is why the human need for God's love is so great. It is this reason that God so loved that He gave of himself.

The initiation to salvation is God's gift. Outside of Christ's intervention in human nature, nature will take its course and the curse of Adam will damn the one who remains centered in his sinful self.

The quest to understand the powerful emotion of love, apart from the God of Scripture, has been one of Western man's oldest endeavors. Plato's treatment of human love in his *Symposium*[10] is considered to be one of his premier works. And yet, as perceived from that early analysis of the subject, the ancient Greek understanding of love was faulty. Plato's concept of love was far removed from the Christian concept. In his *Republic*, Plato described what he believed should have constituted the ideal state (i.e., the ideal government). Here he proposed three classes of citizens with the guardians consisting of the educated elite. Plato prescribed the family arrangements for the guardians as follows:

> There's to be no such thing as private marriage between these women and these men [the guardians]: all the women are to be shared among all the men. And that the children are also to be shared, with no parent knowing which child is his, or child knowing his parent.[11]

Certainly Plato's concept of the ideal society was far removed from the Christian ideal. It is the noble emotion of love upon which the successful family is built and, likewise, it is its absence that is the primary cause of the family's demise.

The Love of Eros

After a genuine love of God, the love between a man and a woman is the most important relationship for building a successful family. It is these two loves from which much of the historical strength of Western culture has sprung. As in the love between God and humanity, a genuine love between a man and a woman must be based on the need-love/gift-love concept. Man and woman need each other. Man must give to woman and woman must give to man to produce that healthy and loving relationship upon which strong families are built. But outside of an understanding of God's love for his human creatures, the love upon which truly successful marriages are built cannot be understood.

The erotic love from which all marriages begin, as Lewis pointed out in his *Four Loves*, is not a fail-safe basis for a successful marriage. Though nearly all lovers in their early days of marriage believe that the love of Eros will satisfy their deepest longings, Lewis describes the illusionary reality of that belief:

To be in love is both to intend and to promise lifelong fidelity. Love makes vows unasked; can't be deterred from making them. "I will be ever true," are almost the first words he utters. Not hypocritically but sincerely. No experience will cure him of the delusion. We have all heard of people who are in love again every few years; each time sincerely convinced that "this time it's the real thing," that their wonderings are over, that they have found their true love and will themselves be true till death.[12]

And yet, as Lewis reminds his reader: "Can we be in this selfless liberation for a lifetime? Hardly for a week. Between the best possible lovers this high condition is intermittent."[13]

Dr. Gary Chapman, the Christian marriage counselor who authored the best seller *The Five Love Languages*,[14] dedicated the first chapter of his book to that inevitable waning of those first fires of marriage. Eros must be sustained through an internalization of the gift-love/need-love relationship. The focus of Chapman's book is his unique way of addressing that dynamic. If one, because of self, cannot give, then one cannot love. True love, of necessity by its very nature, must give. The main cause of a failing marriage, be it one where the partners remain together, or one where they part company, is the narcissistic self becoming dominant in one partner, or even worse, in both partners. In modern-day Western culture the inordinate love of self is so rampant that it has become a major problem in all relationships but particularly so in marriage. Marriage therapy is only successful when both partners become once again committed to giving to each other. Both partners have to understand the sin in the tendency to the narcissistic self and, from that knowledge, let go of self so that gift-love might be enabled.

The issue of fallen human nature cannot, therefore, be divorced from an effective treatment of a failing marriage. Truly successful marriages must be built on a Christian foundation. The ultimate fulfillment that Eros promises is not realized in the love of a mere person. Man's deepest longing stems from his need to be reconciled to his creator and no marriage partner can fulfill that desire. While the initial fires of Eros will eventually grow dimmer with the passing of time, a marriage that is built on the model of God's love will indeed grow stronger, because it is only then that one can selflessly give of oneself to one's partner.

A misconception that humanists often perpetrate stems from their failure to understand the differences in the male and female natures. Modern day political correctness insists in the "equality of the sexes," i.e., that men and women, because they are both human, have the same needs and bring to a marriage the same capabilities of giving. There is, of course, equality between the sexes in the fact that all people, independent of their gender, are individual human beings with each possessing unique personality. The Scriptures teach that in the eyes of God one's gender has nothing to do with worth.[15] However, when the male and female personalities are objectively contrasted, one does indeed find gender differences.

In her best-selling book: *You Just Don't Understand: Women and Men in Conversation,* Tannen shows that the male and female minds possess distinct innate differences as they relate to language and behaviors. Tannen wrote:

> The desire to affirm that women are equal has made some scholars reluctant to show they are different, because differences can be used to justify unequal treatment and opportunity. Much as I understand and am in sympathy with those who wish that there were no differences between woman and men—only reparable social injustice—my research, others' research, and my own and others' experience tell me it simply isn't so. There *are* gender differences in ways of speaking, and we need to identify and understand them.[16]

In addition to behavioral differences between the sexes are the obvious physical inequalities. A team of women football players could not be successfully fielded against the poorest American professional football team in existence, or for that matter, perhaps even an outstanding high school boys team. The natural physical differences between the sexes simply prohibit it. No amount of humanist or feminist rhetoric can change that fact. And while those natural physical differences do not contribute nearly as much to the need-give equation as they once did when cultures were becoming established, they nonetheless still come into play. Human strength yet plays a role in warfare and in certain aspects of economic development.

Radical feministic humanists often distort the reality of these naturally based gender differences. Mary Daly[17] has proposed that the proclivity of the male nature for fighting has rendered him as the inferior sex. She contends that the cause of war is thus due to the male nature. Daly wrote:

> Solanas points out that the male is basically disgusted with himself for not being female, (i.e., not having such qualities as emotional strength and independence, forcefulness, courage, integral vitality ... which he misnames "male"), and that one effect of this is War.[18]

Daly concluded: "Clearly, the basic paradigm and expression of the rigid societal structure and role definitions by which males attempt to cover their basic sense of emptiness is military. The military life provides 'meaning' and the needed injections of 'excitement.'"[19]

Daly fails to understand that war is a result of human nature and not maleness *per se*. Human beings fight because they want what they do not have. Wars are due to an aspect of human personality which both men and women have in common, i.e., the will. If it were not for the institution of law, all differences of will would be settled through physical power. When differences of will occur between sovereign states, a condition of lawlessness abides because the laws of either state are not honored by the opposing state. Such differences are settled through military might i.e., physical power. (These issues somewhat touch on the Greek debate between *nomos* and *physis* discussed in Chapters 1 and 2). To imply that the female nature will not fight for what she wants is to be ignorant of human nature. While she might be less willing to fight physically because of inferior physical strength she is yet willing to seek through struggle the means to satisfy her will. The will is a human trait. The male is better adapted to the exertion of will in the absence of law simply because of his greater physical strength. It is probable, however, that superior male physical strength is responsible for certain differences in the male psyche.

The inherent differences between male and female are not detrimental to the human experience, but are beneficial. To remain with the military homily, a justifiable war should depend on a moral issue, as was the case of American involvement in the Second World War. In a situation of lawlessness, the side in the moral right would best have physical power on its side. If Hitler had won WWII, the Jewish people might not today exist.[20] The Islamic militants of al-Qaeda, who are now plotting war against Western targets because of their hate of Western culture, are truly immoral; the most radical of them believe that Americans should die simply because they are Americans. This is the basis on which the World Trade Center, and the hundreds of people trapped inside, were destroyed in New York City on September 11, 2001. Feminists such as Daly who belittle the male nature, which is better adapted for war, should be thankful for the resolve of masculine strength which is being used to destroy those cells of terror. Furthermore, those feminists in the vein of Daly should remember that these same Islamic militants usually have low regard for women. Many of them believe that women should be kept ignorant and oppressed. A report from a human rights organization in Muslim Pakistan stated that in the year of 2002, nearly 500 women were murdered by family members for "sex outside of marriage, dating, talking to men, being raped or even cooking poorly."[21] If radical Islamists were to prevail in military conflict against their Western targets, the women of Western culture would certainly lose the benefits of Western law, historically influenced by Christian morality, which have given them many of the privileges they now enjoy in Western society.

This brief discussion of the inherent differences between the male and female natures does not equate to a judgment of worth, but it does imply that the God given roles between them is an important one. One of the great tragedies of humanism's dominance in modern Western culture is the disregard of this truth. Many Christian leaders have lost the courage to speak about it. Because the family is a working social unit, for proper functioning there must exist structural organization. Any organization that involves people must have a leadership structure. Scripture is clear in its contention that in the Christian family the husband is to assume that role. The modern humanistic ideal of an equal role of leadership shared between the husband and wife has no doubt contributed to the soaring divorce rates, and many other ills plaguing the modern family. Many people who deride the scriptural teaching of male leadership within the family structure do not consider the responsibly that is placed on the husband by that same authority. His supreme obligation is, first and foremost, to genuinely love his family. With the scriptural obligation of male authority in the Christian home comes a responsibility of selflessness, because supreme gift-love demands a true abandonment of self. A man's love for his family should be to the extent that he would sacrifice his own life for the life of his wife and children if a situation called for it, and the husband and father who truly loves his family would do just that. When love goes to that depth, it is a genuine love that is based upon the scriptural model of love, and the rendering of leadership to the husband under those conditions will be a joyful one.

The Issue of Abortion

An issue in Western culture that points to the failure of the human consciousness to know the moral good of its own accord is the issue of abortion. A brief discussion of the subject is included in this chapter because its practice usually has a direct bearing on the family; when it occurs, a potential member of some family is lost. However, I hope to show here that the moral issues revolving around abortion, from my understanding of Scripture, are not as clear cut as many, who are active in the Pro-Life movement, insist them to be.

I have emphasized throughout this work that Scripture must be the ultimate authority for knowing what is pleasing to God and that the human conscience (when divorced from Scripture), reason and will, i.e., the function of one's personality, cannot be relied upon as the primary means to knowledge of the moral absolute.

Boa and Bowman[22] recently reviewed the traditional conservative Christian approach to the subject of abortion. They promote the view that abortion is always morally wrong except in the case where the life of the mother is in jeopardy. The introduction of this exception is the implicit acknowledgment that the *act* of abortion is not *of itself* the moral evil. (The reader should stay with me here. I am not disagreeing with Boa and Bowman's injection of this exception to the practice of abortion but only pointing out that the conscience is determining morality if the immorality of this issue is determined to be in the *act* of abortion itself.)

In an earlier chapter of their book, Boa and Bowman discussed the source of absolute morality. In their well-written chapter entitled *The Graying of Morality*, they wrote:

> We need, then, a more direct and definitive expression of the moral law than can be gained from introspection or from a consideration of the world's great moral stories and maxims. In short, we need to hear from God himself. It is the Christian claim that God has in fact spoken, and that he has given us a definitive expression of the moral law in the Bible.[23]

Here the authors very succinctly identify the correct source for an absolute knowledge of what is acceptable and pleasing to God. As such, they must apply this standard to the issue of abortion. The Scriptures are complete for equipping one with knowledge of moral right and wrong. As the authors acknowledge, the Bible does not address the issue of abortion directly. The lack of direct mention of abortion in the Old Testament may be why, as they pointed out, that Jewish tradition has never been adamantly opposed to it. They write, "The rabbis were uncertain when the soul became joined to the body of a human being (conception, formation, and birth were all suggested), and no definite position was set forth in the Talmud."[24] Exodus 21:22-25 relates the premature loss of an infant to moral law, but this passage is concerned with accidental loss and not with intentional abortion. Likewise, the practice of abortion is not specifically addressed in the New Testament. It was practiced in the Greek cultures in which the apostles ministered, but, unlike the simple common lie, the apostles did not directly address the issue. I do not think that the inspired writers of Scripture inadvertently failed to address it. That the Scriptures do not speak directly to its practice is for a specific reason, and I think that that reason is because in some instances—as in when the life of the mother is at stake—abortion is not immoral. Therefore, the immorality of abortion must lie apart from the act itself.

Where then is the moral absolute in the issue of abortion? The moral absolute regarding abortion is in the sixth commandment where God specifically forbids murder. Murder, is the unlawful taking of life. Note that the taking of human life is not always murder. The taking of human life and murder are not the same. One who believes that they are the same is determining his morality from a conscience based in human reason, which is a primary characteristic of a humanistic philosophy. The immorality of abortion must lie in the issue of murder. Abortion must be declared wrong on the basis of it being a murderous act. Boa and Bowman wrongly attempt to create two categories for abortion, one an immoral category and the other a murderous category. They write, "Although testimonies to the Christian judgment of abortion as at least immoral and typically as murder are not wanting throughout church history, the subject came up rarely until modern times because abortion was quite rare."[25] This is a philosophically inconsistent position. If abortion is immoral it must be because it is a murderous act.

The Roman Catholic Church, of course, views absolutely any abortion for any reason as murder. This is a result of humanistic influence where the human conscience takes precedence over Scripture as the source of absolute moral truth. In speaking of the practice of abortion and contraception, Bonhoeffer[26] reminded his reader that the Catholic Church identified contraception with murder (Cat Rom., 2.8.13).[27] Today, the official Catholic position is somewhat different. Now the Church deems contraception as immoral but not as immoral as abortion. In his encyclical letter on abortion, euthanasia and the death penalty, Pope John Paul II stated:

> Certainly, from the moral point of view contraception and abortion are *specifically different* evils: the former contradicts the full truth of the sexual act as the proper expression of conjugal love, while the latter destroys the life of a human being; the former is opposed to the virtue of chastity in marriage, the latter is opposed to the virtue of justice and directly violates the divine commandment "You shall not kill".[28]

The Roman Catholic Church misappropriates the sixth commandment when it substitutes the word "kill" for the correct word "murder." Indeed the entire argument of Pope John Paul's letter is built on that misrendering of the Scripture. But the two words are not the same. It is for this reason that the Catholic views of capital punishment are wrong. Capital punishment is not murder. Likewise, the taking of life in war is not always immoral, as I pointed out earlier in this chapter. The Catholic Church's views of morality remain corrupt because, as shown in Part One of this work, its views of reality are yet largely influenced by a humanistic view of reality. Whenever one's views of human nature are based on a model that is incompatible with Scripture, that one will interpret reality within the framework of a humanistic model no matter what they might claim to believe about God. Bonhoeffer spoke correctly when he stated that "Luther's great discovery of the freedom of the Christian man and the Catholic heresy of the essential good in man combined to produce the deification of man."[29, 30]

So when, one might ask, is abortion murder and when is it not? In most cases I believe that abortion fits into that category. However, in my opinion, the innocent young woman who is raped at gunpoint by a vile, dirty and despicable criminal who finds herself pregnant and decides to immediately abort the pregnancy should not be judged as an immoral murderer. And those who think that that scenario is unlikely are not too knowledgeable about the current state of affairs in modern society. These things happen on a more regular basis than what one might wish to believe.[31] Christians who would be quick to point the finger of shame at such a young lady would best look at their own purposes for making the Pro-Life movement their main concern. The bulk of abortions today are happening among young women who need to know of the saving love of Jesus. When people truly find their reason for living in the love and mercy of Christ Jesus, they will neither need, nor want, to resort to abortion.

With that said, certainly the rampant practice of abortion does reflect a society that has long abandoned the God of Scripture. It is indeed a shame to a people where the rights of animals are more heralded than the rights of the unborn. I have witnessed numerous news broadcasts where a person is shown being led off in handcuffs, on his way to jail for kicking a dog or killing a cat, yet a doctor can crush the skull of a fully viable infant and barely have an eyebrow raised. We truly live in a culture that has lost its sense of morality. However, those who think that the Pro-Life movement is all about morality need to remember some of the atrocious crimes that have been committed in the name of that cause. The Pro-Life movement is not entirely about morality. Some of it has its roots in pure political power. There is danger in always joining forces with those who might agree on a given moral issue but who might be coming to that issue from a different philosophical perspective. The issue of abortion, in my opinion, is one of those issues where the genuine Christian must seek much wisdom on how to face this growing problem.

The Effect of Humanism on Philosophies of Child Rearing

An indicator of humanism's current dominance within modern West-ern culture is the success that humanistic sociologists and psychologists (and even some theologians as we will later see) are having in changing the per-ceptions of what constitutes effective parenting. There is a growing ten-dency in Western culture to associate any form of corporal punishment with child abuse. Swedish law now forbids the use of corporal punishment in child disciplinary practice. In societies where it is yet permitted, a miscue by a well meaning parent that might leave any mark on the child's body can be cause for arrest. The push for exclusion of all corporal punishment is osten-sibly, of course, for the elimination of physical child abuse. However, the ultimate contention between those who would ban corporal punishment in child rearing and the Christian proponents who back its responsible use, is in their respective views of human nature. To distinguish genuine child abuse from responsible and loving corporal punishment should not require any unusual skills of discernment.

One physician arguing for the complete abolishment of corporal pun-ishment stated that "We need to help parents give up the notion that chil-dren are inherently evil and need to be beaten."[32] This statement shows his lack of understanding of the Christian view of human nature and discipline. Such statements misrepresent the Christian position of child rearing be-cause if a child is punished such that the verb "beaten," in its modern sense applies to that punishment, then any sane person would concur that such punishment is wrong. Proverbs 23:13-14 reads:

Do not hold back discipline from the child/Although
you beat him with the rod, he will not die/You shall beat
him with the rod/And deliver his soul form Sheol.[33]

If one has a problem with the wording of this passage, instead of dis-carding the principle of discipline rendered here, one should turn to a mod-ern translation of Scripture where the same thought is conveyed by substi-tuting the word punish for beat. A Christian parent who uses corporal pun-ishment properly is not beating the child in the modern sense of the word. Furthermore, the use of corporal punishment would not be called for if the child were not truly doing wrong. This physician's statement reflects his failure to understand that wrong and evil are synonymous. All of us do wrong. Every man since Adam has had that propensity.

The humanist's exultation of self facilitates the view that strict corporal punishment creates an avenue for injuring the concept of self that he so reveres. The humanist sees self as an essentially good entity which is empow-ered to determine for itself, apart from the knowledge of the one and only true God, the essence of morality. The humanist refuses to acknowledge the words of Scripture that states in no uncertain terms that the intent of man's heart is evil from his youth.[34] The genuine Christian parent, whose philosophical roots are in Scripture, knows that in certain instances, where the will remains bent of wrongdoing, corporal punishment is the most effective way to guide the child's nature towards godly change.

Dr. James Dobson, the noted Christian psychologist, has emphasized that even the toddler can be destructively bent on self.

A defiant toddler can become so angry that he is capable of holding his breath until he loses consciousness. Anyone who has ever witnessed this full measure of willful defiance has been shocked by its power. … Why have so few child development authorities recognized this willful defiance? Why have they written so little about it? My guess is that the acknowledgement of childish imperfection would not fit neatly with the humanistic notion that little people are infused with sunshine and goodness, and merely "learn" the meaning of evil.[35]

In his book entitled *The Heart of Parenting: Raising an Emotionally Intelligent Child*, John Gottman shows himself to be a representative of that philosophy to which Dobson here refers. In that book Gottman referred to a particular social psychologist whose observations in the 1930s "showed that most small children are, by nature, primarily altruistic and empathetic toward one another, particularly toward another child in distress."[36] Gottman used this conclusion to justify his own observation, "With this growing belief in the intrinsic goodness of children, our society has been evolving since mid-century into another new era of parenting."[37]

The conclusion of social scientists, that children are intrinsically good, lends credence to the inference from Chapter 2 that the social sciences are not equipped for the objective study of human nature because they cannot take into account the spiritual nature of man. One cannot accurately conclude from a psychologist's observation of children over a period of a few hours that human nature is intrinsically good. The Scriptures teach that outward appearances do not always correspond to the inward condition of the human heart.[38] There is no reason why this truth would not apply to children.

The story is told about a young mother who was preparing pancakes for her two sons, Kevin, 5, and Ryan, 3. The boys began to argue over who would get the first pancake. Their mother, seeing the opportunity for a moral lesson, stated, "Boys, if Jesus were sitting here, He would say, 'Let my brother have the first pancake, I can wait.'" Kevin turned to his younger brother and said, "Ryan, you be Jesus!" While Kevin's cleverness might provoke a smile from the reader, the story nonetheless shows just how even a young child can be bent to the selfishness that, if left unchecked, can result in the birth of the destructive narcissistic personality. Children cannot be engineered into emotionally healthy and morally upright people simply through a humanistic understanding and manipulation of human nature.

Social scientists sometimes reduce complex social phenomena into simple scenarios by compartmentalizing behaviors into major groupings. While this strategy makes it convenient to label certain behaviors, it prevents taking into account the many intricacies of the particulars within that broad grouping. Whether parents who use corporal punishment realize it or not, many social scientists have put them into a category that classifies them as detrimental to society. In 1971, Baumbrind published a study entitled *Current Patterns of Parental Authority*[39] where she outlined three categories of parenting which have become somewhat of a standard for categorizing parental disciplinary behaviors. These categories are permissive, authoritarian, and authoritative. While the last two categories, at first glance, might appear to be similar, they are, in the mind of the social scientist, as different as night is from day. If you are someone who subscribes to spanking your child you have been labeled by some social scientists as authoritarian which means that you tend to show little emotional warmth and that you lack the appropriate skills to respond to your child's emotional needs. On the other hand, if you are an authoritative parent you refrain from corporal punishment and are "considerably more flexible," providing your "children with explanations and lots of warmth."[40]

As I mentioned in Chapter 2, I doubt if any social scientist could have predicted the outcome of Jeffery Dahmer's life from any outward "clinical" observation throughout any of his formative years, either of him or his parents. Even if an in-depth psychological analysis of Dahmer's mind may have shown problems, humanistic psychology would not have been able to truly address his sickness. Dahmer's problems were internal and spiritual in nature. Obviously he put out few external signs as to the depths of depravity to which he would sink. Dahmer would probably have appeared very normal if he had been "scientifically observed" in a social setting during any part of his life. Social scientists are limited in their ability to understand human nature because they want so much to apply the scientific method to their studies, so as to give them an air of legitimacy, that they are forced to ignore the spiritual nature of man. Science is only equipped to study pure physical reality, and that limitation severely restricts the knowledge that can be gathered on the true nature of man.

A scripturally based knowledge of human nature recognizes that even for someone as vile as Dahmer there is hope for genuine healing and forgiveness. When anyone acknowledges his sin, no matter to what degree it may be present, then that one can be put on the road to true healing. There is some indication that Dahmer came to that point before his death. How ironic that Jeffery Dahmer may today be whole with Jesus Christ while innumerable people who hold to their humanistic philosophies of life and, who ostensibly have upstanding positions within their communities, will have to endure those horrible words "I never knew you; Depart from Me,"[41] simply because they could not acknowledge and seek Christ's forgiveness for their sin. The Scripture is plain in its contention that every person comes into the world already on the road to spiritual death.

The humanistic doctrine that pronounces man as basically good obviates one's sense of his need for God. All people inherently have that need, whether they acknowledge it or not. The Christian approach to child rearing and discipline is to enable the child to understand that the road he is naturally on will one day condemn his soul, or his true self. It is to help him come to a realization that he desperately needs the God of Scripture for forgiveness of his sin. A life that is characterized by true success is always, first and foremost, based upon a relationship with the God of Scripture and that relationship cannot develop unless one first becomes aware of his need.

In the next chapter we look at how both modern Judaism and a Christianity that is becoming increasingly divorced from Scripture have moved Western culture to humanistic ideals. As a bridge to that chapter, we here examine a humanistic philosophy of child rearing that, while falling under the guise of Christianity, is actually undermining a true biblical approach to that subject. In 1991, Professor Capps of Princeton Theological Seminary, delivered a presidential address to the Society for the Scientific Study of Religion entitled *Religion and Child Abuse: Perfect Together.*[42] In that address he made a link between the Proverbial[43] motives for Christian support of corporal punishment in child rearing with the ominous act of child abuse. This is a particularly sinister correlation because true child abuse is, and should be, a criminal offense. To lend credence to his argument Capps used two quotes from Frady's biography[44] of Billy Graham. Frady rendered an episode that occurred between Billy and his father that ended with his father sustaining two broken ribs from Billy's kicks of resistance. Capps used this illustration because it obviously points to a breakdown in the effective use of corporal punishment. If a child has enough strength to fight back to that extent, he is obviously past an acceptable age for such punishment. Capps also presented a quote from Billy's mother where she was apologetic for the severity of the discipline of their children. So Capps presented an example from the life of a highly visible evangelist where perhaps the discipline was less than ideal. To that, one should say, so what? Are we to use an example of human imperfection and throw away the scriptural injunction to effective child rearing? Has Capps totally overlooked the fruit of Graham's life? His parents must have done something right. I dare say that Graham would not today scorn the discipline that he received at his parent's hands. I am sure that nearly every person can relate to at least one incident where his or her parents were less than perfect in their handling of a disciplinary problem. Are Christian parents who want to model their disciplinary methods from the precepts of Scripture sinless and perfect? I do not think so. But to correct a problem of sin with more sin is not the answer. Anyone who rejects the inspired words of Proverbs is doing just that. This is a perfect example of a humanistic determination of morality from the precepts of one's own reasoning and conscience.

But even more disturbing in this same address is Capps' inference that belief in the virgin birth of Christ can cause people to trivialize childhood trauma. Capps writes:

> The possibility that … Jesus might have had a human father, is rarely mentioned or discussed among Christian adults. While this idea might also be one that is inherently tormenting for children, I would rather draw attention to the fact that this idea legitimates adults' emotional detachment from the pain and distress that children experience; it encourages them to treat their own experience of childhood trauma as insignificant or as never having happened.[45]

Capps puts forth the proposition that Jesus suffered as a child because he was born illegitimately. Capps states, "Jesus surely became aware of the fact of his illegitimacy and began to suffer its consequences on an everyday basis."[46] Capps reasoned that people who believe the scriptural teaching of Jesus' virgin birth are responsible for callousness towards children who have been traumatized. By believing wrongly that Jesus was virgin born, he reasons, they fail to acknowledge Jesus' suffering because of his illegitimacy. That prevents them from viewing Jesus as a sympathetic figure to those who likewise have undergone abuse.

Capps was correct in one aspect of his contention. The majority in political power in Jewish society during Jesus' ministry probably believed that He was illegitimate. The Apostle John gives us that indication in the following contentious dialogue between Jesus and the Pharisees.

Jesus: I know that you are Abraham's offspring; yet you seek to kill Me, because My word has no place in you. I speak the things which I have seen with My Father; therefore you also do the things which you heard from your father.

Pharisees: Abraham is our father.

Jesus: If you are Abraham's children, do the deeds of Abraham. But as it is, you are seeking to kill Me, a man who has told you the truth, which I heard from God; this Abraham did not do. You are doing the deeds of your father.

Pharisees: We were not born of fornication.[47]

This dialogue was indeed confrontational as one familiar with this passage knows. It ended with an attempt on Jesus' life. When Jesus referred to the Pharisee's father, the Pharisees knew that He was accusing them of being in league with the evil one, Satan (See verse 44 of John 8). The Pharisee's comeback, paraphrased in a modern context, perhaps reveals better the psychology that motivated it. Their internal attitude was probably along the lines, "Don't *you* accuse *us* of having an illegitimate father, *you* are the one who was born of fornication." But while most of the Jewish leaders believed in his illegitimacy, Jesus knew who His Father was. Jesus did not suffer emotionally because of any knowledge of illegitimacy. If anything, He suffered from knowing that those who thought that He was illegitimate, did not truly know Him. One can almost hear the pain of that rejection in his words to that same people, "O Jerusalem, Jerusalem, who kills the prophets and stones those who are sent to her! How often I wanted to gather your children together, the way a hen gathers her chicks under her wings, and you were unwilling."[48] And this is exactly why Jesus is able to sympathize with the victim of any type child abuse. Often a victim of child abuse suffers because he knows that others have judged him falsely. With that suffering Jesus can truly identify and therefore sympathize. So Professor Capps has it wrong. The ones who have put their faith in the Jesus of Scripture, the Jesus who indeed was born of a virgin, will not propagate any form of child abuse, because they, like their master was, will be a true friend to children.

10

Modern Humanism and Religion

It is not because the truth is too difficult to see that we make mistakes. It may even lie on the surface;
but we make mistakes because the easiest and most comfortable course for us is to seek insight where it
accords with our emotions-especially selfish ones.
Alexander Solzhenitsyn (1918-   )

Humanistic philosophy is not in the sole domain of the atheistic worldview, but its determining characteristic is in its inference that moral good can be arrived at from within the confines of human nature, apart from the revelation of Scripture. The atheistic teachings of the ancient Greek Sophists and the non-secular teachings of Socrates, Plato and Aristotle were all fundamentally humanistic, because in them was the belief that movement to the moral good came solely from within the functioning of human personality.

As I stressed in Chapter 7, the ultimate aim of humanism is to a secular extreme, where the existence of the supernatural is denied. While Western culture may be witnessing a growth in secular humanism, atheism is nonetheless not self-sustaining, as the deterioration of communistic societies is proving. As Calvin taught, the fact of God's existence is so indelibly woven into the fabric of the human consciousness that even the most tenacious attempts to erase its traces have always failed. Atheistic systems of thought breed a hopelessness and disillusionment that eventually give rise to a quest for spirituality. The atheism of modern Western culture, spawned by the belief that all reality is within the domain of science, will eventually give way to non-secular thinking in the same way that the secular humanism of the ancient Greek Sophists did centuries earlier. Unfortunately, however, the bankruptcy of atheism that often drives the human quest for spiritual knowledge does not always lead to the God of Scripture. Man's natural tendency, because of the severity of Adam's sin, is not towards the moral good, the one true God, but is towards the exultation of self.

Therefore, while humanistic influences in modern Western culture are often aligned with atheistic viewpoints, the preponderance of humanistic thought comes from within a perspective of monotheism. Although one might readily perceive the humanistic characteristic of secular atheistic thought, it is more challenging to understand how religiously clothed ideas, particularly those coming from the Judeo-Christian heritage, can be fundamentally humanistic in nature.

That man's inclination is away from the one true God is apparent in modern-day Judaism where the basic thought processes that were responsible for the Jew's rejection of their Messiah two thousand years ago remain operational today. In this chapter we first examine some of the ideas espoused by two different voices in modern Judaism and show that, in spite of the fact that Judaism had its origin in the one true God, Judaism must yet today be regarded as a humanistic system of morality.

After discussing modern Judaism, I briefly discuss the humanism of Dr. Wayne W. Dyer, a psychologist whose books and lectures have become popular in recent years. While Dr. Dyer's teachings are clothed in a language of God and spirituality, they reveal a humanistic philosophy that is in opposition to the God of Scripture. Dr. Dyer's philosophy, in my opinion, is leading many people to false perceptions of God and morality.

Finally, perhaps the greatest evidence for the fact that the human inclination is away from the God of Scripture is apparent in the trends of modern Christianity. We here consider why the issue of homosexuality provides an excellent barometer for judging the extent to which humanism has penetrated modern Christianity. I then conclude with a discussion of two examples of teaching that have recently appeared in the conservative Christian community. Here I show how these teachings have the potential to lead to the same thought processes that have shaped the humanistic views of human nature that are now prevalent within Judaism, Catholicism and most of the liberal Protestant Christian denominations.

The Humanism of Modern Judaism

Perhaps no book better characterizes the humanistic philosophy that lies buried within modern-day Judaism than that of Rabbi Harold S. Kushner's *How Good Do We Have to Be?* : *A New Understanding of Guilt and Forgiveness*. Kushner's approach to guilt and forgiveness is not, however, new. His thinking is simply a humanistic philosophy that is wrapped in a cloak of religion. Kushner maintains that since we all are imperfect, God does not expect sinlessness or perfection. In Kushner's view, personal hang-ups result from believing that one is separated from God's love because of one's sin. Kushner teaches that a person is worthy of God's love and grace even though he sins. Unfortunately, Kushner believes that Adam's disobedience was not responsible for man's separation from God but was only responsible for the "Birth of Conscience."[1] In regards to Adam's disobedience, Kushner stated, "I don't believe that eating from the Tree of Knowledge was sinful. I believe it was one of the bravest and most liberating events in the history of the human race."[2] Kushner's words are damning because he promises hope to the sinner where there is none. No person will get to God without utilizing God's provision for sin's atonement. Based on the authority of Scripture, Kushner's statement that "We need to be told that God loves us because we are in fact lovable people, because we deserve love, because we have earned it"[3] is simply false. God's love for the sinner is real, but one must come to God on God's terms. When one rejects God's provision for the atonement of his sin, then no means exist to atone for sin.

While certainly God's love for all people is infinite, all, in their natural condition, have rejected that love and have proven to be unworthy of it. The Scripture teaches that "God so loved" that He sent Jesus, "His only begotton son," so that whoever believes that Jesus has atoned for his sin will not "perish, but will have eternal life."[4] That is the only way to the grace of God. Without the grace which comes to one through *that* faith there is no hope for human redemption. Just as Abraham was saved by faith in God's word, so today, one's sins are atoned for by believing that Jesus was God's son who was sent to atone for those sins. In commenting on Abraham's offering of Isaac, Kushner confides that this biblical story always bothered him.[5] Kushner called God's demand of Abraham "outrageous" and stated that he only came to terms with it when he realized, through the teachings of a particular physician, that Isaac was probably a retarded child since people from that era often sacrificed their imperfect children to the gods. Kushner fails to see both the significance of Abraham's faith and the fact that a true faith demands the abandonment of one's selfish sinful will. The Scriptures teach that Abraham believed God, and because of that faith, God imputed righteousness to him. In refusing to believe God's Word, *(Jesus was God's Word, because he was God)*, all those in the vein of Kushner are cut off from the God in whom they claim to worship.

The fact that Kushner's understanding of morality remains inconsistent with Scripture is further illustrated in his interpretation of the nineteenth chapter of *Numbers*. Here God required the sinner to purify himself by sacrificing a "perfect" red heifer. Kushner claims that this is proof that God does not expect perfection because the "perfect" animal is "slaughtered to make the point that perfection has no place in this world."[6] Certainly,

Kushner has missed the point of the perfect sacrifice. While God knows full well that no mere person can be perfect, could it be anymore apparent that God requires a perfect sacrifice to atone for sin?

Although Kushner's Judaism is not congruous with the secular humanism which views human nature apart from the concept of sin, it is yet a humanism that is based in a false perception of human nature. In the final pages of his book Kushner identifies the difference between a biblical perspective of human nature and his humanistic perspective. In relating a discussion between him and a Christian friend in which they focused on their "theological differences," Kushner states that their differences were primarily in the doctrine of human depravity.[7] This is always a major parting point between a genuine biblical worldview and a humanistic one. The scriptural teaching on human depravity clearly holds that man, in his natural condition, is incapacitated in his ability to move himself to the moral good. While Kushner has obviously owned up to human imperfection, he wrongly suggests that man, within the functioning of his own capabilities, can achieve the goodness required by God. According to Kushner, the fact that most people (psychopaths excepted) are troubled by their wrongdoing and therefore seek to atone for it, proves that people are basically good, even though they occasionally sin. Kusher's reasoning implies that one can atone for one's own sin. However, there is only one way for which sin can be atoned, and Kushner rejects that means.

Similar to the Judaism of Kushner is that of Dennis Prager. Prager is a Jewish moralist who has, in the last two decades, become a popular author and radio talk show host. His mission, in his own words, is "to get people obsessed with what's right and wrong."[8,9] While Kushner believes that all people sin, he views man as basically good. Prager, however, believes that the traditional humanistic view that man is basically good is in error. While Prager's thinking is closer to a biblical doctrine of human nature, it falls short because he believes that a person, in the strength of his own personality, can make himself acceptable to God through his own effort and ability to obey God's law. This view goes against scriptural teaching since inherent in the scriptural view of human nature is the understanding that one cannot, in the power of one's own personality (i.e., one's own nature) change that nature.

In late 1995, a nationally broadcasted call-in radio program[10] featured a cordial dialogue on ethics between a Christian broadcaster and Prager. In response to a caller who asked Prager about the *Psalm* reference to the *absence* of moral good in the natural human condition,[11] Prager asked the caller to tell him "how Noah was called a righteous man?" Prager was obviously implying that here existed an example of one acknowledged by God as a righteous person and therefore was a prime example of one who had made himself into a good person. The caller rightfully responded by saying that he supposed that Noah was righteous on the basis of his faith. Noah was not sinless; his sin is well documented. Noah's righteousness was obviously not one based upon his own goodness but one *imputed* to him because of the faith that he had placed in God's word. God had told Noah that the earth would be destroyed and told him how to escape the coming destruction. Just as Abraham did, Noah believed God and acted on his belief, even in the midst of overwhelming ridicule.

Prager, like Kushner, simply does not understand that the mechanism for salvation is imputed righteousness because of *faith* that one places in God's word. Prager fails to understand that Jesus was God's Word and by rejecting Him as God's Word he has demonstrated a lack of faith in the God he claims to believe in. Both Abraham and Noah had righteousness imputed to them because of their faith in God's word.

In his book, *Think a Second Time*, Prager presents a chapter entitled *Headlines I Would Like to See*. His first on the list is: *Jerry Falwell Declares That All Good People Can Attain Salvation.* Prager constructed the hypothetical news article to read:

> The Reverend Jerry Falwell announced here yesterday that the Lord had communicated with him, telling him that the Fundamentalist Protestant belief that salvation is attainable only by those who affirm a specific belief in Jesus Christ is mistaken. ... Reactions to the Reverend Falwell's announcement were immediate and mixed. Some Protestant ministers declared Falwell a "heretic," while others said that prayerful consideration should be given the reverend's communication from above. Catholic bishops welcomed the call, as they have been preaching for some time that salvation is open to all individuals who follow their consciences in obedience to God's will. And Jews were especially delighted.[12]

If such a headline were to occur, anyone with a proper understanding of Scripture would certainly pronounce Falwell's new teaching as wrong. God has plainly communicated on this subject and the message is clear. It is ironic that Jesus spoke directly to the Jews who then believed as Prager believes today. Consider Jesus' words:

> The works which the Father has given Me to accomplish, the very works that I do, bear witness of Me, that the Father has sent Me. And the Father who sent Me, He has borne witness of Me. You have neither heard His voice at

any time, nor seen His form. And you do not have His word abiding in you, for you do not believe Him whom He sent. You search the Scriptures, because you think that in them you have eternal life; and it is these that bear witness of Me; and you are unwilling to come to Me, that you may have life. I do not receive glory from men; but I know you, that you do not have the love of God in yourselves. I have come in My Father's name, and you do not receive Me; if another shall come in his own name, you will receive him. How can you believe, when you receive glory from one another, and you do not seek the glory that is from the one and only God? Do not think that I will accuse you before the Father; the one who accuses you is Moses, in whom you have set your hope. For if you believed Moses, you would believe Me; for he wrote of Me. But if you do not believe his writings, how will you believe My words?[13]

Both Kushner and Prager fail to realize the purpose for which God gave the law. The law was given to show the extent to which sin affected human ability to freely choose the moral Good. Human nature was so damaged from Adam's disobedience that no one can change himself through his own determination to please God. Human nature must *be changed* to become acceptable to God and the attempt to follow God's law, in the strength of one's own willpower, cannot accomplish it. C. S. Lewis taught this in the opening chapters of his renowned *Mere Christianity*, where he stressed that not even the law that is naturally written on the human conscience can be obeyed in its purest sense. Therefore, as I wrote in Chapter 2, the righteousness required by God for reconciliation unto Himself cannot be gained through the function of human will alone. Righteousness is imputed to the believer because of his faith in the God of Scripture. Modern Judaism ignores the fact that it was Abraham's *faith in God's Word* that produced his justification and *not* his "doing."

The Humanism of Dr. Wayne Dyer

While a plethora of books by Dr. Dyer are in the marketplace, a brief comment regarding his *Manifest Your Destiny: The Nine Spiritual Principles for Getting Everything You Want* will suffice to point out the essence of the humanism behind his teaching. Dyer's appearances on the PBS television

215

network has in recent years made him popular, especially among the educated who seek meaning and purpose in a culture where the emptiness of secular humanism is ever growing.

Dyer is not adverse to using an occasional verse of Scripture to support his views, but a careful perusal of those instances show them to always be taken out of context. For example, he begins *Manifest* with John 10:34. . . "Is it not written in your law, 'I have said, you are gods?'" and John 14: 20, "On that day, you will know that I am in my Father, and you in me, and I in you." Dyer uses these words from the Scripture to support his contention that God and man are one in essence.

I have emphasized throughout this book that the humanist, no matter what he claims to believe about God, always fails to understand how human sin has separated humanity from the one and only true God manifested in Scripture. Until one can understand this truth, one cannot gain a true knowledge of God. In *Manifest Your Destiny,* Dyer's first principle is *Becoming Aware of Your Highest Self.* Dyer states, "With the realization of God within yourself, you not only dissolve your ego's identification as separate from God, but you leave behind the old ways of seeing yourself."[14] Dyer encourages his readers to view themselves as trustworthy because of their divine natures. Dyer states that when people believe that they are not in charge of their lives, but believe that a transcendent God is in charge, that view prevents them from materializing what they desire. Dyer thus encourages his reader to, "trust that the vital force of the universe is exactly what you are."[15] Dyer wants his readers to view themselves as one in essence with God.

However, before anyone can experience the power of God, one must be reconciled to Him through the forgiveness of sin. Therefore, when anyone speaks of knowing God in a life changing way, unless the sin problem, which every person possesses, is dealt with—and God has provided only one solution to that problem—then that one is speaking falsely. The prophet Isaiah wrote,

> But your iniquities have made a separation between you and your God/And your sins have hid His face from you so that He does not hear. For your hands are defiled with blood/And your fingers with iniquity/Your lips have spoken falsehood/Your tongue mutters wickedness.[16]

Homosexuality and Religion

The issue of homosexuality in modern Western society is a topic that is particularly appropriate to the subject of humanism and religion because wherever its practice is dismissed as a serious moral issue, either in word or deed, a dominant humanistic influence is present.

The humanist usually does not view homosexuality as a moral issue. Often he openly approves of its practice or, perhaps more often, is indifferent to it. As I stated in Chapter 2, because of conscience's power, many behavioral standards which are upheld by people of all creeds are congruous with scriptural standards of behavior. Theft and murder are two obvious examples. However, the secular humanist does not view theft or murder as morally wrong because God has decreed them as such. The humanist sees these as wrong because he has a personal interest in their prohibition. No one wants to die at the hands of his neighbor and most people, no matter what their philosophical persuasion, do not want to lose their material possessions to a thief. But the issue of homosexuality is different because the humanistic mind often does not view this practice as wrong, since his conscience does not convince him that its practice, by others, is harmful to himself.

The Scriptures teach that homosexuality is a perverse desire that God has allowed to overtake peoples who have intentionally turned away from Himself. The avowed secular homosexual might attempt to prove this statement erroneous by arguing that he was never a believer in the "God of Scripture." However, such reasoning would only demonstrate his failure to understand that human nature is somewhat a function of that which has come before. One inherits human nature from parents, and parents inherit human nature from their parents, etc. This fact is ultimately, of course, why all human nature is traced to the first parents of the human race. While one may be the first with distinct homosexual nature to appear in a particular family line, that nature has ultimately arisen because it has proceeded from a nature that has become progressively divorced from the God of Scripture. All have inherited a nature that separates them from God. But it would appear, based on the teaching of Scripture, that as people stray farther and farther from the one true God, there are greater repercussions in the human nature that is passed from generation to generation. So when the homosexual proclaims that he cannot help himself because he was born that way, there is a certain degree of truth to that statement. Although all people come into this world with a propensity to sin, it can probably be argued that some people possess a greater propensity to certain types of sin than do others because of what has come before them. It is well known that the offspring of an alcoholic is more likely to become an alcoholic than is one with no family history of alcoholism.

But inherited nature does not excuse anyone from acknowledging his sin and turning from it. Jesus came to give new nature to anyone who will confess his sin and put his faith in the God of Scripture for new life. As stressed throughout this book, *all* that belong to Christ have had to come to an understanding that the nature they brought with them into the world condemns them before God. This is precisely why Jesus told Nicodemus, 'You must be born again.' Jesus stated that the one who does not believe in Him is already condemned or already judged.[17] Condemnation comes with birth. All people, homosexual or not, need to acknowledge Jesus' admonition to spiritual birth.

Whenever the sin of homosexuality becomes prominent—the direction that modern Western culture certainly appears to be heading—it is always a reflection of a society that has become dominated by humanism. The Scriptures teach that God gives the mind and conscience "over to degrading passions" as a result of man's failure to honor him as God. A people that have been so "given up" become characterized by the sins of greed, malice, envy, murder, strife, deceit, gossiping, slander, insolence, arrogance, boastfulness, disobedience, a lack of understanding, untrustworthiness, and unloving-unmerciful spirits.[18] Personalities in Western culture appear to be headed more resolutely toward natures describable by these narcissistic character traits.

In Chapter 3, I pointed out that Scholastic thought, highly influenced by the Greek humanism discussed in Chapter 1, affected Roman Catholic thought towards that same Greek humanism. And in Chapter 5, we saw how the Roman Catholic Church remained opposed to Luther's effort to turn the Church from the error of that teaching. The fact that the sin of homosexuality is today so prevalent within the ranks of modern Catholic leadership is not a happenstance. This fact only confirms the truth of the Apostle Paul's letter to the Romans. Cozzens[19] acknowledged that the Catholic hierarchy realizes that it has a disproportionate number of homosexual priests and seminarians. He cited research that estimates homosexual orientation within the priesthood and Catholic seminaries as high as fifty percent. Cozzen stated that the numbers should be in the 5-10 percent range, if they were proportionate to the general population. (This statement, however, seems out of place since one should expect a leadership grouping within a Christian organization to be free from this practice.) The fact that the Roman Catholic Church has this serious problem within its ranks of leadership is consistent with the untold number of lawsuits stemming from homosexual sex abuse perpetrated by these priests. In 1998, for example, the Roman Catholic Diocese of Dallas agreed to pay more than twenty million dollars to settle a case involving nine altar boys who had been sexually molested by their priests.[20] Anyone following current events knows that this is, to use a trite analogy, only the tip of the iceberg in relationship to the overall problem of homosexuality within Catholicism.

But the infiltration of humanism into Western Christianity is not just a Catholic problem. Much of the thinking in the liberal American Protestant denominations is now dominated by humanistic reasoning. However, the issue of homosexuality is different in the liberal Protestant denominations than in the Catholic Church. Because the Catholic Church officially views the practice as the sin which it is, it forces those within its ranks who practice it into a life of deception and secrecy. In the Protestant denominations there are those in leadership who simply refuse to call homosexuality a moral wrong. In the American Episcopal Church, for example, Bishop John Shelby Spong has attempted to move the practice into full acceptance within that Church. In his autobiography, Spong scoffs at the idea that homosexuality is a moral evil and he actively voices his support for the ordination of openly practicing homosexuals. He has even attempted to prove the Apostle Paul was a repressed homosexual.[21]

Even the Presbyterian Church (PCUSA), which has its roots in the Reformational teachings of John Calvin, has been invaded by those who would change the perception of homosexuality as a morally wrong practice. In his book *The Great Evangelical Disaster,* the late Francis Schaeffer briefly described the humanistic infiltration into this denomination. Here, Schaeffer attributed the ideas stemming from the Enlightenment (see Chapter 6) to its degradation. Schaeffer wrote:

> In the late nineteenth century it was these ideas [ideas of the Enlightenment] which began to radically transform Christianity in America. This started especially with the acceptance of the "higher critical" methods that had been developed in Germany. Using these methods, the new liberal theologians completely undercut the authority of Scripture. We can be thankful to those who argued strenuously against the new methods and in defense of the full inspiration and inerrancy of Scripture. One would remember especially the great Princeton theologians A. A. Hodge and B. B. Warfield, and later J. Gresham Machen. But in spite of the efforts of these men and scores of other Bible-believing Christian leaders, and in spite of the fact that the vast majority of lay Christians were truly Bible-believ-

ing, those holding the liberal ideas of the Enlightenment and the destructive methods of biblical criticism came into power and control in the denominations.[22]

Princeton University, of course, has its roots in the Presbyterian Church and Schaeffer was also a Presbyterian. The thought processes of Princeton's Capps on child rearing, as we discussed in the previous chapter, is indicative of the extent to which the standards of Princeton Theological Seminary have strayed from the teaching of Scripture.

A minister in the PCUSA in the northeast Ohio region of my home recently challenged his denomination's leaders regarding their lax enforcement of its ban of homosexual practices. To protest that laxity, a petition was presented to those officials, in accordance with PCUSA bylaws, to force the convening of a special session to address the issue. Some PCUSA officials, however, attempted to thwart his efforts by influencing certain petitioners to remove their names from the original petition. The minister lamented in the local newspaper how the denominational hierarchy resorted to "contemptible tactics" to avoid the confrontation that meeting would have spawned. Regarding the PCUSA's effort to remove names from the necessary petition, he said: "They are using the worst, lowest, most despicable kind of politics. … What is this kind of politicking even doing in the church?"[23]

The PCUSA, however, as a result of that petition, did eventually convene a trial of one of their ministers for violating church law in marrying same-sex couples and ordaining homosexuals who refused to remain chaste. The result of the trial was little more than a hand-slap. The court acquitted the minister of the ordination charge and only rebuked him for the marriages. It did not remove him from his office. The minister appealed the conviction, and he continued both the ordinations and marriages. Unfortunately he was successful with his appeal.[24] This outcome is certainly indicative of the undue humanistic influence in the PCUSA and the other liberal Protestant denominations. Calvin, if alive today, would certainly be ashamed of this branch of the Church that has evolved from his labor. He would certainly denounce its movement to the humanistic philosophies that he so strongly fought against. Calvin's words, repeated from Chapter 5, seem most appropriate for those who today within that Church do not have the wisdom to understand the evil of homosexuality.

> Pride and vanity are discovered, when miserable men, in seeking after God, rise not, as they ought, above their own level, but judge of him according to their carnal stupidity, and leave the proper path of investigation in pursuit of speculations as vain as they are curious. Their conceptions

of him are formed, not according to the representation he gives of himself, but by the inventions of their own presumptuous imaginations.[25]

This same humanistic influence is now present in many of the other liberal Protestant Christian denominations. From the Associated Press in the Spring of 2003 came the report that the United Methodist Church's 2004 General Conference will witness an attempt to eliminate the church's official statement, "We do not condone the practice of homosexuality and consider this practice incompatible with Christian teaching." It was reported that the Board of Church and Society wants to change it to read, "Although faithful Christians disagree on the compatibility of homosexual practice with Christian teaching, we affirm that God's grace is available to all."[26] God's grace, however, is not available to the homosexual who chooses to remain in his sin whether or not he is a member of any church.

The Humanism that Threatens Biblical Christianity

In this final section I present two topics that have more of a philosophical bent than what has come before. However, I hope to keep the promise I made in the *Introduction*, where I stated that I would not venture too far into philosophy while, at the same time, addressing two important issues that are coming from a Christian philosophical perspective which, in my opinion, are creating avenues for humanistic thinking to become prominent in Christian communities which were once free of that danger.

The Reformers (Chapter 5) were primarily responsible for leading Christianity back to a scriptural view of human nature within Christendom. Their teaching on human depravity was critical to the Reformation, not because they (the Reformers) invented it, but because they realized that its teaching was a foundational truth of Scripture and that the Church's error in failing to properly recognize that truth was largely responsible for the Church's moral decline. The Reformers simply believed God's word on the subject. No more appropriate Scripture upon which the doctrine of human depravity is based can be found than in Genesis 8:21 where God's own words are recorded. *The Jerusalem Bible* states "the impulse of man's heart is evil from his youth." *The King James Version* states "the imagination of man's heart is evil from his youth." *The New American Standard* reads "the intent of man's heart is evil from his youth." *The New International Version* renders it, "every inclination of his heart is evil from childhood." That the meaning of this statement can stand on its own (i.e., can be taken at face value) can be proven from other portions of Scripture. These words are unlike those that Jesus used when he told the rich young ruler to keep the commandments to enter eternal life. Those words do not stand alone because Jesus was not teaching that one can save himself by keeping the law. (For the previous discussion of this conversation see the Kant section in Chapter 6.) But the words of Genesis 8:21, based on the whole teaching of Scripture, can be taken at face value.

The Reformers did not teach that all vestiges of the imprint of goodness were removed from human nature with Adam's sin. I am here reminded of a lecture from one of my undergraduate theology courses where we learned that depravity

> does not mean that every sinner is devoid of all qualities pleasing to men; that he commits, or is prone to every form of sin; that he is as bitterly opposed to God as it is possible for him to be. The ruins of the great cathedrals in Europe left by World War II still bear traces of their original beautiful architecture.[27]

But universal human depravity *does* mean that every person in his natural condition

> is totally destitute of that love to God which is the fundamental requirement of the law ... that he is supremely given to a preference of himself to God ... that he has an aversion to God which on occasion becomes active enmity to Him ... that his every faculty is disordered and corrupted; that he has no thought, feeling, or deed of which God can fully approve ... and that he has entered upon a line of constant progress in depravity, from which he can in no wise turn away in his own strength.[28]

A recent book by Dewey Hointenga, Jr. entitled *John Calvin and the Will: A Critique and Corrective*, is an attack on the biblical doctrine of human depravity. Because Calvin treated the doctrine of human depravity so extensively and effectively, Hointenga puts Calvin in his sights and attempts to destroy a foundational teaching of the Reformation. Hointenga, a Harvard trained professor of philosophy at Grand Valley State University states:

> His [Calvin's] claim, however, that the fallen will is inclined to nothing but evil is mistaken and must be remedied by accepting that both the will's inclination to moral goodness and its capacity to choose it over evil survive in the fallen state.[29]

The average reader might have difficulty following Hointenga's logic because his mind is immersed in the language and techniques of philosophy. Since his conclusion flies in the face of Genesis 8:21, his assault, in my opinion, is not so much on Calvin as it is on God's word. Calvin's view of fallen human nature is consistent with Scripture and therefore Hointenga's conclusions regarding Calvin's thought are, again in my opinion, wrong.

That Hointenga is attacking the very foundation of the historical orthodox view of human depravity is evident in his book. As I have pointed out in Chapters 3 and 5, Calvin and the Augustine that emerged after having wrestled with the Pelagians were essentially united in their view of the human will. Hointenga acknowledged that "Augustine's thought harbors the same inconsistency about the will that I purport to find in Calvin, so that it would be as important to point out the inconsistency in Augustine as in Calvin.[30]

In setting forth his first main point, Hointenga writes, "The inconsistency in Calvin's account of the human will as God created it is this: he claims that the intellect governs the will and yet clearly implies that it does not."[31] Calvin, however, did not claim that Adam's unfallen intellect was by necessity *forced* to govern his will. Calvin only claimed that Adam's intellect correctly provided the knowledge of right from wrong and was therefore *capable* of governing his will. It obviously did not. That proper functioning was lost in the fall. After the fall, the intellect was no longer even capable of enabling the will to the moral good. Hointenga makes the false assumption that because Calvin maintained that in its unfallen state the intellect was capable of knowing right from wrong, he was forced into the ancient Greek position, i.e., that the will must, of necessity, follow the findings of the intellect. In this case the will would have no true freedom. Hointenga states that "the notion of the will as a separate power is not even part of Plato's analysis of the soul,"[32] but as I have shown in Chapter 1, this is not the case, since Plato clearly subscribed to a three-component model of human personality, consisting of the volitional, intellectual and emotional parts. However, *before the fall*, Adam had true freedom of the will and Calvin points that freedom out. It appears to me that Hointenga has set up a straw house to knock down.

Hointenga's second major criticism of Calvin is closely related to the first. It is what he calls Calvin's inconsistency between his (Calvin's) descriptions of the created and fallen wills versus what he actually believed. However, this so-called "inconsistency" is only Hointenga's disagreement with Calvin. Hointenga's argument is that although Calvin in one passage of his *Institutes* states: "The natural gifts in man were corrupted, but the supernatural were stripped from him", Calvin actually believes that the natural gifts were destroyed."[33] By the "natural gifts" Calvin is referring to human intellect and will. The "supernatural" gifts refer to those that proceed from a true knowledge and genuine fellowship with the one true God. Hointenga simply does not agree with Calvin's conclusion that the human personality became totally depraved with Adam's fall. Man's intellect before the fall had the capability of distinguishing moral right from wrong, and the will was free to move according to that judgment. With Adam's disobedience, human reason became darkened in its ability to know absolutely the moral absolute. Calvin did not teach that the human will became a nonentity, but that it lost its freedom to choose the moral good, in and of itself, from the functioning of a fallen human intellect.

The claim that the natural human heart is inclined to nothing but evil, while espoused by Calvin, was not of his origin. These are the very words of God as revealed in Genesis 8:21. One's view of human nature cannot be shaped from one's own power of reason. Attempting to arrive at metaphysical (spiritual) truth through that means will lead to the same type of mistakes that Aquinas made, where his teachings are largely responsible for the humanism that is yet present within the Roman Catholic Church. The cry of the Reformers became *solo scriptura*, the principle of which demands that one's view of reality first and foremost be formed from the teachings of Scripture. While Hointenga uses Roman 2:14-15 in his attempt to show a natural inclination to moral good in human nature, I have emphasized throughout this work that the function of human conscience alone cannot get one to the moral absolute. These verses only show that the unseared conscience will naturally condemn immorality. If the natural human conscience could move one to the moral absolute, the sin of homosexuality would not today be invading every aspect of Western civilization with its dressing of moral neutrality.

A new movement called Open Theism or Free-Will Theism has in recent years become influential in the evangelical Christian community. Open Theism is a dangerous teaching because it subtlety appeals to man's natural tendency towards belief in a sovereign self. And as both Aristotle and Aquinas taught, a small philosophical error will over time lead to disastrous results.[34] The leader of the movement, Clark Pinnock, an emeritus professor of theology from McMaster Divinity College, authored in 1994 (with four others) the book entitled *The Openness of God: A Biblical Challenge to the Traditional Understanding of God*,[35] which helped to propel this new teaching into notoriety.

One theme that I have emphasized in this book is the importance of understanding how the volitional aspect of human nature should exist in relationship to the nature of God. As I stressed in Chapter 2, the only acceptable role of human volition, in relationship to the will of God, is a *responsive* one. Human will must be a *responsive will* to God's will. Sovereignty lies in God's will, *not* in human will. A defining characteristic of humanism is its belief that human volition exists as a sovereign entity. A scriptural understanding of human nature is therefore important for possessing a scriptural understanding of the nature of God. The two go hand in hand. Jesus' own words recorded in the Gospel of John are helpful for understanding the sovereignty of divine will over human will. Jesus stated that "No one can come to Me, unless the Father who sent Me draws him."[36] This is simply an authoritative statement of one of the main theses of this book, which is that no one can come to the moral good on his own terms or solely within the power of his own personality. The Reformation teachings of Luther and Calvin returned to Christianity a scriptural understanding of human nature, which the Church had largely lost following Augustine's defining struggle with the Pelagians.

However, because there is in Scripture clear indication of the *function* of human will in the formation of one's relationship to the God of Scripture, there are those Christians who have traditionally put more emphasis on the significance of human will. Human will is certainly not a nonentity. When one emphasizes that one has to choose Christ for salvation, he is speaking truth. Human volition is always involved in saving faith, as is evident in Abraham's choosing to do what God asked him to do. Human will *responding* to divine will is witnessed throughout Scripture. The function of human will is seen in Joshua's stirring exhortation to God's people:

> Choose for yourselves today whom you will serve: whether the gods which your fathers served which were beyond the River, or the gods of the Amorites in whose land you are living; but as for me and my house, we will serve the Lord.[37]

It is well known that the most notorious opponent to Calvin's view of volition and predestination was Jacobus Arminius, a 17th century Dutch theologian. His followers stressed that election was conditioned by faith, that Christ died for all people, and that believers could, if they so chose to do—because of will's freedom—reject the grace they once had. One can understand how Arminius concluded some of his main ideas since some Scriptures do show a *role* of human will in one's relationship to God. For example, the Apostle Paul wrote to the Colossians:

> And although you were formerly alienated and hostile in mind, engaged in evil deeds, yet He has now reconciled you in His fleshly body through death, in order to present you before Him holy and blameless and beyond reproach— *if indeed you continue in the faith firmly established and steadfast, and not moved away from the hope of the gospel that you have heard* [italics added], which was proclaimed in all creation under heaven, and of which I, Paul, was made a minister.[38]

The preceding passage of Scripture seems to imply that the reconciled one, formerly alienated and hostile in mind, could discontinue his faith if he so chose.[39] Even more persuading words towards this end are from the writer to the Hebrews who states:

> For in the case of those who have once been enlightened and have tasted of the heavenly gift and have been made partakers of the Holy Spirit, and have tasted the good word of God and the powers of the age to come, and then have fallen away, it is impossible to renew them again to repentance, since they again crucify to themselves the Son of God, and put Him to open shame.[40]

Furthermore, the Scripture states in various places that whosoever wills to come to the truth can do so. For example the *Authorized Version* of Scripture renders Revelation 22:17 as "And whosoever will, let him take the water of life freely." (It is interesting to note how the *New American Standard* puts these words in a slightly different light with its rendering, "let the one who wishes take the water of life without cost.") It is because of these passages—and others, of course—that Arminian theology has traditionally commanded the respect of many Christians.

While Open Theism has its basic roots in Arminian theology, it nonetheless holds ideas that are incompatible with Arminius' teachings. Arminius acknowledged the inability of human will to move one of its own accord towards the moral good. Arminius wrote:

> Man is not capable, of and by himself, either to think, to will, or to do that which is really good; but it is necessary for him to be regenerated and renewed in his intellect, affections or will, and in all his powers, by God in Christ through the Holy Spirit, that he may be qualified rightly to understand, esteem, consider, will, and perform whatever is truly good.[41]

While human volition is not a nonentity, it nonetheless cannot operate sovereignly in the movement of one to God—the true moral Good.

Some influential Christians have leaned more towards the Arminian views of human nature and the nature of God than those of Calvin. As I mentioned in the introduction, C. S. Lewis' views, particularly in his earlier writings, were not particularly aligned with Reformed theology. However, it is interesting to note that shortly before his death in 1963, Lewis granted an interview to Sherwood Wirt of the Billy Graham Evangelistic Association where he stated:

> I wrote in *Surprised by Joy* ... that "before God closed in
> on me, I was in fact offered what now appears a moment
> of wholly free choice." But I feel my decision was not so
> important. I was the object rather than the subject in this
> affair. I was decided upon.[42]

While Lewis perhaps would have, even then, identified his position with
one of free will, he certainly had a proper sense of where the true sovereignty
of choice lay. And this was the point of the "science fictional" allegory I
constructed in Chapter 3. One can speak of free will if one puts it in its
proper perspective. Lewis, as I showed in Chapter 7, certainly had a scriptural perspective of human depravity although he may not have been comfortable with that terminology. When one's view of human nature is based
in Scripture, a scriptural understanding of human volition cannot be too far
behind. When a scriptural perspective of fallen human nature is not accepted, a misunderstanding of human volition is almost always the result of
that deception. Therefore, as I stated in the *Introduction* to this book, when
a scriptural understanding of the basic nature of both God and human nature are held to, the differences between Christians who disagree on the
nature of free will should be somewhat inconsequential to genuine Christian unity.

However, the biblical view of God's sovereignty is rejected by Open
Theists. They reject the idea that the only proper function of human will is
a responsive will to God's will. Open Theists believe that while man may
respond to God's will, God in turn may respond to human will. This teaching causes the sovereignty of God to be shared with a falsely perceived human sovereignty, which renders the teachings of Open Theism a subtly disguised humanism that is clothed in the garb of scriptural Christianity. In
the Preface to *The Openness of God* the authors state:

> We respond to God's gracious initiatives and God responds
> to our responses ... and on it goes. God takes risks in this
> give-and-take relationship ... God works with human de-
> cisions, adapting his [*sic*] own plans to fit the changing
> situation. ... he [*sic*] is open to receiving input from his
> creatures ... God invites us to participate with him [*sic*] to
> bring the future into being.[43]

One practical effect of the Open Theist viewpoint is, therefore, in its
misrendering of the function of prayer. Open Theism promotes the legitimacy of praying "let my will be done" instead of "thy will be done" as Jesus
taught His own to pray. As the great evangelist Charles Finney taught, prayer
does not change God, but

produces such a change *in us* and fulfils [*sic*] such conditions as renders it consistent for God to do as it would not
be consistent for him [*sic*] to do otherwise. ... Whenever
this change takes place in them, and they offer the right
kind of prayer, then God, without any change in himself
[*sic*], can answer them.[44]

Open Theists like to emphasize the nature of God's love to the exclusion of the nature of his created beings. They fail to understand that man in
his fallen condition of rebellion is not lovable. As C. S. Lewis stated in the
aforementioned interview, it was as if he heard God say to him, "Put down
your gun and we'll talk."[45] While God *is* love, He does not negotiate with
the natural terror of the human heart that remains in rebellion against him.
Man does not come to God on his own terms but he must come on God's
terms. Open Theists, as do all humanists, fail to understand the severity of
the helplessness of fallen human nature.

In a radio interview featuring a dialogue between Clark Pinnock and
Michael S. Horton, in the days before the movement gained its current
notoriety, Pinnock stated that he rejected the doctrine that Adam's sin imputed guilt to all his posterity. Pinnock stated, "My father being an alcoholic certainly affected me in my home and my life, but to think that I'm
guilty as an alcoholic like he was is nonsense."[46] These words demonstrate
Pinnock's failure to understand the biblical concept of "original sin." While
Pinnock believes in "original sin" he does not understand the correlation
between "original sin" and human nature. It is similar to those who believe
that infant baptism takes away "original sin." Anyone believing that infant
baptism automatically frees an infant from the damnation of "original sin"
simply lacks an understanding of that same correlation. To use Pinnock's
own example, while he is not guilty of the sins of his father, he inherited
from his father the same nature that enabled his father's sin to occur. Whether
it is admitted to or not, all have inherited a nature that is so corrupt that it
prevents them in the sole power of *their own* will to move themselves to the
moral good.

The debate over Open Theism's compatibility with Scripture has been
quietly proceeding for many years. Although recently the *Evangelical Theological Society* declared Open Theism incompatible with Scripture, the movement will not likely fade away.[47] The temptation to believe in human sovereignty is today stronger than it ever was. And it is this view that will become
increasingly prevalent as Western culture moves ever more resolutely towards a society that is dominated by humanistic principles.

11

Summary

Unless the Lord builds the house, they labor in vain who build it.
Psalm 127:1

In this book I have shown why the perception of ultimate good that stems from humanistic thinking is in opposition to that which the Scriptures portray as necessary for the same. A humanistic philosophy, be it one coming from a conscious secular perspective—or one coming from a conscious or unconscious non-secular perspective, always perceives that the highest good can be attained apart from a genuine knowledge of, and submission to, the God of Scripture.

The idea that the intellectual aspect of human personality could enable moral living was birthed in the ancient Greek world. The non-secular Greek model of morality espoused by Socrates, Plato and Aristotle reigned in Western culture until the triumph of Christianity displaced the dominance of that thinking. The Greek philosophers taught that man was born morally neutral. They wrongly believed that man possessed a natural inclination to virtue and that he could arrive at true happiness and contentment if his powers of reason were properly cultivated.

Jesus appeared in the midst of a Judaism that had been overtaken by a form of humanistic thinking. He wanted those so deceived to understand how they had abandoned the faith of Abraham. It is only the type of faith exemplified in the life of Abraham which produces the imputed righteousness necessary for salvation. Such faith involves human will only as it is *responsive* to God's will and it is only *that* type of faith that produces true good. Jesus attempted to show his people that the humanistic pursuit of the moral good through their attempt to obey God's law, solely in the power of human nature, was a faulty one. While the Jews insisted on their loyalty to Abraham, Jesus plainly told them that if they had had the faith of Abraham they would have recognized Him as their Messiah.

At the root all humanism is its failure to acknowledge the severity of the helplessness of fallen human nature. Wherever this truth is not comprehended, humanism always thrives. It is because fallen human nature is so far removed from the nature of God that the only effectiveness of human volition towards the true good is in its response to God's word. Because the Jewish people as a whole did not respond to that Word (Jesus, as God, *is* God's Word), salvation was opened to the gentiles. The gentiles of the Western world were then steeped in the humanism of Greek philosophies.

The Hebrew Scripture foretold of salvation's offer to the gentile. Consider the inspired words of Matthew's gospel:

> But the Pharisees went out, and counseled together against Him, as to how they might destroy Him. But Jesus, aware of this, withdrew from there. And many followed Him, and He healed them all, and warned them not to make Him known, in order that what was spoken through Isaiah the prophet, might be fulfilled, saying,
>
> > Behold, My Servant whom I have chosen;
> > My Beloved in whom My soul is well-pleased;
> > I will put My spirit upon Him,
> > and He shall proclaim justice to the Gentiles.
> > He will not quarrel, nor cry out;
> > Nor will any one hear His voice in the streets.
> > A battered reed He will not break off,
> > And a smoldering wick He will not put out,
> > Until he leads justice to victory.
> > And in His name the Gentiles will hope.[1]

The rise of Christianity in the Western world is, of course, the fulfillment of Isaiah's prophecy.

While the Greek philosophers prepared the Western mind for accepting the reality of a transcendent Hebrew God, their ideas regarding both God and human nature were incompatible with the God of Scripture. Augustine's first writing on human volition had been influenced by Platonic ideas of human nature, but he later came to terms with those erroneous views as a result of his struggle with the unscriptural teachings of the Pelagians. Pelagius had failed to understand the incapacitating effects of Adam's sin, and modern humanists struggle with this same issue. Whenever anyone fails to understand the extent to which Adam's sin adversely affected human nature, that person's view of personality's power is also adversely affected.

Despite Augustine's triumph over Pelagianism, humanistic thinking eventually found its way back into the Church. The knowledge that one is justified only through faith in the one true God, the God of Scripture, was again eventually lost. When Jesus told Nicodemus that rebirth was needed for one to come to God, He was implying that achievement of a moral existence was outside the capability of human personality. This was a shocking revelation to Nicodemus and it is a teaching that, even today, is impossible to comprehend for those who cannot understand the devastation of Adam's sin.

Because Aquinas was obsessed with unifying Christian thought with the humanism of Aristotle, his understanding of the effect of Adam's sin on human nature became corrupt. Although Aquinas believed in a concept of original sin, a careful reading of his writing on the subject of spiritual birth (or the new birth) and human volition shows that he did not fully understand the extent to which Adam's sin incapacitated human nature for movement to the moral good. Aquinas wrote, "Man needs regeneration or rebirth which is brought through the Sacrament of Baptism: 'Unless a man be born again of water and the Holy Ghost, he cannot enter into the kingdom of God.'"[3] Aquinas did not comprehend that the new-birth is synonymous with imputed righteousness as a result of one's faith in God's Word. The new birth really has nothing to do with the physical act of baptism. The physical act of baptism is only an outward symbol of the inward spiritual process.

By the time of the Renaissance, the Church had completely lost its spiritual bearings. The writings of Erasmus show particularly well its dire spiritual condition. The Renaissance humanists responded to that crisis by rebelling against the Scholasticism of that era. They attempted to move learning from the theological realm into the secular, and made the pursuit of knowledge, through what we now call the humanities, their primary goal. However, this new thrust to better understand language and the arts triggered in Luther an intense desire to better understand the writings of the Apostle Paul to the Romans. That study led Luther to a better understanding of fallen human nature and the means to salvation from the damnation of which that nature yields.

When Luther rebelled against the teachings of the Church on the issue of indulgences, the Reformation was born. The disputation of that issue soon turned to the subject of human nature, particularly to the aspect of human volition. The true colors of Erasmus were revealed when he was forced to choose between the Church and Luther's teachings. Erasmus had made his reputation by criticizing Church corruption, but it soon became apparent that his interest in the subject did not center on true Godliness, but upon protecting himself from the scorn of a corrupt Church. Erasmus chose that corrupt Church over the liberating message of salvation by faith alone.

The delineation between a humanistic and scriptural view of human nature was continued in the ministry of John Calvin. Calvin further strengthened the drive to bring Christianity back to a proper understanding of the relationship between God's perfect nature and fallen human nature—an understanding that had been lost since the days of Augustine.

After the Reformation, the swing back to humanistic domination was triggered by the phenomenal successes of science. Although many of the first truly noteworthy scientists were genuine products of the Reformation, their achievements ultimately resulted in the false belief that science would emancipate man from his need of God. This age became known as the Enlightenment or the Age of Reason. A deistic concept of God became popular in this period, and the belief that unjust humankind stood naturally condemned before a just and holy God was again lost in Enlightenment thinking.

The Enlightenment gave rise to modern secular humanism, the humanism that is now commonly associated with the term. In the minds of secular humanists, science has proven the irrelevancy of God. This is well exemplified in the recent comments of James Watson, the co-discoverer of the double helix structure of DNA. In a recent interview that celebrated the anniversary of his 50 year old discovery, Watson stated:

> Every time you understand something, religion becomes less likely. Only with the discovery of the double helix and the ensuing genetic revolution have we had grounds for thinking that the powers held traditionally to be the exclusive property of the gods might one day be ours.[4]

It should not be too surprising how, from Watson and Crick's minuscule bit of scientific discovery in relationship to the vastness of the yet unknown, can come such a sense of arrogance and pride against the supremely intelligent and infinitely wise God. This is simply more evidence of the pride that ultimately caused man's separation from God. Why would not God distance himself from such nonsense? This, of course, is not to deride the importance of scientific knowledge. Science is a noble profession, but failure to acknowledge the ultimate source of all knowledge and wisdom is the tragic result to which the pride of science is susceptible.

Watson made another statement consistent with the secular humanism of Nietzsche. He claimed that the two stupidest sentences in the English language are "Love thy enemy" and the "Meek shall inherit the earth," stating that his successes were due to his self-promotion and lack of meekness.[5] From Watson's mind-set one can understand the far reaching ramifications of modern secular humanism. In moving humanism again to a Sophistic ideal, Nietzsche propelled the perception that the sum total of reality is only that which can be perceived by the senses. The Enlightenment humanists, who championed the methods of reproducible scientific experimentation, believed in a sense of supreme being. Their philosophy was yet steeped in the philosophy of Hellenistic rationalism. Although Watson's and Crick's primary scientific achievements were in that vein, their atheistic reasoning shows the drift to the secular humanism in which what is *imagined* becomes more important than what *is*. Modern-day scientists often subscribe to atheism because the science that seeks to prove the origins of life often revolves more around *imagination* than it does around fact.[6]

A perception of a reality based more on *imagination* than fact has now permeated every facet of Western culture. The American space program, administered by NASA, operates on a philosophy of atheism where image takes precedence over substance. One can only wonder if NASA's unprecedented number of catastrophic failures over the last few decades is a result of that agency's humanistic philosophical approach to its mission. NASA is an organization that could do a good service to truth if it kept humanistic philosophy out of its science. But NASA's leaders have chosen the popular path, and secular humanistic scientists are so good at intimidation that there is little chance for change in that governmental agency. And in the corporate world, image is so important in decision making that many companies put more emphasis on building an image for their products than they do on improving them. They do this because they know that simply by affecting perception they can actually sell an inferior product over a better, but non-hyped, product—although the companies that practice such methods will eventually pay the price for that deception. Truth has the uncanny ability to eventually come to the surface. And should one be surprised that the pop psychologists now promote this dangerous Sophistic philosophy? In his book: *Life's strategies: Doing What Works, Doing What Matters,* Phil McGraw presents his 10 laws of life. Law number 6, presented in Chapter 7 reads: "There is no reality, only perception." However, contrary to what Dr. Phil believes, there *is* a reality and only when one's perceptions are congruous with reality can one properly function. Unfortunately, those in Western culture are increasingly making important decisions based on perception and image with little regard to what is real.

Modern humanistic man has primarily turned to two basic pursuits for his sense of fulfillment. First is his bent to seek his personal fulfillment in a quest for material wealth. Secondly, he is becoming increasingly prone to seek sexual fulfillment outside the confines of loving monogamous marriages.

It was Marx's belief that the human drive for material gain was the dominant driving force that shaped human nature. Communism became a reality because outside of God's remedy for fallen human nature, material gain usually *does* become a primary reason for living. Communism is the *humanistic* solution to this aspect of fallen human nature. But communism fails because human nature has no true sovereignty over itself. There is more theft, greed and deception in communistic countries than there is anywhere else. Communism cannot—as it seeks to do—change the nature of man. Outside of God, man will always seek life's meaning primarily in material things. Only when one's material resources come as a result of God's blessing can they be truly enjoyed because then the beholder does not have the goal of wealth as his primary reason for living.

With the modern humanistic standard of "individual choice and consent" as the "guiding norm sanctioning sexual expression," the false perception that man can determine his own sexual morality has become dominant in Western culture. The so-called sexual revolution has removed sex from its proper role as an expression of love within the confines of marriage and has made sex mainly a means to self-gratification. Sex is now a tool for the narcissist as he unabashedly proclaims, "It's all about me." The primary love upon which the family is structured is becoming undermined and, the family, a major building block of Western culture, is thereby becoming subtly weakened.

The Enlightenment not only led to a secular humanism in Western culture but it also propelled forward the non-secular humanism that now exists within a Protestant Christian framework. Humanism, as I have emphasized throughout this book, is not confined to a secular reality. The non-secular humanism that now exists within Western Christianity is ultimately not much different from the secular humanism that denies the existence of God. Many who call themselves Christian are seeking their sense of fulfillment from the same wells as do the secular humanists. The pursuit of wealth remains the primary goal of many who profess Christianity. From this non-secular humanism proceeds the idea that one can, apart from Scripture, determine one's own standard of morality. This is nowhere more evident than in the movements within the liberal Christian denominations that are attempting to remove the stigma of moral wrong from the practice of homosexuality. And certainly, if such attitudes regarding so obvious a sin abound, can one wonder about the tolerance of any other sin that might prevail within these same ranks?

Hopefully the reader has recognized from this work the cyclic aspect of humanism's dominance in Western culture and the thought processes that are responsible for bringing that thinking into dominance. A former Presbyterian minister turned Unitarian—whose thinking well represents a non-secular humanistic philosophy—summed up the spirit of humanism rather succinctly:

> From the myth of the Garden of Eden has come the notion that humans are tainted with original sin. The truth of the myth is that the freedom to choose (eat of the fruit of knowledge of good and evil) permits us to select evil over good, good over evil.[7]

A culture of humanism always replaces a spirit of trust in the one true God when any people fail to understand the bankruptcy, the helplessness, the folly, the sickness, the utter ruin of the human spirit that Adam's sin perpetuated on the human race. As Calvin said of the Greek philosophers, they sought "for an edifice among ruins and for beautiful order in the midst of confusion." Malachi told the humanistic Jew of his day: "You have wearied the Lord with your words. Yet you say, 'How have we wearied Him?' In that you say, 'Everyone who does evil is good in the sight of the Lord, and He delights in them.'"[8]

One's only option to get to the true moral good, to the one true God of Scripture, is to use his will to respond to God's will as He has plainly revealed it in Scripture. I quoted C. S. Lewis' poignant words from *The Great Divorce* to begin this work, and those same words, slightly paraphrased, present an appropriate ending. These hold the essence of the message of both this book and the message that Malachi gave the Israelites of his day. Lewis' declaration is appropriate for every person that has ever existed since Cain and Abel: "There are two kinds of people; those who say to God, 'Thy will be done' and those to whom God says, 'All right then have it your way.'" The first way leads to life everlasting, the second to everlasting destruction. It is my hope that this book has helped the reader identify with the former group.

Notes

Preface

1 See for example, *Christianity: The True Humanism* by J. I. Packer and Thomas Howard, Word Publishing, 1985 and *The Majesty of Man: The Dignity of Being Human* by Ronald B. Allen, Multnomah Press, Portland, 1984.

2 I use the masculine pronoun for convenience throughout this book to denote humankind instead of male gender exclusively.

3 Although becoming increasingly rare, there is yet some biblically sound Christian influences left in these schools. Only recently—before his death—the Dean of the Princeton University Chapel was Dr. Ernest Gordon. Gordon possessed an admirable Christian faith as his book *Me, Myself and Who? Humanism: Society's False Premise*, clearly shows. (Haven Books, Logos International, Plainfield, N.J., 1980.)

4 *Webster's New Dictionary*, Russell, Geddes & Grossset, Windsor Court, New York, 1990.

5 Chapter 81.

Introduction

1 *Letters of C.S. Lewis, Revised and Enlarged Ed.*, ed. W. Hooper, Harcourt Brace and Co., 1993, Letter of March 31, 1928, p. 252.

2 The Tower of Babel, described in Genesis 11, is probably the ziggurat of Etemenanki whose structure was described by the Greek historian Herodotus in the 5th century B.C. and whose foundation is extant in modern Iraq.

3 D. M. Alstadt, *A Tribute to Greatness; A Few Personal Comments on the Life of Herman Mark*, J. of Polym. Sci.: Polym. Symp. 75, pp. 105-108, 1993.

4 While the three-component model is a convenient and somewhat realistic generalization, in reality, personality cannot be compartmentalized in quite that simple a fashion. Freud's model has components of volition located in the id, and the scriptural designation of the "heart" also seems to include a volitional component.

5 The reader should not conclude that I am defending Freud's humanistic teachings. I put Freud's system of thought into its proper perspective in Chapter 7. However, it is simply erroneous to believe, as some do, that all of Freud's work towards understanding the human psyche is of no value.

6 For example see Philippians 4:7.

7 In these chapters I frequently use the phrase *ultimate reality*. While philosophers often use this term when discussing metaphysics, it is nonetheless an appropriate expression for the Hebrew God Jehovah. I have, therefore, used this term interchangeably with the terms used in Scripture to describe the Hebrew God.

8 Colossians 2:8. The Apostle here exhorts his reader not to be misled by vain philosophy.

9   While humanists usually insist on the total freedom of the human will, there have been some notable exceptions. Voltaire and Nietzsche are two such examples, discussed in Chapters 6 and 7 respectively.

10   Steven R. Covey, *The 7 Habits of Highly Effective People: Restoring the Character Ethic*, Simon and Schuster, New York, 1998.

11   John 14:6.

12   Proverbs 14:12.

13   Walter Lippmann, *A Preface to Morals*, Macmillan, New York, 1929, p. 137.

Chapter 1

1   See reference 4 of the *Preface*.

2   For a review of Greek mythology see Robert Graves, *The Greek Myths*, Vol. 1, Penguin Books, London, 1995.

3   Aristotle, *Metaphysics*, 983b.

4   Aristotle, *De Anima (On the Soul)*, 411a.

5   Robert Flint, *Anti-Theistic Theories*, Wm. Blackwood and Sons, Edinburgh, 1879, p. 336. (Flint was a noted professor of theology at the University of Edinburgh in the late 19th century. This work, because of its age, may be difficult to find, but those who do will find it rewarding.)

6   Simplicius, *Physics*, 24, 13.

7   For example see Aristotle, *Physics*, 187a, 203b.

8   For example see Radoslav A. Tsanoff, *The Great Philosophers*, 2nd Ed., Harper and Row, 1964, p. 12. ⸽

9   Aristotle, *Metaphysics*, 986b.

10   Ibid.

11   Tsanoff, p. 18.

12   William K. C. Guthrie, *A History of Greek Philosophy*, Vol. II, Cambridge University Press, 1965, p. 479.

13   Tsanoff, p. 18.

14   *Philosophic Classics*, 2nd Ed., Vol. 1: Thales to Ockham, ed. Kaufmann, Prentice-Hall, Englewood Cliffs, New Jersey, 1968, p. 46.

15   Guthrie, Vol. III, p. 234.

16   Ibid., p.186.

17   Ibid.

18   Plato, *Theaetetus*.

19   See Guthrie, Vol. III, Chapter IV for a thorough discussion of the *nomos* vs. *physis* debate.

20   This topic is further discussed in Chapter 2.

21   Guthrie, Vol. III, p. 68.

22   Many general texts treat the Greek idea of *areté*. For example see A. Weber and R. B. Perry, *History of Philosophy*, Charles Scribner's & Sons, New York, 2nd Ed., 1925, p. 48.

23   One who has held an upper position in any major modern organization knows that it is not always truth that wins an argument. Image often takes precedence over facts in corporate decision making. The modern corporate debater who casts himself in the best image often wins the debate even though his position

might be the furthest from the truth. This phenomenon is due to the increasing influence of modern secular humanism which, as we will see in Chapter 7, largely stems from Nietzsche.

24 Plato, *Republic*, 442a, trans. Robin Waterfield, Barnes & Noble by arrangement with Oxford University Press, 1993.

25 Secular Western humanism is becoming increasingly influenced by the teachings of Nietzsche, who, as we will see in Chapter 7, denigrated this traditional model of humanism. Nietzsche sought to give the will precedence over the intellect. However, Western humanism is yet highly influenced by this traditional model of Plato.

26 As pointed out by the translator, in Greek culture the temple often served as does our modern bank.

27 Plato, *Republic*, 443a.

28 Ibid.

29 For a concise explanation of this thought see Edgar L. Allen, *From Plato to Nietzsche*, Fawcett, Greenwich, Conn., (First printed in Great Britain, 1957, by the English Universities Press Ltd. under the title *Guide Book to Western Thought*), pp. 12-17.

30 Plato, *Republic*, 532b.

31 Plato, *Republic*, 389c.

32 I am referring to the scandal of 1997-98 that led to President William Clinton's impeachment.

33 Aristotle, however, rejected his teacher's *Theory of Forms*.

34 Aristotle, *Nicomachean Ethics*, 1094b, trans. Harris Rackham, The Loeb Classical Library, Harvard University Press, 1946.

35 The same priority is often observed in the thinking of modern humanists. For example, Hillary Clinton, the American First Lady of the 1990's, basically subscribed to this philosophy when she chose to entitle her book, *It Takes a Village to Raise a Child*. This ordering is opposite to that found in Christianity. Christianity begins with the moral condition of the individual, which then, if properly dealt with, yields positive repercussions in society. (I discuss this further in Chapter 2.)

36 Aristotle, *Nicomachean Ethics*, 1094a.

37 Ibid., 1098a.

38 Ibid., 1103a.

39 Ibid., 1103b.

40 Ibid.

41 Ibid., 1104b.

42 Ibid.

43 Ibid.

44 Ibid.

45 C. H. W. Johns, *Babylonian and Assyrian Laws, Contracts and Letters*, Charles Scribner's Sons, New York, (#229), 1904, pp. 44-66.

46 Ibid. (#'s196, 198).

47 For example see Guthrie, Vol. III, p. 116.

48 Ibid., p. 117.

49 Paul Johnson, *Intellectuals*, Harper and Row, 1988.

50 Allen, p. 34.

51 Aristotle, *Politics*, 1253a, trans. Harris Rackham, The Loeb Classical Library, Harvard University Press, 1967.

52 Aristotle, *Nicomachean Ethics*, 1106a.

53 Ibid., 1113b.

Chapter 2

1 Exodus 3:14, *The Jerusalem Bible*, English text revised and edited by Harold Fisch, Koren Publishers LTD, Jerusalem, Israel, 1992, p. 65. (As I stated in the *Introduction*, the Hebrew-based Scripture quoted in the first part of this chapter is taken from the Jewish authorized *The Jerusalem Bible*. I have in this chapter included the transliteration of the Hebrew names rendered in the source.)

2 I am not here purporting a deistic view of reality, but only precluding a pantheistic position.

3 The grossly perverted young man, convicted of serial murder in 1992, who was reared in a seemingly solid upper-middle-class environment.

4 *The Jerusalem Bible*, Genesis 11:27-8, p. 11.

5 Ibid., Genesis 15:20, p. 15.

6 Ibid., Genesis 12:1-4, p. 12 (*Note that Avram is the transliteration of Abram, as rendered in the source. See note 1).

7 Ibid., Genesis 15:1, p. 14.

8 Ibid., Genesis 15:6, p. 14.

9 See Genesis 22:1-19.

10 Søren Kierkegarrd, *Fear and Trembling* (A good English translation: Hong and Hong, Princeton University Press, Princeton, New Jersey, 1984.)

11 Ibid., (Kierkegarrd here taught that Abraham's faith was in the knowledge that Isaac's life would be spared. But this view is not consistent with Scripture because we know that Abraham would have brought the knife down, if God had not intervened, fully believing that God had the power to raise Isaac. See Hebrews 11: 17-19).

12 Carol Delany, *The Humanist*, Vol. 59, No. 3, 1999, pp. 14-18.

13 I am not implying that such a response should be the usual one to a young inquisitive mind. But in cases where parental authority is being challenged on a point that is outside the intellectual grasp of the child, it may indeed be the most appropriate response.

14 Hansen has implied that Plato studied the writings of Jeremiah while in Egypt, but I have not been able to substantiate that claim. See Norman Hansen, *A Cultural History of the Enlightenment*, Pantheon Books (Random House), New York, 1968, p. 18.

15 Adam Fox, *Plato for Pleasure*, Fawcett, New York, 1963, p. 82.

16 Some of the ideas of the "might makes right" thinking can be observed in the works of Nietzsche, Marx and Darwin, discussed in Chapter 7. They teach that human nature, if freed from the imposition of external manipulation (religious or otherwise), will through the strength of human will and natural selection, arrive at an ideal or improved state. Marx's philosophy was actually very close to

the *physis* model in that he believed that in a communistic society the need for government would eventually cease. Here, naturally strong individuals should evolve to lead humanity in its quest for perfection. However, the humanistic naturalist model leaves much to be desired because of the false presumptions of human nature under which it operates.

17   Aristotle, *Politics*, 1253a, trans. Harris Rackham, The Loeb Classical Library, Harvard University Press, 1967.

18   M. C. Townsend, *Psychiatric Mental Health Nursing*, 2nd Ed., F. A. Davis Company, Philadelphia, 1996, p. 834. (I owe this reference to my wife, a surgical registered nurse who came upon this poignant example during the course of her training.)

19   Marcus Tullius Cicero, *De Legibus (Laws)*, bk. 1, ch 16, sct. 45, trans. C. W. Keyes, The Loeb Classical Library, Harvard University Press, 1948.

20   Aristotle, *Nicomachean Ethics*, 1107a, trans. Harris Rackham, The Loeb Classical Library, Harvard University Press, 1946.

21   See Reference 32 of Chapter 1.

22   I am not implying by this statement that circumcision, as well as many other issues of Jewish custom yet practiced today as a result of God given law, is today a moral issue. This is an example that falls into the subject of the relationship of the Mosaic Law to Christianity, which is not in the scope of this work.

23   *The Jerusalem Bible*, Exodus 20:13, p. 86.

24   I discuss this issue more thoroughly in Chapter 9.

25   Ibid., Genesis 3:7, p. 3.

26   C. S. Lewis, *The Problem of Pain*, Macmillan, 1962, p. 100.

27   *The Jerusalem Bible*, Genesis 8:21, p. 9.

28   Ibid., I Kings 8:46, p. 415, II Chronicles 6:36 p. 992.

29   Ibid., Psalm 53:2-3, p. 752.

30   Ibid., Psalm 143:2, p. 796.

31   Ibid., Psalm 130:3, p. 791.

32   Ibid., Isaiah 53:6, p. 527.

33   Ibid., Isaiah 64:6-7, p. 536.

34   Many other examples show this idea, See Deuteronomy 31:17-18 and Deuteronomy 32:19-21.

35   C. S. Lewis, *Mere Christianity*, Chapter 1, Macmillan, 1943.

36   Many examples in the Hebrew Scripture show this. See Leviticus 4.

37   Genesis 4:2-11.

38   Luke 4:16-21, Jesus' reading was from Isaiah 61:1-2. The wording in Luke is slightly different from that found in Isaiah. (Jesus' synagogue quote adds "and recovery of sight for the blind" discussed later in this chapter).

39   John 4:25-6.

40   Deuteronomy 6:4.

41   Genesis 1:1.

42   *The Jerusalem Bible*, Genesis 1:26, p.1.

43   Ibid., Genesis 11:7-9, p.11.

44   For example, the egg (shell, white and yolk) sometimes used for illustration of this principle is a poor example, since a single essence is not there illustrated.

45 *The Holy Scriptures (According to the Masoretic Text)*, The Jewish Publication Society of America, Philadelphia, 1955, Genesis 3:15, p. 6.

46 *The Jerusalem Bible*, p. 3.

47 Ibid., Isaiah 7:14-15, p. 485.

48 M. Rosen, *Y'SHUA*, Moody Press, Chicago, p. 17, 1982.

49 *The Jerusalem Bible*, The Song of Songs 1:3, p. 857.

50 Ibid., Micah 5:2, p. 700.

51 Ibid., Isaiah 53: 4-5, 8-9, p. 527.

52 The reliability of God's written word is further discussed in Chapters 4 and 6.

53 John 10:30.

54 Ibid., John 8:58.

55 Ibid., John 1: 1-5, 14a.

56 C. S. Lewis, *Mere Christianity*, Macmillan Publishing, New York, 1952. p. 56.

57 *The Jerusalem Bible*, Isaiah 61: 1-2, pp. 533-534.

58 John 8:31-58.

59 John 1:29.

60 Luke 5:20-25.

61 John 3:3.

62 John 3:17-18.

63 Bill Moyers, *Genesis, A Living Conversation*, Doubleday, New York, 1996.

64 This subject is further discussed in Chapter 7 when dealing with the philosophy of Darwin.

65 By "destroy" I mean the destruction of human life apart from that which was preserved the ark.

66 Proverbs 1:24-33, Wording from *The Jerusalem Bible*, p. 801, (phrasing mine).

Chapter 3

1 Tacitus, *The Annals of Tactitus,* trans. A. J. Church and W. J. Brodribb, The Franklin Library, Franklin Center, Penn., 1982, p. 344.

2 Clark Pinnock, et al., *The Openness of God: A Biblical Challenge to the Traditional Understanding of God*, InterVarsity Press, Downers Grove, IL, 1994. (This is a tenet of Open Theism which is discussed further in Chapter 10.)

3 Augustine, *The Confessions of St. Augustine*, trans. J. G. Pilkington, Liveright Pub. Co., New York, 1943, p. 41.

4 Ibid., pp. 45-46.

5 Ibid., p. 163.

6 Ibid., p. 147.

7 Augustine, *On Free Will (De libero arbitrio)*, trans. John H. S. Burleigh, in *Library of Christian Classics, Vol. VI, Augustine: Earlier Writings,* The Westminster Press, Philadelphia, 1953, p. 113.

8 Ibid., p. 127.

9 Ibid.

10 Ibid.

11 Ibid., p. 107.

12 Romans 5:12.

13 Luke 16:19-31.

14 Jeremiah 17:9.

15 Augustine, *The Problem of Free Choice*, (This is a different translation of *De libero arbitrio*, chosen because of its clarity) trans. Dom Mark Pontifex, in *Ancient Christian Writers*, No. 22, The Newman Press, London, p. 193.

16 Ibid., pp. 194-195.

17 *Confessions*, p. 99.

18 *Confessions*, pp. 96-97.

19 Ibid., p. 47.

20 Ibid., p. 57.

21 Ibid., p. 69.

22 Augustine, *Grace and Free Will*, in *The Fathers of the Church, A New Translation*, Vol. 59, trans. Robert P. Russell, The Catholic University of America Press, Washington, D.C. 1968, p. 287.

23 Augustine is probably referring to Psalm 37:23 (Not 26:33 as rendered in the source) and Phil. 2:13.

24 Augustine, *The Problem of Free Choice*, p. 222.

25 Ibid., pp. 222-225.

26 The Apostle is here referring to Isaiah 8:14 and 28:16.

27 Romans 5:12 and 9:30-33.

28 Aquinas, *Summa Theologiæ*, trans. W. A. Wallace, Vol. 10, 67, Blackfriars, McGraw-Hill, 1967, pp. 55-57.

29 Light travels at the finite speed of 186,282 miles per second. Light also has properties that are foreign to particles, in that it also behaves as electromagnetic radiation. While light possesses properties of a wave it also possesses properties a particle and therefore today we speak of light's dualistic nature.

30 Modern humanists maintain that modern scientists who hold to the truth of Scripture are making the same error when they refute the ability of science to prove the mechanisms by which life began. However, it seems more reasonable, based on both the theory of science and the philosophical nature of the subject of origins, that modern humanistic scientists are meddling in areas where they have no expertise. It must be remembered that certain subjects can be, and other subjects cannot be, studied in the laboratory through reproducible experimentation. Science is best equipped to deal with the former, and philosophy, aided by science, is best equipped to deal with the latter. Darwin wrote that he could not prove in any single case where any given species changed into another species, yet this unproven theory is taught as fact.

31 If the reader finds this statement difficult he should study John 6:32-65. This subject is further treated in the Renaissance discussion of the next chapter. The Renaissance was largely a reaction to Scholastic theology.

32 Romans 1:19-23.

33 C.S. Lewis, *The Weight of Glory and other Addresses,* ed. W. Hopper, Touchstone, Simon and Schuster, 1996, p. 39.

34 I Cor. 2:14.

35   Aquinas, *The Summa Theologica,* trans. Fathers of the English Dominican Province, Revised by Daniel J. Sullivan, Vol. 2, 94, Encyclopaedia Britannica, Great Books of the Western World, 1952, p. 222. (The reader will note that for purposes of clarity I have used two different editions of Aquinas' *Summa.*)

36   Aquinas, *Summa Theologiæ,* trans. H. McCabe, Vol. 3, 12, Blackfriars, McGraw-Hill, 1964, p 17.

37   Jeremiah 17:9.

38   II Cor. 5:21.

39   Aquinas, *Summa Theologiæ,* trans. T.C. O'Brien, Vol. 14, 105, Blackfriars, McGraw-Hill, 1975, p. 85.

40   II Cor. 5:17.

41   John 3:3.

42   Romans 5:12-21.

43   Matthew 7:13-14.

44   Aquinas, *Summa Theologiæ,* trans. J Fearon, Vol. 25, 71, Blackfriars, McGraw-Hill, 1969, p. 7.

45   Ibid., p. 23.

46   Aquinas, *The Summa Theologica,* trans. Fathers of the English Dominican Province, Revised by Daniel J. Sullivan, Vol. 1, 83, Encyclopaedia Britannica, Great Books of the Western World, 1952, p. 437.

47   Aquinas, *Summa Theologiæ,* trans. T Gilby, Vol. 5, 23, Blackfriars, McGraw-Hill, 1967, p. 111.

48   1 John 5:13.

Chapter 4

1   Paul O. Kristeller and John H. Randall Jr., *The Renaissance Philosophy of Man,* ed. E. Cassirer, P. O. Kristeller, J. H. Randall, Jr., The University of Chicago Press, Chicago & London, 1948, p. 3.

2   See Chapter 1, reference 12.

3   Eugenio Garin, *Italian Humanism,* trans. Peter Munz, Harper and Row, New York, 1965, p. 25.

4   Ibid., p. 23, (Petrarch is referring to Romans 11:34).

5   *The Renaissance Philosophy of Man,* p. 125.

6   *The Renaissance Philosophy of Man,* pp. 103-104.

7   Petrarch is referring to John 4:14.

8   *The Renaissance Philosophy of Man,* pp. 104-105.

9   Ibid., p. 105.

10   Ibid., pp. 113-114.

11   Ernest Hatch Wilkins, *The Life of Petrarch,* The University of Chicago Press, 1961, pp. 251-252.

12   Ibid., p. 47.

13   Garin, p. 24.

14   Richard Tarnas, *The Passion of the Western Mind,* Ballantine Books, NY, 1991, p. 210.

15   For example see Will Durant, *The Renaissance, A History of Civilization in Italy from 1304-1576*, Simon and Schuster, 1953, p. 351.

16   Paul Oskar Kristeller, *Eight Philosophers of the Italian Renaissance*, Stanford University Press, Stanford, California, 1964, p. 32.

17   Ibid., p. 32.

18   Note that this title is identical to the work of St. Augustine discussed in Chapter 3.

19   *The Renaissance Philosophy of Man,* p. 155.

20   Ibid., pp. 168-169.

21   Ibid., From Romans 9 (The translator used the KJV), p. 176.

22   Ibid., p. 177.

23   Ibid., pp. 177-178.

24   G. C. Berkouwer in *Revelation and the Bible*, ed. Carl F. H. Henry, General and Special Divine Revelation, Baker, 1958, p. 14.

25   Ibid., p. 17.

26   Geoffrey W. Bromiley in *Revelation and the Bible*, ed. Carl F. H. Henry, Church Doctrine of Inspiration., Baker, 1958, p. 209.

27   Hermon Ridderbos in *Revelation and the Bible*, ed. Carl F. H. Henry, The Canon of the New Testament, Baker, 1958, p. 190.

28   J. I. Packer, *"Fundamentalism" and the Word of God*, London: InterVarsityFellowship, 1958, p. 90. (The current publisher is Wm. B. Eerdmans, Grand Rapids/Cambridge) F. F. Bruce was Professor of Biblical Histroy and Literature in Sheffield University, England.

29   I have not be able to find an English translation of this work.

30   Garin, p. 16.

31   Ibid.

32   Rene´ Pache, *The Inspiration and Authority of Scripture*, trans. H. I. Needham, Moody Press, Chicago, 1969, p. 189.

33   Durant, p. 571.

34   George Faludy, *Erasmus*, Stein and Day, New York, 1970, p. 1.

35   For details surrounding these uncertainties see Faludy.

36   J. A. Froude, *Life and Letters of Erasmus, Lectures Delivered at Oxford 1893-4*, Charles Scribner's Sons, New York, 1894.

37   Froude, p. 30.

38   Faludy, pp. 97-98.

39   Froude, p. 24.

40   Alister McGrath, *The Intellectual Origins of the European Reformation*, Baker, 1993, p. 42.

41   Faludy, pp. 82-83.

42   It is possible that Erasmus, based upon some of his later writings, altered his view of the Old Testament since he used passages from it frequently in his first published attack against Luther. (See next chapter)

43   Froude, p. 119.

44   Jacob Burckhardt, *The Civilization of the Renaissance in Italy*, First Modern Library Ed., Random House, 1954, p. 389.

45   Ficino was a Renaissance theologian who attempted to revive the status of Plato within the Catholic Church.

46 LeoX was also the Pope under whom Luther was excommunicated.
47 Froude, p. 50.
48 Ibid.
49 Froude, pp. 67-68.
50 Ibid., p. 68.
51 Ibid., p. 132.
52 Ibid., pp. 121-122.
53 Ibid.

Chapter 5

1 Jacob Burckhardt, *The Civilization of the Renaissance in Italy*, First Modern Library Ed., Random House, 1954, p. 320.
2 Ibid., p. 341.
3 Leopold Von Ranke, The Beginning of the Reformation in *Luther: A Profile*, ed. H. G. Koenigsberger, Hill and Wang, New York, 1973, p. 5.
4 Ephesians 2:8.
5 Habakkuk 2:4.
6 See Introduction to *Luther's Ninety-Five Theses*, trans. C. M. Jacobs, Revised by H. J. Grimm, Fortress Press, Philadelphia, Reprinted from Luther's Works, Vol. 31, Fortress Press, 1957.
7 *Luther's Ninety-Five Theses*, trans. C. M. Jacobs, Revised by H. J. Grimm, Fortress Press, Philadelphia, Reprinted from Luther's Works, Vol. 31, Fortress Press, 1957.
8 J. A. Froude, *Life and Letters of Erasmus, Lectures Delivered at Oxford 1893-4*, Charles Scribner's Sons, New York, 1894, p. 139.
9 Ibid., p. 229.
10 Ibid., pp. 207-208.
11 Ibid., p. 205.
12 Ibid., p. 210.
13 Ibid., pp. 253-254.
14 See footnote 3 of *Discourse on Free Will (Erasmus-Luther)*, trans. and ed. by Ernst F. Winter, Federick Ungar Publishing Co., New York, 1961, pp. 4-5. (In Article 36 of this document Luther asserted that free will was mere fiction)
15 *Discourse on Free Will (Erasmus-Luther)*, trans. and ed. by Ernst F. Winter, Federick Ungar Publishing Co., New York, 1961, p. 6.
16 This tactic is still today used by humanists in their attempts to discredit Christians who frame their view of reality in the truth of Scripture.
17 *Discourse on Free Will (Erasmus-Luther)*, pp. 7-8.
18 Ibid., p. 9.
19 Ibid., pp. 10-11.
20 Ibid., pp. 8-9.
21 Ibid., pp. 97-98.
22 Ibid., p. 104.
23 Ibid., pp. 105-106.
24 Isaiah 64:6.
25 Jeremiah 10:23.

26 *Discourse on Free Will (Erasmus-Luther)*, p. 65.
27 Matthew Henry, *Commentary on the Whole Bible*, Vol. IV, MacDonald Publishing Co., McLean, VA, p. 477.
28 John 6:44.
29 *Discourse on Free Will (Erasmus-Luther)*, p. 129.
30 Froude, pp. 388-389.
31 Alister McGrath, *The Intellectual Origins of the European Reformation*, Baker, 1993, p. 54.
32 Ibid., pp. 94-98.
33 Ibid., pp. 54-56.
34 John Calvin, *Commentary on The Book of Psalms*, Vol. 1, (from the *Preface*), Wm. B. Eerdmans, New York, 1963, pp. xl-xli.
35 John Calvin, in *The HarperCollins Encyclopedia of Catholicism*, ed. R. P. McBrien, Harper, San Francisco, 1995.
36 See McGrath, p.55 for details on Ganoczy.
37 John Calvin, *Institutes of the Christian Religion*, trans. John Allen, Vol. 1, Presbyterian Board of Christian Ed., 7th Ed., Philadelphia, 1936, pp. 274-275.
38 Ibid., pp. 296-297.
39 Ibid., p. 54.
40 Ibid., p. 56.
41 Ibid., p. 66.
42 Ibid., p. 58.
43 Ibid., pp. 68-69.
44 Ibid., pp. 78-79.
45 Ibid., p. 58.
46 Romans 1:21.
47 Calvin, *Institutes*, p. 215.
48 Ibid., p. 281
49 Ibid., p. 299.
50 Ibid.
51 Ibid., p. 67.
52 Ibid., p. 299.
53 Ibid., p. 287.
54 Ibid.
55 Ibid., pp. 287-288.
56 Calvin, *Commentary on The Book of Psalms*, p. xxxvi.
57 Calvin, *Institutes*, p. 52.
58 Ibid.
59 Romans 9:10-20.
60 Calvin, *Institutes*, p. 82.
61 Ibid., p. 83.
62 Ibid., pp. 86-87.
63 Ibid., p. 282.
64 Ephesians 2:8-9.

Chapter 6

1   *Introduction to Contemporary Civilization in the West (I)*, Columbia University Press, New York, 1946, p. 557.

2   In systems at the atomic scale, the classical mechanics based on Newton's work does not hold, and quantum mechanics must be resorted to.

3   Isaac Newton, from *Opticks* in *The Portable Enlightenment Reader*, ed. Isaac Kramnick, Penguin Books, 1995, p. 97.

4   Peter Gay, *Age of Enlightenment*, Time-Life Books, Time Inc., 1966, p. 20.

5   Michael White, *Isaac Newton: The Last Sorcerer*, Addison-Wesley, Reading, Massachusetts, 1997.

6   Issac Newton, *Observations Upon the Prophecies of Daniel and the Apocalypse of St. John*, Darby and Brown, London, 1733, pp. 13-14.

7   Francois-Marie Arouet De Voltaire, in *Letters Concerning the English Nation*, 1733, quoted from *The Portable Enlightenment Reader*, 1995, pp. 51-52.

8   Ibid., p. 54.

9   Ibid., p. 57.

10   Ibid., p. 58.

11   Francois-Marie Arouet De Voltaire, *Philosophical Dictionary*, 1764, English trans. 1765, quoted from *The Portable Voltaire*, ed. Ben Ray Redman, Penguin Books, 1977, p. 222.

12   Ibid., p. 187.

13   Voltaire, in letter to Frederick William, Prince of Prussia, quoted from *The Portable Enlightenment Reader*, p. 132.

14   Ibid., p. 131.

15   Voltaire, *Philosophical Dictionary*, quoted from *The Portable Voltaire*, pp. 195-196.

16   Ibid., p. 193.

17   John 3:19-21.

18   Acts 7.

19   A specific modern day example of such atrocities has been documented in the stunning video: *Sudan: The Hidden Holocaust* by D. J. Kennedy, Coral Ridge Ministries, Ft Lauderdale, FL.

20   Voltaire, *Philosophical Dictionary*, quoted from *The Portable Voltaire*, pp. 124-125.

21   Ibid., p. 226.

22   Ibid., pp. 93-95.

23   I Cor. 5:17.

24   Voltaire, *Philosophical Dictionary*, quoted from *The Portable Voltaire*, pp. 109-110.

25   *The Portable Enlightenment Reader*, ed. Isaac Kramnick, Penguin Books, 1995, p. 1.

26   Immanuel Kant, *Fundamental Principles of the Metaphysic of Ethics*, trans. Thomas K. Abbott, Longmans, Green and Co., London, 10th Ed., 1946, p. 10.

27   Ibid., p. 11.

28   Ibid., p. 14.

29   Ibid., p. 18-19.

30 Ibid., p. 74.

31 Ibid., p. 19.

32 As in Chapter 2 when discussing the "law of God", the reader should remember that with this statement, I am not addressing the relationship between the Mosaic law and the "New Covenant."

33 Kant, *Metaphysic of Ethics,* p. 21.

34 Matt. 5:17-19.

35 Matt. 22:35-40.

36 Kant, *Metaphysic of Ethics,* p. 28.

37 Ibid., p. 29.

38 Ibid., p. 30.

39 A parallel passage is in Matthew 19.

40 Immanuel Kant, *Religion within the Limits of Reason Alone*, trans. T. M. Greene and H. H. Hudson, Harper & Row, New York, 1960, p. 16.

41 Ibid., p. 17.

42 Ibid., p. 40.

43 Ibid., p. 47.

44 John 14:6.

45 However, just as the evangelical Christian community has sometimes misunderstood the American philosophy of government, so has it more often been misunderstood by many modern humanists who believe that American government should be intolerant to true Christian faith.

46 Thomas Paine, *Common Sense* (the closing sentences), in *The American Tradition in Literature*, 3rd Ed. Grosset & Dunlap, New York, 1967, and p. 171.

47 Thomas Paine, *The American Crisis*, in *The American Tradition in Literature*, 3rd Ed. Grosset & Dunlap, New York, 1967, p. 175.

48 Thomas Paine (emphasis is Paine's), quoted from *The Portable Enlightenment Reader*, p. 178-179.

49 Ibid., p. 175.

50 Isaiah 55:7-9.

51 Thomas Jefferson, quoted from *The Notes on Virginia*, 1787, in *The Portable Enlightenment Reader*, p. 161.

52 Thomas Jefferson, quoted from a letter to Benjamin Rush, 1803 in *The Portable Enlightenment Reader*, p. 165.

53 Joseph Priestley, quoted from a letter to Dr. Horsley, 1783, in *The Portable Enlightenment Reader*, pp. 155-156.

54 Ibid., p. 156.

55 John 8:55-58.

56 Benjamin Franklin, quoted from a letter to Joseph Preistley, 1780, in *The Portable Enlightenment Reader*, p. 73-74.

57 Benjamin Franklin, quoted from a letter to Ezra Stiles, 1790, in *The Portable Enlightenment Reader*, p. 167.

Chapter 7

1 The Franklin Covey Co. (Copyright, 1998), March 2002.

2 Jack Cuozzo, *Burried Alive, The Startling Truth About Neanderthal Man*, Master Books, Green Forest, AR, 1998.

3 Alfred Russel Wallace, like Darwin, was a British naturalist whose ideas were similar to Darwin's. Together they issued a joint publication on the subject in 1858, about a year before Darwin published his *Origin of Species*.

4 Gillian Beer, in Introduction to Darwin's *The Origin of Species*, (1859), Oxford University Press, 1998, p. ix.

5 Charles Darwin, *The Autobiography of Charles Darwin*, ed. Nora Barlow, W.W. Norton & Co., 1993, pp. 56-57.

6 See reference 13.

7 I Cor. 2:14.

8 Charles Darwin, *The Origin of Species*, (1859), Oxford University Press, 1998, p. 391.

9 Darwin, *Autobiography*, p. 85.

10 Matthew 24:37-8, 1 Peter 3:20 and 2 Peter 2:5.

11 Darwin, *Autobiography*, p. 86.

12 John 3:18, KJV.

13 Darwin, *Autobiography*, p. 87.

14 Ibid. p. 90.

15 C. S. Lewis, *The Problem of Pain*, Macmillan, New York, 1971, pp. 47-48.

16 Ibid., p. 56.

17 Ibid.

18 Ibid. pp. 56-57.

19 Ibid. p. 58.

20 Ibid.

21 Ibid., p. 75. Lewis here refers to Augustine's *De Civitate Dei XIV*, xiii.

22 Ibid., p. 76.

23 Ibid., p. 85.

24 Ibid., p. 68.

25 Ibid., p. 85.

26 Darwin's wife.

27 Adrian J. Desmond & James R. Moore, *Darwin*, Warner Books, 1991, p. 384, p. 387.

28 Lewis, *The Problem of Pain*, p. 95.

29 Daniel C. Dennett, *Darwin's Dangerous Idea: Evolution and the Meanings of Life*, Simon and Schuster, New York, 1995, p. 145.

30 William S. Sahakian and Mabel L. Sahakian, *Ideas of the Great Philosophers*, Barnes & Noble, New York, 1966, p. 48.

31 Arthur Schopenhauer, *The World as Will and Idea*, trans. R. B. Haldane and J. Kemp, Routledge & Kegan Paul Limited, London, 1948 (first published 1883), pp. 253-254.

32 Augustine, *The Confessions of St. Augustine*, trans. J. G. Pilkington, Liveright Pub. Co., New York, 1943, p. 1.

33 Friedrich Nietzsche, *Beyond Good and Evil*, trans. R. J. Hollingdale, Penguin Classics, 1990, p. 192.

34 Ibid. p. 193.

35 Ibid. p. 195.

36 Ibid. p. 197.

37 Ibid.

38 Friedrich Nietzsche, *Twilight of the Idols*, trans. R. J. Hollingdale, Penguin Classics, 1990, p. 41.

39 Ibid. p. 87.

40 Friedrich Nietzsche, *The Anti-Christ,* trans. R. J. Hollingdale, Penguin Classics, 1990, p. 128.

41 II Cor. 12:10.

42 I Cor. 1:27.

43 Nietzsche, *The Anti-Christ*, pp. 148-149.

44 Ibid., pp. 166-167.

45 Ibid. pp. 133-134.

46 John 4:24.

47 John 8:43-45.

48 Calvin S. Hall, *A Primer of Freudian Psychology,* The World Publishing Company, 1954, pp. 11-12.

49 Breuer and Freud were colleagues early on. Together they published *Studien über Hysterie (Studies on Hysteria),* but they parted ways when Freud began to espouse some of his more radical sexual theories.

50 Sigmund Freud, *The Origin and Development of Psycho-Analysis (First Lecture)* in Great Books of the Western World, The Major Works of Sigmund Freud, Encyclopedia Britannica, Inc., 1952, p. 4.

51 Ibid.

52 Ibid., *(Second Lecture)*, p. 7.

53 Ibid.

54 Ibid., *(Fourth Lecture)*, p. 14.

55 Ibid., pp. 14-15.

56 See for example, *Unauthorized Freud: Doubters Confront a Legend*, ed. Frederick C. Crews, Viking: Penguin Putnam, Inc., 1998.

57 Freud, *Origin and Development of Psycho-Analysis (Fourth Lecture)*, p. 16.

58 Ibid.

59 Ibid., p. 17.

60 Sigmund Freud, *Civilization and Its Discontents,* in Great Books of the Western World, The Major Works of Sigmund Freud, Encyclopedia Britannica, Inc., 1952, p. 791.

61 *Unauthorized Freud: Doubters Confront a Legend*, ed. Frederick C. Crews, Viking:Penguin Putnam, 1998.

62 Sigmund Freud, *Civilization and Its Discontents,* p. 774, p. 776.

63 T. Rockmore, in *The Columbia History of Western Philosophy*, ed. R.H. Popkin, Columbia University Press, NY, 1998, p. 550.

64 Sigmund Freud, *The Ego and the Id,* in Great Books of the Western World, The Major Works of Sigmund Freud, Encyclopedia Britannica, Inc., 1952, p. 702.

65 Ibid., p. 707.

66 Sigmund Freud, *Civilization and its Discontents*, p. 792.

67 1 John 4.

68 Sigmund Freud, *The Origin and Development of Psycho-Analysis (Fifth Lecture)*, p. 20.

69 *Karl Marx: On Society and Social Change: With Selections by Friedrich Engels*, ed. Neil J. Smelser, University of Chicago Press, Chicago and London, 1973, p. vii.

70 Some biographers claim that the conversion to Christianity happened before his birth.

71 Karl Marx and Friedrich Engles, *The Communist Manifesto*, The first sentence of the first chapter. English translation edited by Engels, 1888.

72 Friedrich Engels in *Karl Marx: On Society and Social Change: With Selections by Friedrich Engels*, ed. Neil J. Smelser, University of Chicago Press, Chicago and London, 1973, (from *The Origin of the Family, Private Property and the State*), p. 22.

Chapter 8

1 Matthew 6:24.

2 Matthew Henry, *Commentary on the Whole Bible, Vol. 5*, MacDonald Publishing Co., McLean VA, p. 81.

3 Laura Berman Fortgang, *Living Your Best Life: Ten Strategies for Getting from Where You Are to Where Your're Meant to Be*, Jeremy P. Tarcher/Putnam, New York, 2001.

4 Ibid., Introduction, p. ix.

5 Ibid., p.xiii.

6 Steven R. Covey, *The 7 Habits of Highly Effective People: Restoring the Character Ethic*, Simon and Schuster, New York, 1998.

7 Ibid., pp. 18-19.

8 Ibid., Steve Labunski, Executive Director, International Radio and Television Society, Introductory pages.

9 Ibid., p. 21.

10 Ibid., p. 34.

11 Ibid., p. 319.

12 Ibid., pp. 46-47.

13 *Akron Beacon Journal*, Sports Commentary, Jim Litke, Assoc. Press, *A Rose by any other name still is a gamble*, January 30, 2003.

14 *Celebrate Your Self: Enhance your self-esteem*, Dorothy C. Briggs, Doubleday, New York, 1977, p. 3.

15 Genesis 8:21.

16 Isaiah 57: 20-21.

17 Jerry Sherk to P. McManamon in *Life after football is not so super, Akron Beacon Journal*, Akron, Ohio, Jan 24, 2003.

18 By this I mean that the extraordinary physical abilities of an athlete are only temporary. For example, any high school all-star baseball player could have out hit either Mantle or Williams by the time they reached 50 years of age.

19 CNNSI.com news release, July 8, 2000.

20 I Timothy 6:10.

21 Robert T. Kiyosaki with Sharon L. Lechter, CPA, *Rich Dad/Poor Dad*, Warner Books. 2001, p. 165.

22 I Timothy 6:10.

23 Proverbs 11:28.

24 Matthew 6:25-33.

25 Robert H. Bork, *Slouching towards Gomorrah: Modern Liberalism and American Decline*; Regan Books, 1996.

26 John D. Ashcroft, Attorney General, et al., Petitioners v. The Free Speech Coalition et al. 535 U.S. 795 (2002).

27 *Sexual Values: Opposing Viewpoints Series*, ed. Charles P. Cozic, Greenhaven Press, Inc., San Diego, CA., 1995, pp. 23-28.

28 Romans 7:15.

29 I Corinthians 7:9.

30 *Psychology Today*, December 2002.

31 D. Zillmann and J. Bryant, *Journal of Applied Social Psychology*, Vol. 18, No. 5, 1988, pp. 438-453.

32 II Corinthians 12:21.

33 Steven Seidman, *Embattled Eros: Sexual Politics and Ethics in Contemporary America* Routledge, NY, 1992, p. 188.

34 While most humanists reason from conscience (and correctly so) that a child cannot rationally willingly participate in sexual activity, some, in their depraved minds, have even begun to depart from that exception.

35 Reported in *The Plain Dealer*, Cleveland, OH, July 20, 2002.

36 James Lehman, Letter to the Editor of *The Akron Beacon Journal*, Akron, Ohio, August 19, 2002.

37 Mr. Lehman is, of course, referring to Romans 1:18-32.

38 *Time*, Vol. 140, Issue 9, August 31, 1992, p. 59.

39 George Anastasia, *The Summer Wind: Thomas Capano and the Murder of Anne Marie Fahey*, Regan Books, 1999.

40 Mathew 23:27.

Chapter 9

1 See the Chapter 7 discussion of Freud. See also Isaiah 53:6 and Phil. 2:21.

2 DSM-III is the American Psychiatric Association's, *Diagnostic and Statistical Manuel of Mental Disorders*, 3rd Ed., revised 1987.

3 See Chapter 7, reference 16 and related discussion.

4 Alexander Lowen M.D., *Narcissism: Denial of the True Self*, Macmillan, New York, 1983, p. ix.

5 Ibid.

6 Ibid., pp. 49-50.

7 *Parade, The Sunday Newspaper Magazine*, ed. L. Kravitz, Parade Publications, New York, December 1, 2002.

8 C. S. Lewis, *The Four Loves*, Harcourt Brace Jovanovich, New York, p. 12.

9 John 3:18

10 Some authors have attempted to use Plato's *Symposium* to support their contention that Plato was sympathetic to homosexuality. However, this should be questioned since it is clear from Plato's *Laws* that he *did not* view homosexuality as a legitimate form of human love. See Plato, *Laws*, VIII, 841.

11 Plato, *Republic*, 457d, trans. by Robin Waterfield, Barnes & Noble by arrangement with Oxford University Press, 1993.

12 Lewis, *The Four Loves*, p. 158.

13 Ibid., p. 159.

14 Gary Chapman, *The Five Love Languages*, Northfield Publishing, Chicago, 1995.

15 Galatians 3:28.

16 Deborah Tannen, *You Just Don't Understand: Women and Men in Conversation*, Ballantine Books, (Random House), New York, 1990, p. 17.

17 Daly was a faculty member of Boston College until she clashed with the school's administration, in the late 1990's, over many of her feministic tenets.

18 Mary Daly, *Gyn/Ecology: The Metaphysics of Radical Feminism*, Beacon Hill Press, Boston, 1978, p. 360.

19 Ibid., pp. 360-361.

20 Of course, this is a hypothetical illustration used only for the sake of logic. One who knows the teaching of Scripture on this subject cannot accept that contrary as a true possibility.

21 Reported in the *Akron Beacon Journal*, Akron, Ohio, December 12, 2002.

22 Kenneth D. Boa and Robert M. Bowman Jr., *An Unchanging Faith in a Changing World: Understanding and Responding to Critical Issues that Christians Face Today*, Thomas Nelson Publishers, 1997.

23 Ibid., p. 189.

24 Ibid., p. 229.

25 Ibid., p. 233.

26 Dietrich Bonhoffer, *Ethics*, trans. H. H. Smith, Macmillan, New York, 1965, p. 176.

27 Bonhoffer agreed with the Catholic Church on the issue of abortion but not on the issue of contraception.

28 John Paul II, *The Gospel of Life*, Times Books, Random House, New York, 1995, pp. 23-24. (For prior comments on the morality of "sex within marriage", see *The Pursuit of Sexual Pleasure* in Chapter 8.)

29 For those who may be reading this section apart from the rest of this book, it may be difficult to appreciate the context of this thought.

30 Bonhoeffer, *Ethics*, p. 103.

31 I recommend the reader thoroughly review the case of the State of Kansas vs. the Carr brothers of Wichita, Kansas concerning their crime spree of December 2000. If want wants a primary example of the Catholic Church's wrong position concerning capital punishmenet this, in my opinion, is an excellent one.

32 *American Academy of Pediatrics NEWS*, Sept. 1990.

33 Proberbs 23:13-14.

34 Genesis 8:21.

35 James Dobson, *The Strong Willed Child: Birth Through Adolescence*, Tyndale House, Wheaton, IL, 1978, p. 77.

36 John Gottman, *The Heart of Parenting: Raising an Emotionally Intelligent Child*, Simon & Schuster, New York, 1997, p. 32.

37 Ibid.

38 I Samuel 16:7.

39 Diana Baumrind, *Developmental Psychology Monograph*, Vol. 4, 1971, pp. 1-102.

40 Gottman, p. 32.

41 Matthew 7:23.

42 Donald Capps, *Journal for the Scientific Study of Religion*, Vol. 31, 1992, p. 1.

43 Proverbs 10:13, 13:24, 22:15, 23:13-14, 26:3, 29:15.

44 Marshall Frady, *Billy Graham: A Parable of American Righteousness*, Little, Brown and Co., Boston, 1979.

45 Capps, p. 10.

46 Ibid., p. 11.

47 John 8:37-41.

48 Matthew 23:37.

Chapter 10

1 Harold S. Kushner, *How Good Do We Have to Be?: A New Understanding of Guilt and Forgiveness*, Little, Brown and Company, New York, 1996, p. 21.

2 Ibid., p. 31.

3 Ibid., p. 44.

4 John 3:16.

5 Kushner, p. 74.

6 Ibid., p. 170.

7 Ibid., p. 175.

8 Dennis Prager, *Think a Second Time*, Regan Books, HarperCollins, New York, NY, 1995.

9 Ibid., See Chapter 34 entitled: *Why Aren't People Preoccupied with Good and Evil?*, p. 197.

10 *Openline*, Moody Broadcast Network, Hosted by Chris Fabry, aired November 1995.

11 Psalm 53:3-4.

12 Prager, p. 74.

13 John 5:36b-47.

14 Wayne W. Dyer, *Manifest Your Destiny: The Nine Spiritual Principles for Getting Everything You Want*, HarperCollins, New York, 1997, p. 13.

15 Ibid.

16 Isaiah 59:2-3.

17 John 3:18.

18 Romans 1:18-32.

19 Donald B. Cozzens, *The Changing Face of the Priesthood*, The Liturgical Press, Collegeville, MN, 2000, p. 98.

20 I am aware that there are voices in Catholic leadership who truly lament the presence of homosexuality within the church's ranks and are raising their voices against it.

21 John Shelby Spong, *Here I Stand, My Struggle for a Christianity of Integritiy, Love, and Equality,* Harper San Fancisco, 2000, pp. 362-363.

22 Francis A. Schaeffer, *The Great Evangelical Disaster,* Crossway Books, Westchester, IL, 1984, p. 34.

23 Rev. William Pawson, *Akron Beacon Journal,* February 1, 2003, p. A12.

24 *Akron Beacon Journal,* April 22, 2003 and May 4, 2004.

25 John Calvin, *Institutes of the Christian Religion,* trans. J. Allen, Vol. 1, Presbyterian Board of Christian Ed., 7th ed., Philadelphia, 1936, p. 58.

26 *Akron Beacon Journal,* April 5, 2003, p. A11.

27 Henry C. Theissen, *Introductory Lectures in Systematic Theology,* Wm. B. Eerdmans, Grand Rapids, MI, 1949, p. 267.

28 Ibid., p. 268.

29 Dewey J. Hoitenga Jr., *John Calvin and the Will: A Critique and Corrective,* Baker, 1997, p. 126.

30 Ibid., endnote 2, Chapter 3.

31 Ibid., p. 23.

32 Ibid., p. 28.

33 Ibid., p. 70.

34 Mortimer J. Adler, *Ten Philosophical Mistakes,* Collier Books, Macmillan, New York, 1985, p. xiii.

35 Clark Pinnock, et al., *The Openness of God: A Biblical Challenge to the Traditional Understanding of God,* InterVarsity Press, Downers Grove, IL, 1994.

36 John 6:44.

37 Joshua 24:15.

38 Colossians 1:21-23.

39 I do not think that the purpose of the words in this Scripture and those from the verses which follow are meant to teach this, but I do understand how one might interpret them as such. I think that these verses are to accommodate the truth exemplified in Jesus' parable of Mark 4. Some seed appearing to be alive is, in reality, dead.

40 Hebrews 6:4-6.

41 *The Writings of James Arminius,* trans. James Nichols and W. R. Bagnall, Vol. 1, Baker Book House, 1956, p. 252.

42 C. S. Lewis, *God in the Dock:Essays on Theology and Ethics,* ed. Walter Hooper, W. B. Eerdmans, Grand Rapids, 1970, p. 261.

43 Clark Pinnock, et al., *The Openness of God: A Biblical Challenge to the Traditional Understanding of God,* p. 7.

44 Charles G. Finney, *Lectures on Revivals of Religion,* Lecture IV, Fleming H. Revell Company, New York and London, 1868, p. 48.

45 C. S. Lewis, *God in the Dock,* p. 261.

46 Broadcasted on KBRT, Los Angeles, September 1990. (Complete Text available at www.modernreformation.org) Horton is Associate Professor of Theology at Westminster Theological Seminary, Escondido, CA.

47 *Christianity Today,* December 2002.

Chapter 11

1 Matthew 12:14-21. The Isaiah passage is from Chapter 42.
2 For an in-depth answer to this charge see Michael S. Horton, *Journal of the Evangelical Theological Society*, June, 2000, p. 317.
3 Thomas Aquinas, *On the Articles of the Faith and Sacraments of the Church, The Catechetical Instructions of St. Thomas*, trans. Collins, p. 120.
4 James D. Watson in *Do our genes reveal the hand of God?*, interview with the *London Telegraph*, March 20, 2003
5 *Idea No. 37: The New Celebrity, Seed Magazine*, March/April, 2003, pp. 80-83.
6 For the scientific reader who desires compelling evidence of this statement I recommend Jack Cuozzo's book, *Buried Alive: The Startling Truth about Neanderthal Man*, Master Books, Green Forest, AR, 1998.
7 Joseph S. Willis, *Finding Faith in the Face of Doubt*, Quest Books: Theosophical Publications, Wheaton Ill, 2001, p. 104.
8 Malachi 2:17.

Index

A

Abel 32, 192, 235
abortion 28, 200–203 *See also* Pro-
Life movement
Abraham v, viii, 22, 22–25, 38, 139,
195, 208, 212, 214, 225, 229
God's choosing of, 22, 23, 63
his offering of Isaac 23, 24, 30,
212
his response to God 23, 25
his uniqueness 22
Jesus' reference to, 39, 40
the faith of, 22, 32, 38, 39, 40,
58, 215, 229
the God of, 20, 33, 36, 58
Ur (Ur-kasdim) and, 22
Abram *See* Abraham
abstinence 181
Adam 38, 52, 59, 98, 102, 103,
104, 106, 108, 109, 185, 223
free will and, 49
the sin of, 29, 31, 49, 51, 54, 62,
178, 182, 183, 210, 212, 224
his offspring and, 49, 51, 76,
163, 204, 215, 235
human nature and, 49, 63,
146, 186, 193, 195, 222
adultery 27, 186
Ahaz 36
al-Qaeda 199
Allen, Woody 190
almah 36
Ambrose *See* Augustine: Ambrose
and,
American Psychiatric Association
193
Anaximander 3, 4

apeiron, the 3, 4
Aquinas, Thomas ix, 56–64, 115,
119, 224, 256
Albertus Magnus and, 56
Aristotle and, 12, 57, 58, 62
free will and, 62
Greek philosophy and, ix, 231
his definition of sin 62
his early life 56
natural inclination to good and,
60, 105, 107, 149
natural law and, 60
Natural Theology and, 57, 72, 76
"original" sin and, 59, 231
predestination and, 63
Scholasticism and, 19, 66, 67,
231
science and, 57
spiritual birth and, 61, 231
Summa Theologica 57, 62, 243
areté See Greek philosophy
Aristotle 2, 5, 9–14, 69, 70, 107,
115, 116, 119, 121, 180, 194,
210, 224, 229, 231
Anaximander and, 3
Aquinas and, 12, 56, 57, 58, 60,
62
De Anima 237
free will and, 19
habit and, 13, 54
happiness and, 12, 13
Metaphysics 237
moral excellence and, 13, 62
moral good and the state 12, 26
moral neutrality at birth and, 19,
32, 48, 62
moral virtue as distinct from
Sophist's 14
natural inclination to good and,
12, 19, 60
natural law and, 27
Nicomachean Ethics 11, 12, 69,
238, 239, 240

265

the Reformation and, 66, 67
righteousness
  imputation of, 23, 25
  faith and, 32, 33, 40, 43, 212, 214
Roman Catholic Church *See* Catholic, (Roman Church)
Rose, Pete 181

S

salvation 32, 35, 43, 51, 61, 88, 98, 107, 146, 172, 189, 196, 213, 214, 229, 230 *See also* redemption
Schaeffer, Francis 219, 255
Scholasticism 19, 56, 66, 67, 68, 69, 72, 76, 77, 85, 87
  extra-biblical views of sin and, 89, 186
Schopenhauer, Authur 127, 151, 249
  Nirvana and, 152
science iv, 5, 7, 17, 21, 56, 76, 77, 115, 116, 143, 232
  evolutionary thought and, 143, 242
  Petrarch's view of, 72
  scientific method x, 57, 58
  social 21, 205, 206
Scripture
  accuracy of translation and, 78
  as only source for true knowledge of God 20, 32, 193, 200
  as source of moral truth 187, 192, 201
  authorized Jewish renditions of, viii
  Hebrew 33
    first promise of redemption 35
    humanism's incompatibility with, ii, vii, 141
    Jesus' use of, 33
    The Septuagint 38

human personality and, vi, 21
human sexuality and, 185, 187
its supernatural character i, 77, 79, 82
male authority in the family and, 200
Renaissance philosophy of, 82
the humanist's view of, 21
ultimate verification of its truth 21
Seidman, Steven 188, 252
self-determination 177
self-help books 176
September 11, 2001 199
sexual lust
  vs. sexual desire 185
sexual pleasure 175, 185–190
sexual revolution 185
Simplicius 3, 237
sin
  acknowledgment of, 216
  as the root cause of hopelessness 29
  atonement for, 32, 37, 93
  Augustine's teaching on, 48
  Genesis 3:15 and, 35
  gravity of, 29, 146, 148
  imputation of, 49
    Adam and, 51, 62
  its definition 29 *See also* Augustine: sin defined
  its result and, 49, 141, 195
  selfishness and, 193
  universality of, 30, 42, 182
Skinner, B. F. 188
Society for the Scientific Study of Religion 207
Socrates 2, 5, 7, 8, 9, 11, 14, 15, 17, 24, 26, 27, 46, 123, 194, 210, 229
  self knowledge and, 17, 46
Solzhenitsyn, Alexander 210
Sophists viii, 2, 5, 6, 7, 8, 9, 14, 15,

Order this book by mail: Photon Publishing
P. O. Box 2201
North Canton, OH 44720

by website: www.photonpublishing.com

by email: photonpublishing@spearnet.net

by phone: 330-699-2694